FOR THE LOVE
OF PLEASURE

Lauren Rabinovitz

Rutgers University Press

New Brunswick, New Jersey, and London

For the Love of Pleasure

WOMEN, MOVIES AND CULTURE IN TURN-OF-THE-CENTURY CHICAGO

Library of Congress Cataloging-in-Publication Data

Rabinovitz, Lauren, 1950–

    For the love of pleasure : women, movies, and culture in turn-of-
the-century Chicago / Lauren Rabinovitz.

      p.   cm.

    Includes bibliographical references and indexes.

    ISBN 0-8135-2533-0 (cloth : alk. paper).—ISBN 0-8135-2534-9 (pbk. : alk. paper)

    1. Motion pictures and women.   2. Women in motion pictures.
3. Women—Illinois—Chicago—Social conditions.   4. Chicago (Ill.)—
Social conditions.   5. Popular culture—Illinois—Chicago—
History—19th century.   6. Popular culture—Illinois—Chicago—
History—20th century.   I. Title.
PN1995.9.W6R33   1998
791.43' 082' 0977311—DC21   *97-45724*
                                                                   CIP

British Cataloging-in-Publication data for this book is available from the British Library

Manufactured in the United States of America

For Jeanette Rabinovitz,

Jill Santivasi,

and Mara Santivasi

CONTENTS

ILLUSTRATIONS

ACKNOWLEDGMENTS

THE IDEA FOR THIS BOOK was sparked more than ten years ago when I was a Chicago resident trying to answer questions from students, friends, and colleagues at the University of Illinois at Chicago about the beginnings of the local motion picture business. What had begun as a simple investigation into industrial and economic matters took several twists and turns, not the least of which was my own relocation to Iowa. If I started my journey sincerely trying to satisfy the questions posed by others, I soon turned their curiosity to my own advantage by remapping their original inquiries onto a new plan that fit my interests. But I am indebted to all those who started me down this track in the first place because it set off what has become a passion for early cinema. Among my Chicago guides, none supported me more than my dear friend Richard de Cordova. He was always on the research lookout for me; he supplied me with many helpful sources; and he provided ample hospitality in Chicago whenever I returned to do my work. His death last year has robbed me of the joy of his friendship and of the satisfaction of showing him the completed work in which he took so much pleasure.

Portions of this work benefited as well from opportunities to air my ideas before interested audiences, whose feedback strengthened the overall project. I am grateful to Lucy Fischer and the entire University of Pittsburgh English Department; Tom Gunning, Mark Sandberg, and the Chicago Film Seminar; and Jim Lastra and the University of Chicago Mass Culture Workshop for inviting me to present my work and for their responses. In addition, an earlier version of chapter five appeared in *Camera Obscura: A Journal of Feminism and Film Theory*, no. 23 (Spring 1991) as "Temptations of Pleasure: Nickelodeons, Amusement Parks, and the Sights of Female Sexuality." In editing that piece for publication, Lynn Spigel helped me to see how to make my argument better.

The most delightful preparation for the book's overall shape came when I got to participate in the summer 1992 Obermann Faculty Research Seminar, "The Image in Dispute: Visual Cultures in Modernity," held at the University of Iowa's Obermann Center for Advanced Studies. Each of the Obermann Fellows contributed to my thinking in a variety of ways. Dudley Andrew, the seminar's director, generously edited and especially helped to hone my argument in several chapters. Earlier versions of chapters one and two appeared as "The Fair View: Female Spectators and the 1893 Chicago World's Columbian Exposition," in *The Image in Dispute: Art and Cinema in the Age of Photography,* edited by Dudley Andrew (Austin: University of Texas Press, 1997). For their continuing support throughout the seminar and since, I owe much to Jay Semel, the Obermann Center's congenial director, and to Lorna Olson, his most gracious and extraordinary assistant.

I have also benefited from the advice and careful readings from a remarkable group of friends and colleagues. I am especially grateful to Leo Charney, Rich Horwitz, and John Raeburn. Richard Maltby maintained an unflagging enthusiasm for this book and provided many valuable suggestions; he generously shared his work, compared film notes with me, and commented on the entire manuscript. Rick Altman traded research discoveries and read portions of the manuscript; our animated conversations regularly kept fresh the joys of productive scholarship. Students in two graduate seminars and one undergraduate course nurtured me through the entire development of the ideas in this book. Among the dozens who rewarded me with their critical insights, enthusiasm, and imaginative ways of thinking, I especially wish to thank Melanie Nash for her insight and judgment; Laura Baker, Mary Flanagan, and Rosanna Maule for our many discussions that helped to enliven this book; Alison Kibler and Sharon Wood for writing remarkable dissertations and for sustaining my intellectual growth in important ways. Chrys Poff was a wonderfully resourceful research assistant in helping me to get this volume ready for publication. The American Studies and Communication Studies departments at the University of Iowa provided continuing support and assistance.

I would also like to express my gratitude for the assistance of Rosemary Hanes at the Library of Congress, Division of Motion Pictures, Broadcasting, and Recorded Sound; Linda Ziemer, Assistant Curator in Prints and Photographs, Chicago Historical Society.

At Rutgers University Press, Leslie Mitchner actively supported this work from the beginning, when it was just an idea, through to the final stages of completion. Her advice was always both perceptive and prudent. The counsel and conscientiousness of Marilyn Campbell and Tricia Politi saved me on a number of occasions in readying the volume for publication.

One of the most gratifying aspects of my sojourn into turn-of-the-century culture was imagining that I was coming into contact with the world my grandmothers knew. Although this book is not about them and covers the years just before Bertha Levi and Sarah Rabinovitz, Jewish Eastern European immigrants, each stepped off the train in Chicago, I like to think that my desire to know something of their past fueled the directions I took. Neither of them went immediately to live in Chicago, and neither of them ever experienced America as independent single women. But their lives were lived out as mothers, wives, workers, and Jews in midwestern cities, and they did love movies, fashion, and social outings. In my own way, I have tried to be true to them.

Greg Easley accompanied me every step of the way. For the better part of a decade, he helped me sort out the ideas germane to this book. Not merely content to depend on his intellectual counsel, I relied upon his advice regarding the book's illustrations and his original cover design. A simple acknowledgment of gratitude does not even begin to cover how much this book owes to him.

Finally, although they do not realize it, three people were always in my thoughts as I worked on this project. They are tied to my own memories of so many pleasure-filled occasions: shopping trips to grand old downtown department stores, excursions to amusement parks long past their glory days, the thrill of visiting the last truly great international exposition in New York in 1964, and countless hours at the movies. Although I grew up not in Chicago but in St. Paul, Minnesota, after World War II, much of the fun of my youth was the legacy of an earlier time. My mother was my first guide and loving escort, and her stories of a Depression-era girlhood at the movies, at the amusement park, and afoot in downtown city spaces also made me feel part of something that did indeed stretch across the century. My sister, Jill, was my partner and co-conspirator in all our adventures. She and I learned together what it meant to roam the neighborhood shopping center; to spend an entire day without adults at the amusement park; to take the bus downtown by ourselves and be fascinated by the department stores, the magnificent public library, and the matinees at movie palaces of a bygone era. Now that we are adults, the times we spend together are not all that different from what we used to do. Happily, my niece, Mara, exhibits an unabashed curiosity about those adventures. But it is difficult to portray and recover for her a world that has largely disappeared or been transformed into suburban shopping malls, multiplex cinemas, and Walt Disneyesque theme parks. Because I want her to feel part of our past and believe the past may animate all our futures, I drew on my mother, my sister, and my niece as the inspiration for this book.

FOR THE LOVE
OF PLEASURE

INTRODUCTION

The danger begins the moment a girl leaves the protection of Home and
Mother.

FLORENCE MABEL DEDRICK, "Our Sister of the Street," 1909

As RECENT CELEBRATIONS of the centenary of motion pic-
tures remind us, the date of cinema's inception and the origins of movies
are still identified as the simple invention of a new apparatus. But even
in 1895, cinema was more than a new technology tied to Renaissance notions of picturing objects in space. As Rick Altman points out, "The *physical phenomenon* which we retroactively label 'cinema' [is not the same
as] . . . the *social phenomenon* which we recognize as cinema. In terms
of technology, the cinema projector [was] simply an accessory added to
the light source and stand already available for lantern slides."[1] From the
outset, cinema was much more than a machine, a mere picturing device,
since its incorporation into industrialized societies was generally as one
among the number of new gathering places at the turn of the century. Its
organization as a social phenomenon within a distinctive niche even more
than its application of technologies old and new made it profoundly ideological, an invention and expression of the society and times. Like its urban contemporaries—the international exposition, the department store,
and the amusement park—cinema was a site specially produced for a
combination of leisure, spectacle, social encounters, commerce, and cultural education. As a social phenomenon, cinema acquired meaning and
purpose through the cultural contexts in which it was embedded and
especially through nineteenth-century frameworks of social and visual
knowledge.

As an emerging cultural institution, cinema shared much with other
commercial forms of theatrical spectacle—the dime museum, the

panorama, the illustrated lecture, vaudeville, the circus. Critics are just beginning to understand the common features and functions of all these
forms of spectacle. But cinema equally employed the aesthetics, rules of
combination, and representational practices of other turn-of-the-century
commercial institutions—the department store, the international exposition, and the amusement park. Yet, no one has shown how cinema was
governed by the social practices it shared with these forms. It is through
just such an examination of specific historical practices that one can gain
a better sense of the field of meanings put into play through and by the
cinema. An analysis of discursive interplay among cinema and contemporary institutions of spectacle and sociability will explain how meanings
were made and organized in a unified historical context. It is possible to
recover not the essential truth of what any single individual experienced,
but the collective rules of cultural governance that shaped how movies
were meaningfully integrated into people's everyday lives and how these,
in turn, contributed to the evolution of the rules and cultural roles of the
movies. From the outset, cinema made its claims upon viewers as a subject fabricated through contemporary institutions of leisure, perception,
and industry.

The study of early cinema, the shape and evolution of movies in the
period before 1907, has recently attracted so much scholarly activity that
what counts as knowledge about the first two decades of motion pictures
has thoroughly changed since the 1980s. Books by Charles Musser, Richard Abel, Miriam Hansen, André Gaudreault, Giuliana Bruno, and Noël
Burch and important essays by Tom Gunning and Judith Mayne have collectively transformed the way western early cinema is understood and
taught as a representational system of meaning.[2] The number of journal
issues and collected anthologies, archival screenings, and museum and
professional film society activities devoted to early cinema are nothing
short of a phenomenon in itself.[3] Much of this work focuses on early cinema as a *new* object that seemingly had not yet had time to establish
its own set standards of practices. Early cinema provides a transitional
stage—it is not only the beginning of prevailing practices but also a place
where possibilities that might get closed down or shut out later were still
permissible. An interesting component of the new scholarship on early
cinema has been the "rediscoveries" of modes of representation in early
cinema—from the integral role of the lecturer who "explained" the images to the practices of the creative exhibitor who uniquely organized the
footage and mixed it with other audio and visual forms. Textual practices,
as well, were marked by heterogeneity and even a possibly confusing sig-

nifying system. Scholars of early cinema have opened up definitions for a new understanding of cinema in the present era.

It is best, though, to understand early cinema as a new object through a three-pronged approach, bringing together methods that have often been used separately. One may still begin by studying extant examples of early movies and, from them, hypothesizing representational practices based on theories of cinema and visual representation. This is clearly insufficient, however, as a solitary focus. While film scholars have always done this kind of work with the understanding that it is through the film text that the object of cinema makes itself primarily known or understood, it is immediately apparent in early cinema that the "film text" is an unstable foundation. Early cinema physically exists in small quantities compared to extant films from later periods, and there are often different versions (different lengths, arrangements, colors or tones) of the same examples. Furthermore, early cinema may have often been more like the theater where each performance had ephemeral elements (e.g., sound effects or music, narration, entr'actes) added to it. This material evidence means that there can never be any definitive standard object of study.

Thus, it is important to examine early cinema within a context of actual historical practices. It was through both historical events and a wider array of shared discourse that the specific rules for cinema's operations were laid out. The context, of course, may begin as narrowly as a consideration of manufacturing, distribution, and exhibition factors. But it may also get as broad as the very societies themselves in which film was embedded.

One might productively turn then to the modes of interaction between the cinema and the earliest moviegoers as the means to bridge the *text* and its *context*. This brings together questions about the *spectator* (the ideal or model of someone who is addressed by the films and who is most often intuited from the study of the films themselves) with those about *audiences*, actual demographic groups of people who are defined through conventional methods of social history. Once these separate designs regarding *text* and *context* are united in one purpose, they become something wholly different and unique: a method of learning the ways that knowledge was constituted. The social practices in which cinema was rooted would have directed or influenced how moviegoers made sense of movies. What is most important about cinema as *history* is how audiences were taught to make sense of such spectacle.

The technology or apparatus of cinema may have been recently "invented," but it was implemented alongside and in comparison to existing technologies and using old representational practices. Furthermore, as a

new object, cinema got put to use most immediately in societies under-
going dramatic urban changes and demographic shifts. The period from
the 1880s until the 1920s fixed the making of a consumer society, the inception of the technological, economic, and social landscape in which
we currently live. For many social historians of this period as well as for
film scholars, cinema played a key role in the changing urban landscape.
For Ray Rosenzweig, it was a "refuge from the time discipline of the factory."[4] For Elizabeth Ewen, it "constituted a major source of new ideas."[5]
However much these historians agree upon the significance of cinema,
they focus less on how cinema made itself meaningful as an emerging
cultural institution than on demographics of attendance, location, and
popularity. However much they have drawn attention to the importance
of cinema in the lives of working class and immigrant city dwellers by citing oral histories, reminiscences and autobiographies, and social reformers' interviews, they have paid only cursory attention to the workings of
cinema as a specific intersection of spectacle and sociability.

    Within such a historiographic framework, even one's conception of
the city must change. Massive population and employment shifts due to
intense growth in industrialization were remaking the physical spaces
and institutions of modern city life. Expansion, bureaucratization, and
commercialization at increasingly rapid rates were the hallmarks of late
nineteenth-century cities. Urban leaders responded with a double vision
of diversity and disunity, heterogeneity and homogeneity, tradition and
the future.[6] Those were the terms of ambivalence and even contradiction
that characterized a wide range of their discussions about modern American life.
    Among urban centers in both Europe and the United States, Chicago
best exemplified an emerging modern society attempting to cope with
massive industrial and social changes. The second largest city in the United
States, Chicago was the fastest-growing city in the world and a national
capital of trade and manufacturing. Its population doubled between 1880
and 1890 from half a million to a million, and by 1900, the population
had reached 1.7 million.[7] Much of this increase came from foreign immigration; in 1900, 34.4 percent of the city's population was foreign-born,
42.8 percent was first-generation American-born; only 1.8 percent was
classified as Negro and 20.9 percent identified as native white.[8] Besides
its overflowing population of immigrants and migrants housed in tene-
ments, the city's rapidly expanding middle class (made possible largely

by the upsurge in commerce and trade) also had strong ethnic ties to foreign cultures.

To Americans of the time, Chicago's newness and growth in the decades following the Great Fire of 1871 epitomized an emerging modern America. Although it may be hyperbole, an 1893 guidebook to Chicago put it most succinctly: "Here was a city which had no tradition but was making them, and this was the very thing that every one seemed to understand and rejoice in. Chicago was like no other city in the world, so said they all. Chicago would outstrip every other American city, New York included, and become first of all American, if not European or world, cities."[9] Because Chicago was a regional, national, and international model studied by many as *the* urban laboratory in which to document the social effects of modern industrialism, there exist rich, varied cultural resources describing the city at the turn of the century. These fertile materials provide a rich ground for analysis of how the new movie culture addressed and defined its new urban subjects.

Of particular importance to the changing city in general and to Chicago in particular was the rapidly expanding rate at which women were entering the work force. In the 1880s and 1890s, the U.S. female urban labor force expanded at a rate that doubled the increase in the female population.[10] Chicago attracted women workers at a rate three times greater than in the nation as a whole.[11] As former Chicago journalist Theodore Dreiser noted in his 1900 novel *Sister Carrie,* "In 1889 Chicago had the peculiar qualifications of growth which made such adventuresome pilgrimages even on the part of young girls plausible. Its many and growing commercial opportunities gave it widespread fame, which made of it a giant magnet, drawing to itself, from all quarters, the hopeful and the hopeless."[12] The dramatic effect was that young women suddenly appeared alone on city streets in such large numbers that their public wanderings became a new mobile visible signifier of an independent female sexuality. Their urban presence, movements, and visual accessibility indicated the degree to which young women's activities had become disengaged from the protection of the family, their public identities increasingly associated with a nonreproductive, eroticized sexuality.[13] An important consequence was that the physical institutions of modern city life were remade into sexually integrated spaces.

Among the rapidly increasing numbers of women who migrated or immigrated to Chicago in the last two decades of the nineteenth century, a sizable number boarded or lodged in houses or apartments away from family, relatives, or employers. Popularly known as "women adrift," these

women may have been designated as wandering, but they were also understood as lost and, therefore, requiring saving. Implicit in the popular
term was the middle-class belief that women on the street were, in fact,
"pure and passive orphans threatened with sexual danger."[14]

The "woman adrift" was an important reinscription and containment
of a threatening figure since women's presence and visibility indicated
that the city offered women freedom and a certain amount of independence. As Elizabeth Wilson says,

> The city, a place of growing threat and paranoia to men, might be a place
> of liberation for women. . . .True, on the one hand it makes necessary rou-
> tinised rituals of transportation and clock watching, factory discipline and
> timetables, but despite its crowds and the mass nature of its life, and de-
> spite its bureaucratic conformity, at every turn the city dweller is also of-
> fered the opposite—pleasure, deviation, disruption.[15]

The term's frequent, common usage in turn-of-the-century planning reports, social welfare studies, and government commissions remade the
working girl lured by the pleasures and freedom of the city into the bodily signifier for the city's dangers. Her presence symbolized the possibility
of what was most feared or desired by others. By remaking her as a potential victim in need of constant supervision and protection, reformers
and civic leaders sought to reassert the rigidly gendered geography and
social practices that had previously sustained an orderly image of the city.

Before the 1880s, women's appearances in public were necessarily
codified and regulated according to a well-defined set of conventions.
The respectable woman made herself a public display only when she was
escorted by a gentleman. She and he strolled or rode within the temporal and spatial terms of the promenade, an elite ritual of public social exchange, as bourgeois couples paraded up and down the street nodding
to each other, seeing and being seen.[16] If loitering and alone, a woman
risked being regarded as a prostitute. Thus, city life was organized and
regulated through rigidly gendered spaces that actually mapped discrete
zones according to the type of women's displays contained within them.
Single women aimlessly strolling or assertively occupying public space
signified the sexual and other socially taboo pleasures that were associated with "red-light" districts filled with brothels, gambling houses, opium
dens, dance halls, and saloons. The nineteenth-century city attempted to
pose the control of women as a solution to moral and political order, and
the result was a rigidly dichotomous geography.

Women's unregulated appearances in the changing urban topography in the 1880s and 1890s, however, began to challenge this order and to erode the male's exclusive right to the city. Judith R. Walkowitz summarizes: "Whatever the precipitating causes, the public landscape of the privileged urban flâneur of the period had become an unstable construct: threatened internally by contradictions and tensions and constantly challenged from without by social forces that pressed these dominant representations to be reworked, shorn up, reconstructed."[17] The politics of sexual difference and a rigidly gendered landscape underlaid the flâneur's cosmopolitanism, his representational practices, and his attitude as manifested in the privileged gaze. Walkowitz adds, "No figure was more equivocal, yet more crucial to the structured public landscape of the male flâneur, than the woman in public."[18] As Walkowitz and other feminist scholars have recognized, sexual difference complicates the politics of loitering.[19]

The flâneur was a wandering gentleman observer who looked into the faces of the nineteenth-century urban crowd and put *his* experience to literary form. In common usage, the flâneur was someone who ambled or strolled through city streets and observed life around him. An 1893 *Century Magazine* article defined the contemporary flâneur, "He does not care for facts or objects as such or for what they teach, but he does care for their momentary effect upon his eyes and nerves. He does not crave knowledge, but he delights in impressions. He likes to idle in the city because, if he keeps himself purely receptive, the city prints each instant a fresh picture in his brain."[20] Walter Benjamin identified the Parisian flâneur of the 1830s as a "panoramically situated" spectator who goes "botanizing on the asphalt."[21] Benjamin's flâneur, who emphasized the randomness of his experience, created the impression that he could accurately interpret the crowds around him.

Several critics have extended Benjamin's discussion of the flâneur to posit a new mode of spectatorship, one that absorbs a "ceaseless succession of illusory commodity-like images."[22] In particular, Susan Buck-Morss has concluded that Benjamin's interest was sparked because the flâneur was a figure of a modern spectatorial consumer: "In the flâneur, concretely, we recognize our own consumerist mode of being in the world."[23] For Benjamin, the flâneur was a dialectical figure who presented himself as open to everything but who actually saved himself from the chaos of randomness through his pretensions to epistemological control.

By reducing the city to a panorama or scale model, he transformed urban diversity into a series of miniaturized, accessible images that could be collected, organized and consumed.

The idea of flânerie as practiced in nineteenth-century European cities—the elite practice of aimless strolls, of joyfully mingling with the crowd as a way of knowing the city—provides an important discursive frame for a new urban subjectivity. How flânerie evolved and transformed from its representational practices in European literature to an American context is a beginning for understanding how the pleasures of a consumerist mode of urban knowledge formerly associated with the elitist European flâneur came to dominate as a gendered subjectivity for all classes in late nineteenth-century U.S. culture.

The flâneur was not just a European form of modern consciousness but was transplanted from London culture to U.S. cities in the middle and later nineteenth century. Literary scholar Dana Brand argues that, in the middle of the nineteenth century, the flâneur formed part of this country's tenuous urbanism and cosmopolitanism.[24] Brand's work challenges other literary critics; they have uniformly favored the western frontier as a symbol for the anti-urban recapturing of a premodern innocence in nineteenth-century American literature rather than recognize the flâneur's American presence as especially important for rethinking the origins of modern subjectivity in American settings.

It is especially important to define the flâneur as a gendered subject, as a male for whom the streets were accessible, unrestricted public spaces that posed no physical danger or taint of unrespectability. The female flâneur or flâneuse was not possible until a woman could wander the city on her own. For a woman to assume flânerie in the nineteenth century was to risk being viewed as a prostitute: "The flâneur was simply the name of a man who loitered; but all women who loitered risked being seen as whores, as the term 'street-walker,' or 'tramp' applied to women makes clear."[25] The female street walker was a paradoxical figure—the central image of so many male urban fantasies but also the symbol of a degraded femininity that conflicted with nineteenth-century ideals of domesticated feminine virtue. In a discussion of the obsessive degree to which so many late nineteenth- and early twentieth-century male writers focused their attention on the prostitute, Walkowitz writes: "Women were presumed to be both endangered and a source of danger to those men who congregated in the streets. In the mental map of urban spectators, they lacked autonomy: they were bearers of meaning rather than makers of meaning."[26]

Women in public spaces were symbols and, although they occupied what Walkowitz calls "multivalent symbolic positions" of conspicuous display as well as of class and sexual disorder, they were most often condensed by male writers to a bodily icon of sexual exchange in a market economy. As Anke Gleber protests, the prostitute was not a flâneuse because she "does not have the streets at her disposal any more than she commands the use of her own body. . . . These women form nothing if not the cynically distorted female images of consumption and flânerie in an age of capitalist and sexist exploitation."[27] For example, the flâneur maintained a *purposeless* gaze whereas the prostitute's gaze needs always to be purposeful. A prostitute's physical mobility on the streets was always limited since it was still subject to the controlling gazes and attentions of male passersby, to prejudgment and to prejudices, as well as to police actions or the threat of police harassment that disciplined the prostitute to regulate and to limit her appearances and movements. In other words, she could neither assume the cloak of anonymity associated with the flâneur nor transcend the techniques of power that regulated her through everything from scrutinizing looks to sexual assaults to police encounters and arrests.

As the obsession of so many flâneurs (including Benjamin describing his own city walks), the prostitute became not only the symbol of the flâneur's desire but also the inversion of his imagined power and freedom. If the flâneur required the figure of the prostitute as a character in his world, it was because she provided an acceptable alternative to women's otherwise unaccounted for and untimely appearances. As Mark Seltzer writes about the novels of the period: "The compulsory visibility of the prostitute—the painted woman, who must catch one's eye—draws on an exciting theatricality or illusionism and a charismatic self-absorption and self-abstraction."[28] Her acceptably timed appearances in certain sectors of the city even contributed to the importance of a sexual geography: discreet districts that allowed for more open displays of sexuality and alternative sexual practices helped to maintain an orderliness to the city landscape as an urban adventure that was both knowable and navigable for the flâneur. The prostitute grafted the flâneur's sexual desire onto his sense of urban spatial order as the embodied projection of his desire to see.

In this situation, the strolling female pedestrian's identity depended upon seeing herself as constantly being viewed, upon forms of surveillance and self-censorship. As Susan Buck-Morss says, "Women in capitalist society—all women—impersonate commodities in order to attract a distracted public of potential buyers, a mimesis of the world of things which by Benjamin's time had become synonymous with sexiness."[29] In describing this as generally the modernist process of female subjectivity, Buck-Morss also accounts for the conventions through which women were represented.

Cinema's development, from the outset, was fundamentally part of the urban process of women's spectacularization through her self-display. Venues for movie screenings—vaudeville, amusement parks, and nick-elodeons—became quickly associated with places of amusement characterized by open displays of female sexuality. In their campaigns against commercialized vice that culminated in the early teens, reformers made few distinctions between movie theaters and dance halls, nightclubs, cheap shows, or amusement parks as places frequented by prostitutes and pimps and where sexual danger lurked.

Cinema's beginnings as a social phenomenon stemmed from the urban imagination in the turn-of-the-century American city. They were intertwined with both the fears and pleasures associated with the rapidly changing city. As Richard Maltby summarizes,

> That fantasy [of the woman adrift and entrapped into becoming a prostitute] located the site of sexuality, pleasure, guilt and excess geographically, in the red-light districts of American cities, and [after the turn of the century] it indicted the commercialisation of pleasure in movie theatres, dance halls and cabarets because they encouraged sexual pleasure to escape its geographical bounds and confuse the Victorian dichotomy of public and private. As a place of commercialised pleasure, the cinema was both social space and the site of narrative, and both those activities came under scrutiny.[30]

Cinema can only be understood as a cultural institution when its gendered politics in relationship to the rest of the urban scene are examined, when the social controls that defined it are evaluated, and when the historical practices that marked it as both a social space and the site of narrative are taken into account. Early cinema was thoroughly infused with questions regarding the new visibility of an independent female sexuality and its attendant issues of sexual victims and male predators, of the evils of prostitution, and of urban institutions that pandered to and promoted sexual behavior.

The chapters of this book represent a shift from thinking about the *production* of systems of representation as connected to the new technologies of the turn of the century (the cinematic apparatus per se) to thinking about the *historically specific* relationships between viewer and object seen. Throughout, gender provides the "wedge" through which subjectivity is both a cultural construction and something that must constantly be reworked, remade, and rewarded. Such active work occurs in the practices of the visible—in photography, painting, and cinema—when they are at the service of cultural institutions, such as the department store, the exposition, the amusement park, and even the movie theater. Of course, gender is just one component of subjectivity operating at any given moment in these interactive processes. But it is a helpful way to think about the social construction of the subject, and one with which turn-of-the-century discourse was obsessed.

Part One of this book prepares for the actual onset of cinema by analyzing how the representational and social practices of particular Chicago institutions—the city thoroughfare, the shopping zone of department stores along State Street, and the 1893 Chicago World's Columbian Exposition—were highly regulated, gendered spaces that were paradigmatic for the articulation of female subjectivity at the cinema. These chapters examine the relationship between women's leisure and the construction of a modern female subject by focusing on women's appearances in Chicago's urban spaces. On the basis of evidence from both visual and printed materials—photographs, paintings and drawings, journalists' accounts, autobiographies, novels, advertisements, tourist guidebooks, and early cinema—Part One examines how in each of these urban spaces a staged female spectatorship reconciled the conflicts of the emerging urban space. In other words, these chapters trace out the efforts to teach women about their proper places within the larger visual culture. The discussions of street life, the department store, and the exposition explain how subjective knowledge was constructed, how the phenomenon and evolving status of the tourist-observer was an important process for addressing racial difference, how power operated on the individual body. These sites became the grounds for the practices that constitute modern gendered spectatorship.

Part Two examines the intersection of urban subjectivity and female sexuality in the cinema after 1900. In general, these chapters enlarge the ways that cinema was organized as a social space and a system of visual representation in order to sort out the confusion of an increasingly chaotic city landscape. In 1907, reformers singled out Chicago's movie houses as a technology and site that lured women into lives of vice. By reducing the complexities of urban disorder to the commercial centers that provided a subculture of independent sexual behavior for the masses of young women living in the city, reform discourse aligned cinema with a range of more manageable targets. In amusement parks and in cheap theaters that became popular between 1905 and 1908, cinema offered women expanded opportunities for companionship with other women and for heterosexual courtship.

The rapidly changing shape of late nineteenth-century Chicago gave to the city an aura of crisis, one that tempted some with new pleasures or scared others with sexual danger. The sharp increase in wage labor that brought myriads of diverse ethnic groups of women to the city bifurcated women's daily patterns of work and leisure, resulting in new public and semi-public commercial centers that catered to women's leisure. Of course, not all women participated fully in leisure activities outside the home since both married women and domestic servants did not experience so sharp a division between work and leisure as those on a time clock in the urban marketplace. But there was a dramatic increase in the numbers of young women who did frequent new commercial entertainment centers. In Chicago, where 40 percent of the population was under twenty years of age,[31] the rise of commercial entertainments in general and cinema in particular did much to redefine women's presence in urban spaces as well as the sexual boundaries of the city.

Between 1890 and 1910 in Chicago, the mass construction of such gendered subjects of visual knowledge was a significant means of cultural hierarchy, a technique—ultimately privileged in cinema—by which men and women assumed both social and self-identities. The city became a place where new commercial centers, new representational practices, and a range of public spectacles and reform activities inspired different groups of men and women to assert publicly their own claims for identity. Cinema played a crucial role in the claims of identity as the invention whose social function brought men and women together in the same locale to see and be seen.

Early movies may have constituted a readable language of sexual danger or pleasure personified in women's bodies. But that language can be understood *only* within the ways that the social environments of the theater and the amusement park located audience participants through coding of masculinity and femininity. The legacy of the fair and the department store in the movie theater and the amusement park encouraged a female film spectatorship only within the discourses of visual knowledge common to all these social spaces.

ONE

Women and Sightseeing

1

URBAN TRAVELS

FANTASIES OF FLÂNEURS AND FLIRTS

It may have been your habit of mind to consider drama as occasional; episodic; an artful presentation merely, as set forth on a stage within an isolated house called a theatre. . . . That is but a little truth. The broader, unescapable truth is that you are ever in the midst of a drama; a drama in the open. You are both spectator and actor therein.

LOUIS H. SULLIVAN, *The Autobiography of an Idea*, 1924

As these overworked girls stream along the street, the rest of us see only the self-conscious walk, the giggling speech, the preposterous clothing. And yet through the huge hat, with its wilderness of bedraggled feathers, the girl announces to the world that she is here.

JANE ADDAMS, *The Spirit of Youth and City Streets*, 1910

Sexual liberation for women under capitalism has had the nightmare effect of "freeing" all women to be sexual objects (not subjects). It must be admitted that women have collaborated actively in this process.

SUSAN BUCK-MORSS, "The Flâneur, the Sandwichman, and the Whore," 1986

THE CULTURAL MAPPING OF CHICAGO as it attempted to cope with rapid growth between 1880 and 1910 occurred across a wide variety of texts, from etiquette books to cartoons, from novels to newspaper sketches, and from photographs to movies. The technological improvements, rapid growth, and dissemination of such cultural production transformed city newspapers, contributed to the expansion of photographic reproduction and book publication, and supplied the basis for cinema. Between the 1880s and 1900s, the rise of a commercial culture merged for the first time with popular culture and even supplanted it. It became the first national popular culture. Within this period, popular culture had no more important function than making the new city legible. It did so predominantly in two ways: it depended upon sight as the primary sense for organizing perceptions of the city, and it articulated a crisis of female sexuality, deeply connected to self-seeking women who traversed urban spaces and who were figured either as sexual victims or as predators. This was the chimera that defined the changing city.

For a new generation of writers who were rising to prominence by writing for the cheap penny press, the dense varieties of Chicago street life and its vast potential for pleasure were the same as for the flâneur. One of the most widely read journalists in the country, George Ade, wrote street fables for the *Chicago Daily Record* from 1893 to 1900. Ade specialized in the urban anecdote, transforming the struggles of the working classes, the disparities of wealth and poverty, and the tensions and uncertainties of modern city life into slang-filled, psychological profiles. In Chicago's daily routines, Ade saw regular disappointments, moral downfalls, and social hypocrisy. In the well-heeled tradition of flânerie, Ade often rendered the abundantly fascinating dangers of the city in the bodies of women.

For example, in "The Stenographic Proposal" it is the female "typewriter" who tempts the young male stenographer every day through her mere presence. For she is a respectable woman adrift, the daughter of an upper-class civic leader who recently bequeathed his family only debts.[1] She agrees to marry her boss before the stenographer has an opportunity to propose marriage. The description of the boss's proposal resembles a primal scene, a conversational exchange silently observed and recorded by the unseen stenographer from an open doorway. By writing down the conversation in shorthand, he masters his sense of the loss of the object of his desire.

Ade's outlook may be similar to the flâneur's. But he no longer writes from a vantage point in the thick of the crowd. He offers up the city and its inhabitants as "characters" largely from the distance of an implied visual frame. He is like the stenographer of his creation. His vantage point is that of the voyeur, the stationary unseen "invisible" spectator who is described as "a guilty eavesdropper."[2] He watches and listens, an observer whose position is like that of the cinema spectator.

In another sketch entitled "From the Office Window," Ade's protagonist is just such a cinematically situated observer, a young Chicago office clerk promoted to a windowed office that allows him to look into four windows in the opposite building.[3] Ade's clerk Ruggles is heir to the flâneur as the interpreter of urban life but, more significantly, father to the cinema spectator as he learns the semiotics of the sun's reflections and shadows on the windows across the court. He has been repositioned and distanced from the thick of the action through the imposition of the glass, which serves both as a frame for a series of images and as a partition that removes him from physical immersion in the events being depicted, keeping him especially apart from the dangers of female sexuality. His social anonymity and invisibility are heightened but at the expense of mobility as he becomes a stationary *seeing* observer for whom life as a panorama rolls by and is theatrically framed as though for his observation.

First, he watches in the lower two windows an old man working. As he listens to the man whistle, he notes that the man's emaciated body, slow-moving gestures, and out-of-date tunes cannot signify newness or modernity. So Ruggles shifts his attention to the upper two windows, where he observes an elderly woman introducing two policemen to a young girl. Rather than watch the repetitive motions of the old man at labor, he observes daily the sexual scenario of competitive courtship in the two upper windows. Work and sexual pleasure are here contrasted as the two poles that the city has to offer a young man. Rather than *listen* to the old man, he is charmed by *watching* the silent narrative unfold. But then the young girl disappears from the scenario, and "for a time Ruggles looked in vain for the girl."[4] After her disappearance, he is transferred to another office "half across the continent" for nearly a year.[5] When he returns, he "slipped into his old seat with a feeling of comfort and satisfaction. The wall and the bit of sky seemed to welcome him."[6] Here, Ruggles plays out the scenario of the cinema spectator, whose relationship to the images before him is figured as a sequence of possession and loss of the female body connected to the possession and loss of light-reflected images. His return to the symbolic "theater of cinema" is represented as pleasurable, and his "sigh of relief that nothing had happened" since his absence—his hope that the narrative waited just for him—is disappointed by the appearance of the girl looking older, "not quite so merry-faced," and with a baby in her arms.[7]

"From the Office Window," like many of Ade's stories, intertwines female sexuality and a hint of illicit sex with the attractions and dangers of the urban environment. But, since the stories are narrated from a safe distance of an invisible male spectator, there is no possibility of contamination. James Gilbert summarizes, "[Ade] emphasizes his [the clerk's] detachment, his vaguely aroused interest, his safe separation through the glass. With his unproven assumptions and his wink at the reader, Ade underscores this point of view and suggests a literary syntax in which to place the most tragic events. Even scandalous incidents in the lives of others could be counted as mere curiosities."[8] The inscribed spectator is not subject to the danger of becoming objectified and consumed by the gaze of another. Gilbert notes the significance of this observational position: "[Ade's stories] provide a glimpse of something illicit; he lights a flicker of salaciousness and then quickly extinguishes it. . . . Diversity, poverty, danger, inhabit the city, he says, but they can be transformed or evaded."[9] The new modern figure of consciousness required a different kind of legitimization, one that conferred upon him the authority for reasserting the social hierarchy that was continuously being challenged in a City of Babel. The voyeur's power of surveillance supports his position of visual superiority in the construction of subjective knowledge while it extends the pleasures of a consumerist mode of knowledge, formerly associated only with the elitist flâneur, to the common man.

Tourist guidebooks also described the changing city and made similar recommendations for how to participate in it. Like Ade's street fables, they encouraged a new type of urban flânerie, strolls that never completely immersed the visitor in the city. Available in expanded numbers for the 1893 Chicago World's Columbian Exposition, guidebooks advised tourists to consume the city through a series of visual impressions received from a distance.

Their ideal was to remake the city as a panorama by offering to men "nocturnal rambles" through the "Bad Lands of Chicago"—its gambling and drinking district, the Chinese quarter and opium dens, the Jewish and Italian ethnic neighborhoods, and cheap hotels and brothels. For women, the books suggested shopping and strolls in parks.[10] Although the flâneur-turned-tourist still wandered the city streets, his ramble was no longer purposeless and had an itinerary that was expressly not for partaking of any of these offerings but solely for observing from a distance the "haunt[s] of color and habitat."[11] One guidebook expressly stated: "If you are in search of evil, in order to take part in it, don't look here for guidance. This book merely proposes to give some hints as to how the dark, crowded, hard-working, and sometimes criminal portions of the city *look* at night" [emphasis mine].[12]

Such harmless sightseeing or "slumming" in dangerous neighborhoods became a common enough occurrence that in 1905 and 1908 two films even satirized it. *Lifting the Lid* (American Mutoscope & Biograph, 1905) begins with an exterior of a busy street scene and a departing tourist motor coach. In a series of subsequent interiors shot on studio stage sets, a

CHICAGO'S STATE STREET AT NIGHT, LOOKING NORTH FROM ADAMS STREET, C. 1907. *Postcard.*

guide with a megaphone ushers the hapless tourists through the very haunts that the guidebooks described. They visit an Irish clubhouse labeled "Mike Duffy Association," a Chinese chop suey house where they try to eat with chopsticks, an opium den where a country bumpkin tries to have a smoke, and a dance hall where prostitutes dance and mingle with the patrons and waiters. At the dance hall, the performance of a Salome dance so excites the country rube that he jumps on stage and grabs the dancer. In the resulting mayhem, the tour guide ushers out his charges. The film then ends simply with the touring coach returning to its initial point of departure and the sightseers disembarking. *The Deceived Slumming Party* (American Mutoscope & Biograph, 1908) pursues an almost identical scenario and offers up the same stock set of characters and "Bad Lands" sights. It introduces an additional satirical element by showing each scene before the tourists arrive and the local inhabitants staging vice for the tourists upon their appearance. In each scene, after the tourists depart, the tour guide returns to the room and pays off the "actors."

Because women's unescorted appearances in the "Bad Lands" typified them as prostitutes, the guidebooks alternatively mapped out proper spaces in which female tourists could wander safely in the city environment. Women tourists apparently followed this advice. For example, when a group of Missouri schoolteachers visited the Chicago World's Columbian Exposition, the only other parts of the city they visited (always accompanied by male chaperones) were nearby parks and architectural landmarks. They took in Washington Park, Lincoln Park, the park-like boulevard along Lake Shore Drive, and they made what one of their male chaperones described as "a very circumspect pilgrimage" to view the downtown skyscrapers.[13] An Iowa farm woman visiting Chicago in the fall of 1893 only took time off from the Exposition to spend a day visiting the department stores on State Street, to walk past Chicago's mansions on Prairie Avenue and Lake Shore Drive, and to ride through Lincoln Park.[14]

The books may have mediated the confusion and noise for which Chicago's ethnically diverse streets were famous. But they also explicitly maintained the strict division of gendered public spaces that was the familiar landscape of the flâneur. For a woman, the model was to restrict her public wanderings to an activity that could both time her appearances according to a regularized schedule and contain her visibility as a symbol of conspicuous display within strict urban geographic boundaries. The guidebooks even included the name and address of a commercial service that existed solely to aid women in following this practice; the "Women's Directory, Purchasing and Chaperoning Society" on Van Buren Street provided escorts to help women who were unfamiliar with Chicago to negotiate the city streets and stores in the appropriate ways.[15]

Such middle-class dicta for city behavior as exemplified by guidebooks or Ade's journalistic sketches may not always have encompassed actual lower- and working class behavior and, indeed, it was the very contrast between what middle-class authorities claimed and working class women's appearances provided that posed a crisis in the 1890s. The more that women were publicly assertive, the more vigorously popular stereotypes for feminine good conduct attempted to exert a fantasy of social control over women's appearances. For example, late nineteenth-century etiquette books were preoccupied with a civic order in which a woman could appear unescorted on city streets but should do so "seeing and hearing nothing. . . . She is always unobtrusive, never talks loudly, or laughs boisterously, *or does anything to attract the attention of the passers-by*" [emphasis mine].[16] In other words, the newly independent respectable woman should neither see nor be seen. She should ideally be both blind and invisible! Guy Szuberla confirms that these books were important not so much as social documents of urban life but as a "careful coding of identity and 'ceremonial expressions' in the city's public places [which attempted to] regulate desire and properly maintain gender divisions."[17] He points out the books' shared assumption that the "mantle of reserve" with which a woman should carry herself on the streets could so outfit her that even if she were walking alone at night her appearance and demeanor would be so thoroughly understood that she could pass unmolested.

But the more that the etiquette books insisted this was so the more that dime novel authors, journalists like Ade, and novelists like Theodore Dreiser contradicted and parodied the ideal of the woman alone on the street, negating the semiotic codes of the etiquette books and reconstructing them. For example, popular novels about women's abduction into "white slavery" or forced prostitution often began with a young—usually working class—girl walking alone in the twilight or early evening, returning from home or school. Although she might circumspectly be wearing her "mantle of reserve," the masher approaches her anyway and effects a seemingly harmless flirtation, as in the 1910 bestseller *The House of Bondage:* "I'm not used to the beesness [of being a traveling salesman], un' I'm lonesome, un' I only vondered if you vouldn't go vit me to a moving-picture show, or something, this evening."[18] The very codes that had been designed to regulate desire are undercut for the purpose of reconfiguring the lower-class girl in particular as a victim of the procurer. The narrator of this novel expresses this in an omniscient voice that editorializes on the girl's vulnerability: "Young life was a period of menial service from which the sole escape was marriage, whether to stranger or to friend. That a stranger should harm her was, to Mary—as it is to most girls of her age and environment—an idea unentertained: strangers were too few, and the world of moral fact too closely shut and guarded."[19] In portraying the young woman singularly "unprotected" by her marital status as an innocent walking alone on the street, the author necessarily participated in a culture that contradictorily urged young women to be independent while they should simultaneously abide by traditional codes of male protection.[20]

The subject of this contradiction was everywhere taken up. Magazine cartoons, in particular, satirized the codes of conduct popularized by the etiquette books. For example, one cartoon entitled "An Idea" shows three dandies collectively admiring a handsome woman. They lean forward in unison to look at her statically posed upright figure. The caption reads: "I say, boys, since she has refused all three of us individually I say we follow her home and try it as a body. She couldn't resist us."[21] The fact of women's public appearances by themselves as provocateurs for new male street behaviors becomes a humorous topical subject for dizzyingly overturned traditions of respectability.

Such cartoons also appropriated the privilege of the gaze for women walking alone on nighttime city streets. As a well-dressed woman waits next to a street lamp for a streetcar in one cartoon entitled "Unprotected Female," she looks off in the direction of a well-dressed man approaching her from the background. The caption reads: "Oh my! I wish that car would hurry. Here comes a man, and I'm just sure he will insult me!" In the next panel, the gentleman stands facing front in the foreground, and the lady gazes at his back: "Humph! He didn't even look at me!" [22] The joke depends upon a satire of codes of conduct and a notion that women appropriate the gaze—the act of seeing—only for the purpose of making themselves *seen* as an object of male desire.

Using timeworn devices, other cartoons play on the presumed reciprocity of seeing as a sexual contract. For example, the well-dressed man, thereby coded as a gentleman, who gazes at the woman standing alone

➤ "AN IDEA." *Cartoon from* Life *8, 23 September 1886, 177.*

AN IDEA.

Cholly: I SAY, BOYS, SINCE SHE HAS REFUSED ALL THREE OF US INDIVIDUALLY I SAY WE FOLLOW HER HOME AND TRY IT AS A BODY. SHE COULDN'T RESIST US.

Unprotected Female: Oh my! I wish that car would hurry. Here comes a man, and I'm just sure he will

Unprotected Female (after gentleman has passed): Humph! he didn't even look at me.

"UNPROTECTED FEMALE." *Cartoon from* Life *11, 12 January 1888, 25.*

with her back to him passes in front of the woman in the next panel so that her face is revealed as a grotesque both to the gentleman and the reader.[23] Another *Life* cartoon depicts the man in one panel so absorbed in watching a woman standing alone on the corner that, in the next panel, he falls into an open manhole.[24] It is interesting that this example's caption, "Ah! She sees me!" uses *her* appropriation of the gaze as the trigger for his literal downfall. Szuberla suggests that the circulation of these representations of street interactions helped to open up a space for the social acceptability of women's flirtations on the street: "The sign systems, which had simply and confidently distinguished a lady from a woman of the street, and a gentleman from a masher, veered off dizzily into contradictions and complexity."[25] Yet, Szuberla does not recognize the degree to which "the flirt" functions as a more socially acceptable stereotype of the urban woman pedestrian than the prostitute because she is a more culturally approved object of desire. Nevertheless, she is equally a construction of masculine desire that both maintains the gendered hierarchy of newly sexually integrated spaces and reconfigures the independent woman as a woman who seeks out or who simply embodies the site of

AH, SHE SEES ME!   —!   —!!—!!!

~ "AH! SHE SEES ME." *Cartoon from* Life 8, 4 November 1886, 274.

masculine desire. She is the woman whose freedom on the city street is expressly designed in order to allow her to remake herself as spectacle.

The photographer Sigmund Krausz extended this newly configured relationship in *Street Types of Chicago with Literary Sketches by Well-Known Authors* (1892). Krausz accompanied three-quarter-length studio photographic portraits of Chicago street types with prose sketches that animated and gave meaning to the wooden, highly theatrical, and artificially lighted poses.[26] "Out for a Stroll" offers a young lady wearing a hat and carrying an open parasol.[27] She looks over her shoulder into the foreground, her eyes slightly cast downward, her face expressionless. She "sees," but it is coded as a demure act of gazing. The prose accompanying the photograph identifies her as a "stenographer and typewriter" who is walking down State Street on her lunch hour and who is smiling "as she turns a side glance at a handsome young fellow."[28] Indeed, the prose narrativizes the photographically static woman's body by locating its agency in an unthreatening sexual "flirtation," a stolen look that harmlessly enriches her few moments of midday leisure in her workday world.

Krausz's flirt makes her appearance actually followed by another photograph, one of a man in suit and top hat.[29] He leans slightly forward in an active posture, his left hand twirling the end of his handlebar mustache, his right hand slung into his pants pocket as he gazes off into the distance. These two gestures and his posture code him as caught in the act of desire, the mustache twirling a sign of delightful anticipation and his body position and hand in pocket an air of casual nonchalance. His gaze provides an eyeline match to the flirt's, and its placement in the book following hers makes it act in modern terms quite cinematically as the reverse shot of her look at him. In other words, his photo returns the

"OUT FOR A STROLL." *Photograph from Sigmund Krausz's* Street Types of Chicago with Literary Sketches by Well-Known Authors, *1892, ICHi-03133. Courtesy of Chicago Historical Society.*

gaze of hers, and its caption locks in such a spatial and temporal connection with its remark of surprised response: "Ah There!" By her juxtaposition to this photograph, the flirt may look but she looks—and with her eyes cast downward demurely at that—only to be held as the object of a male sexualized gaze.

Krausz's flirt is reproduced in Carrie Meeber, the protagonist of Theodore Dreiser's realist 1900 novel, *Sister Carrie,* about one young girl's struggles through the moral confusion of the turn-of-the-century city. Like "the flirt," Carrie also goes "out for a stroll," an act that publicly claims the space and urban rights of the flâneur. Lonely at night in the laborers' flat she shares with her sister and brother-in-law, Carrie stands in the doorway and looks out at the Chicago street. One night she ventures out a bit: "Her easy gait and idle manner attracted attention of an offensive but common sort. She was slightly taken back at the overtures of a well-dressed man of thirty, who in passing looked at her, reduced his pace, turned back, and said; 'Out for a little stroll, are you, this evening?'"[30] Carrie backs off and hurries home since "there was something in the man's look which frightened her."[31] Szuberla celebrates both Krausz's flirt and this passage in Dreiser's *Carrie* as a new scripting for women's public claims to identity. He argues that they "openly look in the faces of the strangers that they meet—as if they were as free as men to do so."[32] Szuberla mistakes the appearances of such public inscriptions for a freedom from or overturning of traditional gender hierarchies.

Carrie is an important reworking of an existing stereotype who does repeatedly appropriate the privileged gaze. Yet in the course of the novel she learns to identify with the carefully controlled, feminized desire of the shopper. Her effort to claim the rights of the flâneur rewrites her in the social terms of the street coding of masculine looks and desires. It is her demeanor, her bodily claim to flânerie in her "easy gait and manner" that Dreiser reconfigures as the embodiment of sexual desire, as the site and origin for attracting sexual attention. The woman alone cannot be a flâneur, a fact further reinforced by her acknowledgment of the gendered organization of looking relations, by her reaction to "the man's look which frightened her." Carrie no more has the streets at her disposal than does the prostitute, and the progress of the novel depends upon her learning to contain her desire to see within acceptable confines.

By the time she hooks up with the traveling salesman Drouet outside the city's big department stores, she has learned, like Krausz's flirt, how to reclaim her public identity and to enjoy the attention her appearance has attracted. She has learned to see amid the act of being seen in a sex-

꘎ **"AH THERE!"** *Photograph from Sigmund Krausz's* Street Types of Chicago with Literary Sketches by Well-Known Authors, *1892, ICHi-03123. Courtesy of Chicago Historical Society.*

ualized context: "Not only did Carrie feel the drag of desire for all of which was new and pleasing in apparel for women, but she noticed, too, with a touch at the heart, the fine ladies who elbowed and ignored her, brushing past in utter disregard of her presence."[33] In this way, Dreiser attaches importance to clothes, to a woman's mimicking a store mannequin, as a prerequisite for visibility. Carrie's *invisibility* to other women in contradistinction to the "fine ladies" around her is an indication of her non-existence, an acknowledgment that ignites a new desire in her for "what the city [holds]—wealth, fashion, ease—every adornment for women . . . for dress and beauty."[34] Once Carrie takes command of the society of consumption by becoming a public object of consumption herself—a theater star who displays herself on the stage and is additionally made into a representation for display on posters and in the newspapers—she is able to feel that her existence is real: "To stare seemed the proper and natural thing. Carrie found herself stared at and ogled. . . . With a start she awoke to find that she was in fashion's throng, on parade in a showplace [the department store]—and such a showplace."[35] Carrie's "rise" to a status of visibility depends upon both her spectacularization and her self-identity as an object of spectacle. While the implications for Szuberla may well be a newly available kind of flâneuserie extended to women, the flirt's gaze is merely a socially broadened analogue of the prostitute's: it still needs always to be purposeful and its meaning is limited by the controlling gazes and attentions of male passersby.

Nowhere was the creation of male desire through the urban politics of seeing and being seen more fully condensed than through the narration and representation of *What Happened on Twenty-third Street, New York City,* a 1901 Edison Manufacturing Company film. Set on an actual city street rather than on a studio stage, the short one-shot film records urban passersby and a couple—not dissimilar to Drouet and Carrie—who walk into the foreground when the breeze from a city grate lifts up the woman's skirt. The film relies upon cinema's heterogeneous origins in commercial amusements for its subject matter and representational strategies—the amusement park ride and burlesque device of air jets that suddenly and surprisingly lift women's skirts, both on stage and on park ride entrances and exits.

But the mimetic representation of public urban space in this film complicates any easy reading of its scenario as mere theatrical artifice. Instead, as an actuality film, it opens a space for women's appearances that sets the real city street as a *stage* for the purpose of a female spectacle. The visual framing signifies both nature and artifice, reality and illusion-

WHAT HAPPENED ON TWENTY-THIRD STREET, NEW YORK CITY
(Edison Manufacturing Company, 1901).

ism through its centering of a city street into which male passersby come and go without ever cutting directly across the central space. Indeed, a young boy starts to cut across the center, but stops and walks around an imagined spatial boundary, an area carved out for the camera by its exclusionary status, an area that seems to appear as an open space defined by its availability, emptiness, and possibilities expressly for the camera's eye. Thus, the couple that starts from the deep background and walks toward the foreground—in a direct rear to front promenade—enters into a space already demarcated, already asserted as a "stage." (Here, I disagree with Tom Gunning's interpretation that "our original attention is . . . diffused across the shot, solicited by many little events, none of which seem to have any narrative purpose."[36]) The city street is made over into a theatricalized stage neither by the apparent artifice of apparatus like lighting effects nor by its psychic distanciation from spectators in the cinema but by an onscreen implied set of internal spatial boundaries. In addition, the formal placement or centered framing of the rectangular grate on the sidewalk reinforces an overall formal composition of weightiness and solidity to the central space. The couple walks into that already demarcated space—that space set up to be a theater of tricks, trick effect, magic, or illusion.

If this is a representation of urban space that purposely defines the street as a *stage* for spectacle, the process of female spectacularization was also complicated by the looking relations established before her appearance by inscribed onscreen spectators who look at the camera. The woman is not party to or a part of these onscreen, knowing spectators who acknowledge the camera's presence. This is markedly different from a film like *Trapeze Disrobing Act* (Edison Manufacturing Company, 1901) in which the woman on a literally figured stage returns the look of both the camera and the onscreen spectators. In this film, a woman performs a striptease on a trapeze swing in front of two country rubes who sit in a box seat on the left and respond in a too enthusiastic fashion to her stage act. The woman's inscribed look back at the camera suggests a tacit contract between her and both real and implied spectators, an agreement to her status as looked-at object. The rubes' responses and return of the gaze contribute to the increased narrativization of the woman's participation in staging herself as spectacle. Her movements, her stripping of clothing as she reveals more of her body, her athletic prowess on the swing make her a different kind of subject from the woman on Twenty-third Street who has no opportunity to acknowledge the presence of a space already marked for spectacle. She "naively" enters into it. Because she does not share the knowledge of other onscreen participants, the film produces a hierarchy of knowledge that casts the spectator in the theater at the top of the hierarchy, the male onscreen observers in the middle, and the woman at the bottom. The lifting of the woman's skirt becomes a moment of voyeuristic pleasure for the spectator in a way that *Trapeze Disrobing Act* cannot: nothing interferes with the direct gaze of the spectator at the eroticized object. Here an erotically charged moment is first authorized temporally by onscreen lookers who then disappear so that

TRAPEZE DISROBING ACT *(Edison Manufacturing Company, 1901).*

nothing interferes with the look of the spectator at the woman's billowing and lifting skirts.

The conclusion of this little vignette is deceptively enigmatic. After she holds down her uplifted skirt, the woman laughs, looks at her male partner, and for a moment glances at the camera. Is this a moment in which her laugh and look express her own delight in the rush of air up her dress, an admission of her sexual pleasure in her own body? Is this an acknowledgment of the look of the camera, breaking or rupturing the voyeuristic situation of which she has been the victim? One might conclude that her look does both: it is a moment of *jouissance* or sexual sensory pleasure in the surface of her own body as well as a retrospective authorization of the rather tacit contract of looking relations demarcated in *Trapeze Disrobing Act.* One might even conclude that her look and laugh put the easiness of that psychic scenario into doubt or question.

It seems equally important, however, that her glance at the camera— it is only there for a second—is followed by her departure into the foreground and offscreen and then by male passersby who traverse at angles from both sides the space that she has just occupied. These spectators do not acknowledge the camera's presence but stare in the direction of the figure of the departing woman. Thus, in a fairly complex move, the scenario repeats the spatialized looking relations with which it started and returns the woman to the object of the male gaze, setting a final temporal marker for the authority of voyeurism. Her laugh and look function within the narrative as a marginal representation at best, a momentary fracture of a scenario of locking her into a tradition of representing male desire. In fact, this film is important precisely because it exemplifies the articulation of gendered looking relations in a rudimentary narration. It differentiates sexual object and looking subject and thus constructs a specifically cinematic *male spectator* as an implied aspect of the text.

Structures of exhibitionism generally guided early cinema, producing films based on their ability to *show* something and characterized initially by the recurring look at the camera by actors and later by their activation of an implied male spectator. This dominant trait in films made before 1906 has led Tom Gunning to label early cinema the cinema of attractions: "The cinema of attractions directly solicits spectator attention, inciting visual curiosity, and supplying pleasure through an exciting spectacle—a unique event, whether fictional or documentary, that is of interest in itself."[37] Within this conception of cinema, the modern display of women occurred in two ways: the self-presentation of the body eroticized in motion and the woman's direct look into the camera.[38]

Some films featured full shots of women dancing before the camera, such as *Annabelle Butterfly Dance* (Edison Manufacturing Company, 1895), *Annabelle Serpentine Dance* (Edison Manufacturing Company, 1895), *Crissie Sheridan* (Edison Manufacturing Company, 1897), *Ella Lola, a la Trilby* (Edison Manufacturing Company, 1898), or *Turkish Dance, Ella Lola* (Edison Manufacturing Company, 1898). *A Nymph of the Waves* (American Mutoscope & Biograph, 1903) features Catarina Bartho in a frilly hat and flouncy long dress as she performs her infamous "speedway" dance in front of a projection of Niagara Falls' rushing waters. In *Karina* (American Mutoscope & Biograph, 1902), a woman in a low backed gown repeatedly lifts her dress up to her waist for a full frontal view of her body as she executes a can-can dance. These films assert the physicality of the women's body surfaces; their entire bodies signify pleasure.[39] These films also offer up women as more than objects or still lives for the camera. The women's constant motion coupled with the moving flow of rising and falling dress fabrics alternately reveals and covers their bodies from view. The subject is a perfect demonstration of the new limits of the technology.

Other films similarly featured women doing exercises for the camera. For example, *Latina, Physical Culture Poses No. 1* (American Mutoscope & Biograph, 1905), *Latina, Physical Culture Poses No. 2* (American Mutoscope & Biograph, 1905), *Latina, Contortionist* (American Mutoscope & Biograph, 1905), and *Latina, Dislocation Act* (American Mutoscope & Biograph, 1905) all show the same performer contorting her body into unusual poses for the camera while she looks directly at the camera. *Her Morning Exercise*'s (American Mutoscope & Biograph, 1902) full frontal shot of a woman in a translucent nightgown as she exercises with a pulley overdetermines the erotic coding of a woman's body. She smiles directly at the camera; her look and the veiling of her body allow for interplay of concealment and revelation that more fully stages the activity of exercise as a highly sexualized spectacle.

The sight of the female body was not the only site of erotic possibility. In such films as *Sandow* (American Mutoscope & Biograph, 1896), *Sandow* (American Mutoscope & Biograph, 1902), *Sandow* (American Mutoscope & Biograph, 1903), *M. Lavelle, Physical Culture No. 1* (American Mutoscope & Biograph, 1905), and *M. Lavelle, Physical Culture No. 2* (American Mutoscope & Biograph, 1905), the sight of the male body in tights displaying muscular development, posing, and rippling chest muscles turned the male body as well into sexualized spectacle. These films, however, were not so much defined through the codes of sexual difference that spectacularize the women through the play of bodily concealment and revelation (as in *What Happened on Twenty-third Street* and other titles) as through the exhibition of a hyper-sexualized body, in these cases, an already known or famous extraordinary body.

Films like *The Physical Culture Girl* (Edison Manufacturing Company, 1903), *The Broadway Massage Parlor* (American Mutoscope & Biograph, 1905), *The Athletic Girl and the Burglar, No. 2* (American Mutoscope & Biograph, 1905) set up physical culture not purely as an activity of exhibitionism but conflate it with flirtation and female sexuality, offering an increasingly fetishistic display of women's bodies. In *The Physical Culture Girl,* the young woman performs for the camera not on a barren stage but within a fictional location of a bedroom. Her activity of exercising is not constructed as self-display through the look *at* the camera; she does not even acknowledge the camera's presence throughout her routine. She awakens in bed, stretches, rises, hits a punching bag, juggles Indian clubs, and performs calisthenics. The film constructs her as an ordinary girl caught unawares in her everyday world. Her body is displayed but not as part of an inscribed reciprocal agreement between spectator and object. In *The Broadway Massage Parlor,* a mother and daughter enter an establishment divided in two by a wall. The daughter gets a facial massage from a man on one side of the wall while the mother lifts weights on the other side. As the man massages the young woman's face, he kisses her, and she reciprocates until the mother enters and bops him on the head with a dumbbell. In *The Athletic Girl and the Burglar, No. 2,* a woman works out while a burglar sneaks by her. She sees him, pummels and subdues him with dumbbells, then stands over him raising her arm and dumbbell in a victorious gesture.

＞┳ THE BROADWAY MASSAGE PARLOR *(American Mutoscope & Biograph, 1905).*

Other films rely on different "natural" pretexts than exercising to put the female body on display for the camera. *Model Posing Before Mirror* (American Mutoscope & Biograph, 1903) simply offers a candid shot of a woman in a body stocking striking a series of poses in front of her looking glass. It theatricalizes the intimacy of a woman's boudoir and allows for a sneaky peek, providing the audience the position of the voyeur. *Must Be in Bed Before Ten* (American Mutoscope & Biograph, 1903), most likely shot around the same time as the previous film, similarly takes place in a woman's bedroom, where a lovely young woman disrobes. She removes her jacket, dress, corset, chemise, underslip, and both stockings as she apparently is caught in the act of getting ready for bed. She does not acknowledge the presence of the camera. For Judith Mayne, this increasing narrativization of women's bodies is an important part of early cinema.[40]

The "naturalization" of such female display reaches its height in early cinema in such films as *What Happened on Twenty-third Street* and *Soubrette's Troubles on a Fifth Avenue Stage* (Edison Manufacturing Company, 1901). The films are interesting companion pieces, especially since they were likely conceptualized at the same time (they were copyrighted on the same day) and feature the same woman. In *Soubrette's Troubles,* a busy street scene offers up an actuality view from the corner of an intersection. A stage pulls up to the corner. A man disembarks, and a woman tries to climb down from the top deck of the omnibus. As the man attempts to offer her his assistance, the wind whips up and lifts up her skirt to reveal her legs from the knees down. She looks behind her and then heads off down the street with the man. Such narrativization denies the actress the look at the camera and her acknowledgment of being seen in an act of self-display. It engenders a psychic scenario connected to the apparatus of cinema that models through the camera's mediation the differentiation of sexual object and looking subject and emphatically segregates filmic and theater or viewing space. It constructs a specifically cinematic *spectator* as an implied aspect of the text—rather than as part of an empirical audience—along gendered divisions.

Of course, the self-display and exhibition of the female body specifically for the spectator as voyeur relies upon the theatrical tradition of burlesque that plays upon frustration of the desire to see. Such films as *From Show Girl to Burlesque Queen* (American Mutoscope & Biograph, 1903) explicitly mimicked the erotic stage show for the camera: a woman smiles at the camera as she takes off various articles of clothing. She bends over and looks into a mirror—all the while unbuttoning her dress—and discards the dress, draping it over a chair. She pulls down one strap of her underslip and then goes behind a screen. She throws the slip over the top of the screen, reaches her arm out slowly from behind the screen and grabs a towel on the dresser, then emerges in a showgirl's scanty costume. She picks up a pointer from under a stack of clothing on the chair and strikes a pose just as a young man in costume walks in from a rear door and looks at her. This film exemplifies a tacit exchange of looking relations wherein the performer understands she is the object of the gaze and performs for it. Yet, unlike the live situation where performer and spectator share the same space although it may be divided between stage and audience, there can be no reciprocal exchange of looks here since

➤ FROM SHOW GIRL TO BURLESQUE QUEEN *(American Mutoscope & Biograph, 1903).*

the presumed male spectator for whom she displays herself is present only through a temporal disjuncture. Thus, the film solidifies her status as the complicit object of the gaze by the onscreen entrance of a male looker whose gaze stands in for the spectator's. (This situation conforms to Benjamin's description in "The Work of Art in the Age of Mechanical Reproduction" regarding the difference between the actor who performs for a live audience and the film actor who performs for the as-yet-to-be-realized presence of a spectator. Although he does not acknowledge how gender contributes to what the terms of the new condition are, Benjamin describes the shift as significant for the spectator's increased identification with the camera rather than with the performer.)[41]

Like Mayne, Janet Staiger says there is no doubt that exotic dance films, stripteases like *Trapeze Disrobing Act,* and even disrobing acts that had a narrative pretext (getting ready for bed, putting on a swimsuit, modeling a corset) were all predominantly understood as having a "wicked nature" in their prurient representation of female sexuality regardless of whether the source material had first been performed in the theater, vaudeville, or lowly burlesque.[42] (However, Robert C. Allen points out that disrobing dancers and performers in this period always stripped down only to flesh-colored body stockings, and bodily "revelation" often occurred behind backlighted opaque screens or translucent screens.[43] This scenario was also true in cinema [e.g., *Birth of the Pearl,* American Mutoscope & Biograph, 1903, *Must Be in Bed Before Ten, Model Posing Before Mirror*] where the nudity was never as complete as is suggested.) These films, according to Staiger and Mayne, are the prototypes for *What Happened on Twenty-third Street.*

Staiger is right that the cinematic apparatus invited a new perceptual closeness to the women's bodily movements and, by extension, offered up a new intimacy. It allowed for a view of the woman's body whereby even if she returned the spectator's gaze, it would always be incommensurable with the spectator's. In this way, cinema transformed the process of mutual looking relations endemic to vaudeville and burlesque and continually being renegotiated on city streets. As Allen observes about the woman dancer's representation in cinema, "Her returning gaze had less power to unsettle since the gulf that separated the displayed woman from the man who looked at her was an unbridgeable, material gulf. He could look; she could only appear to look at him."[44] In this regard, movies made meaning differently than did live shows.

These films were most often shown, however, as part of vaudeville programs. Thus, their meanings were dependent upon their differentiation from other vaudeville acts as a *cinema* novelty *and* their similarity to other acts for their generic rules, performance styles, and gendered conventions. Their historical reception was intertwined with their status as vaudeville entertainment. In fact, most of the performers who made exotic dance films were themselves vaudeville headliners, and their films would likely have been understood as actualities or recordings of their celebrated acts. For example, Catarina Bartho (*A Nymph of the Waves*) performed at Koster and Bial's vaudeville house and at New York City roof gardens between 1896 and 1903, and her act included not only the speedway dance that she filmed but a can-can, a toe dance, and a dance jumping on and off tables at the roof gardens.[45] Her publicity releases credited her with a background in Russian ballet, and she was not the only "ballerina-turned-vaudevillian" whose repertoire mixed forms of high and low culture.[46] Indeed, it is likely that New York film producers located Bartho and such other exotic dancers as Fatima, Carmencita, or Ella Lola at the vaudeville theaters and roof gardens where they were employed. Thus, while it is important to consider the structures of exhibitionistic self-display and uniquely cinematic syntax that guided the depiction of women in early cinema, it is equally important to remember that the shape of cinema could not by any means be understood to be a cinema with its own self-enclosed, internal logic. Cinema neither presented its products nor made its subject matter legible independently from other forms of contemporary entertainment. Many of these subjects—partially clad showgirls backstage or at home, women getting ready for bed, physical culture girls, living picture models—were already popular topics not only in vaudeville and burlesque acts but in other forms of mass commercial entertainment. They were prevalent subjects of stereopticon slides, cards of twin photographs seen simultaneously through a special viewer to produce a three-dimensional appearance. Such stereograph viewing was a popular parlor pastime, reproducing travel landscapes, foreign cultures, and international expositions as well as genre topics of everyday life, jokes, and boudoir intimacies. Indeed, the now well-known early film *The Gay Shoe Clerk* (Edison Manufacturing Company, 1903) was a recapitulation of a stereograph view. What the film versions did was to bring widespread representations of female display out of the private, domestic realm into new social, commercial arenas.

In addition, any discussion of the meanings of early cinema representations must be made within the ways that vaudeville was reorganizing as a middle-class variety of entertainment. As M. Alison Kibler has effectively shown, vaudeville's bid for middle-class respectability depended upon a series of gender renegotiations both in the audience makeup and in how vaudeville addressed its audiences.[47] Before mixed audiences of loons, and restaurants; it was a well-known commercial entertainment district. The Edison Manufacturing Company catalogue's description of the film may well point out that the film was shot outside one of the city's daily newspapers,[52] but, Twenty-third Street was, more importantly, the most famous sex district in New York City. The Tenderloin was known primarily for its numerous brothels, for prostitutes' regular street appearances, and for prostitutes' presence in the many saloons that lined the avenues.[53] Twenty-third Street was also a well-known locale for male loitering. Because it contained some of the windiest corners in New York City, it offered loiterers the possibility of watching women's dresses being lifted up by the breeze.[54] (Indeed, as Gunning points out, policeman later assigned to scatter such onlookers coined the familiar phrase "twenty-three skidoo."[55]) Such facts indicate that the title of the film offers an important signifier and, as Gunning says, "set up an atmosphere of titillation."[56]

Twenty-third Street was also the neighborhood that resident artist John Sloan, one of the Eight or Ash Can School painters, sketched and painted regularly between 1906 and 1913. He portrayed the humanity of the Tenderloin District's thoroughfares, restaurants, dance halls, poorly furnished flats, and movie theaters. Through Sloan's detached observations and point of view, one can catch voyeuristic glimpses of the new urban life at the turn of the century. Deemed vulgar at the time he made them, Sloan's paintings and lithographs dared to depict the well-dressed, often jauntily posed prostitutes of the district without the moralism usually served up with the subject. Neither did he portray them as victims. Instead, for Sloan, the streetwalker functioned as a symbol of the changing urban culture around him. His diaries from the period are dotted with his observations about the prostitutes seen on his walks in the neighborhood.[57] In particular, two paintings from this period, *Sixth Avenue and Thirtieth Street* (1907, private collection) and *The Haymarket* (1907, The Brooklyn Museum) encapsulate his attitude as well as the prostitute's pivotal role for the changing gender politics of urban vision.

Sixth Avenue and Thirtieth Street foregrounds three women on a neighborhood street corner. On the left, a disheveled, somewhat slatternly figure in white carries a pail of beer. (There is a sign over the corner saloon, saying "Lion Brewery.") To the right of this woman, two well-dressed, heavily made-up women walk arm-in-arm and cast their glances backward over their shoulders at the first woman. Their colorful attire, feathered boas, and oversize plumed hats provide a striking contrast to the shabby woman carrying the beer pail. They smile prettily, they

➤ JOHN SLOAN, SIXTH AVENUE AND THIRTIETH STREET, *1907. Private collection. Courtesy of Mr. and Mrs. Meyer Potamkin.*

are young and beautiful, and they are handsomely outfitted. The street facade on the right and the elevated railroad tracks on the left form parallel lines that converge in the deep background of the painting and thus define a triangular space that theatrically frames the three women and makes them the focal point of observation. In this way, they are caught candidly in motion.

The most immediately discernible feature of this painting to the modern eye may be the act of looking: two well-dressed, beautiful, carefree women who are striding up the street turn to smile and stare at their less fortunate sister. Yet, the two young women are prostitutes and are typed by their dress and demeanor as well as by the painting's title. The intersection was a well-known hangout of streetwalkers. According to art historian Suzanne L. Kinser, the title "would have caused the average New York to look closely for signs of the prostitute. Even a stranger to the city would very likely have been alerted to the painting's controversial content by the attire and actions of specific women in it."[58] Thus, the painting also encourages the viewer, from a removed vantage point across the street, to examine the women for outward evidence of their sexual status. This theme is especially encouraged and rewarded by what is depicted to the right and left of the three women. On the right, a group of three men gawks at the two prostitutes. On the left and in the middle ground, a woman dressed remarkably like the young girls walks away arm-in-arm with a man. The dynamics of city sexuality are here summed up by a series of looks.

Sloan's other subject, *The Haymarket,* refers to an infamous dance hall just down the street from this corner. The Haymarket was so notorious that by 1903 American Mutoscope & Biograph had even made a six-scene film of it. *A Night at the Haymarket* loosely sketches the sexual narrative associated with the hall. It begins with the sidewalk crowd in front of the entrance. As a man walks by, a woman of the streets nods at him and tilts her head in a "come hither" gesture. He tips his hat and follows her. She points to the Haymarket, and they walk through its front door. The action moves to the interior where the man and woman join the other couples dancing. A house manager watches and intervenes periodically when a man cuddles up too close to his dance partner. In a third scene, couples sit at tables in a wine room, where they all drink, exhibit much merriment, and frequently engage in sexual intimacies: there is much hugging. In this scene, a man starts a brawl, and the management evicts him. The police enter and escort two other couples out to the street. The film resumes with women dancing a wild and prolonged can-can. But they are interrupted by a police raid. Finally, the film returns again to the facade of the Haymarket to show the results of the raid. Many men file out and are led into a paddy wagon. Several men attempt to cover their faces with their hats or pull up their jacket collars. A line of women marches out separately. Many cry into their handkerchiefs. The last woman to enter the street is the woman from the beginning of the film; she struggles valiantly while two policemen hang on to each of her arms. Indeed, this finish would become its own subject the following year in two one-shot films that each depicted a prostitute being photographed by police while she struggled and made faces.

In Sloan's painting *The Haymarket,* prostitutes are more elegantly attired in white taffeta dresses and large plumed hats. They are what one critic calls "glamorous night creatures" as they approach the brightly illuminated door of the hall that is a rather inviting opening from the dark night beyond it.[59] Seen from the back, the women appear to be caught mid-stride as they sweep into the hall. Their central arrangement within the frame, their brightness, and their bodily carriage make them a bold and commanding center of the picture. Again, Sloan provides a vantage point of detachment, of watching from afar. Again, onlookers reinforce through the act of gazing a central focus on the women as well as additional cues that they are indeed prostitutes.

Sixth Avenue and Thirtieth Street (1908, National Gallery of Art, Washington D.C.) is also the title of one of Sloan's lithographs. It portrays a well-dressed woman putting on her gloves and setting off down the street

JOHN SLOAN, THE HAYMARKET, *1907. The Brooklyn Museum, AccessionNumber 23.60, Gift of Mrs. Harry Payne Whitney. Courtesy of The Brooklyn Museum.*

amid a group of young onlookers. Sloan's diary admits that his subject was "a girl of the streets starting out of 27th Street, early night, little girls looking at her."[60] While a modern audience might not know from either the title or the portrait that the woman is a prostitute, her presentation types her just as much as Sloan's assumption that the simple addresses of his titles would tell on his subjects. By drawing her in the act of pulling a glove up her wrist, Sloan again centers the gesture within a street space hollowed out around her and bathed in bright light. The children who stare at the woman recede behind her into the shadows. The light theatrically illuminates and isolates her. By positioning one foot jutting forward, the figure assumes a forward striding movement. The presentation energizes her, gives her a sense of purpose, an assertiveness, and a bold command of the space. Furthermore, her face is turned to the left so that her right profile is revealed. Her chin stuck out and her lips set in a straight line suggest character traits of determination or defiance while they follow the compositional curve of her arm and elbow, a sweeping line that continues upward to the feathered plume on her hat. The emphasis on this entire sweeping motion that takes in her figure, carriage, bearing, face, and dress all contribute to a unified portrait of feminine defiance, transgression, and even a dignified street bravado.

The geographic contextualization and presentation of the women in Sloan's art are relevant for *What Happened on Twenty-third Street, New York City*. Both the title of the film and the dress of its central female character would have typed her as a prostitute. Her identity or at least her social position within this environment may best be claimed through her dress and demeanor in association with the neighborhood itself. But even this identity might be called into question.

In the morning and afternoon, the same streets were also filled with female shoppers visiting the nearby retail outlets and department stores. At night along the same strip, prostitutes joined the clientele of restaurants, hotels, theaters, and saloons. As Timothy J. Gilfoyle demonstrates in his study of nineteenth-century sex commercialization in New York City, women's appearances along West Twenty-third Street confused the ways that observers were used to understanding prostitution in exclusively spatial terms. In other words, various types of prostitution were integrated into the everyday geography of New York rather than in neighborhoods solely devoted to vice. Gilfoyle claims, "Most often, prostitutes lived and worked in the same neighborhood, making them a noticeable part of the urban milieu. . . . Prostitutes shared the community with shoppers and tourists during the day and with theater and restaurant patrons at night. Residents and visitors alike confronted the demimonde while

➤ JOHN SLOAN, SIXTH AVENUE AND THIRTIETH STREET, *1908.*
Rosenwald Collection, National Gallery of Art, Washington D.C. Copyright
© 1997 Board of Trustees, National Gallery of Art, Washington.

walking along stylish [streets]."[61] Although middle-class residents usually resorted to descriptions of the city neighborhoods that bifurcated them into an ideal city spatially organized by regions of vice and virtue, commercial sex in fact "permeated all parts of the metropolis."[62] As Gunning's remarks about the neighborhood's windy corner show, the location already confused prostitutes with other women since they all became subject to an expectation for sexualized spectacle, an illicit looking as part of the everyday relations of the street. Such illicit looking eventually caught the attention of the cops, with police disciplining onlookers but not to cause the practice to stop: the "twenty-three skidoo" is a mild interruption rather than a more repressive form of police action.

So although Twenty-third Street would have signified a notorious sex district to the film's audiences, the referent itself also symbolized the greater confusion of the city and the breakdown of the bourgeois ideal of orderly city life. Well-dressed women on the streets were not necessarily immediately readable. Almost as if in response, one contemporary critic expressed the importance of visual signification in women's dress and demeanor, rather than the times and locations of their appearances, for differentiating among types of women: "By some indescribable wearing of the sealskin saque [sic] or the jaunty hat, [the prostitutes] gave the impression that they were of the half-world where dwell most of the heroines of your modern French dramatists and romances."[63] Along such streets, the legibility of the demeanor of any woman became doubly important for reasserting urban order and epistemological control over the city.

In this context, *What Happened on Twenty-third Street* is about confusion over how to interpret female sexuality in public spaces, and it provides an answer to the confusion. It authorizes the possibility that the well-dressed woman who enters the emptied out central space is a prostitute. One way to read the film in this light is that her reaction to her skirt being lifted—her hand clapping her mouth and her glance at the camera—is the bemusement of a prostitute who, like the lady in *Trapeze Disrobing Act,* has a tacit agreement about her status as commodified sex object. Thus, the woman's laugh and return gaze may not be transgressive but merely collusive; because she is already presumed to be a prostitute and therefore a sanctioned sex commodity, the final stares after her further validate the spectator's right to enjoy her display and bodily revelation. The name of the street coupled with the initiation of rudimentary narrative action contribute to an expectation that something sexually titillating will occur in the space as it is opened up. The woman-as-prostitute's entrance into that space participates in a larger commercialization of sex in leisure entertainment that sanctions the extension of male sexual fantasy and fulfillment to the very boundaries of the real.

The risk of such an analysis is overgeneralizing a historical cinematic situation in order to conclude that every woman disposed in urban space was surveyed as a possible prostitute—looked over for signs of her dress and behavior—thus establishing a new social practice for policing all woman as potentially dangerous while simultaneously erotic. The point, however, is that this is precisely what did occur. Every woman did not need literally to be "looked over" in actual practice for the notion of a woman's sexual availability by her mere presence on a city thoroughfare to take hold and to become widely circulated in the culture.

The woman who looks back is hardly transgressive since her look is so fully recoupable and recuperated. The woman who looks back at the camera in *What Happened on Twenty-third Street, New York City* is already locked into the hierarchy of subject and object, a hierarchy perhaps not yet fully developed in the cinema but fully articulated through the range of popular cultural representations that addressed modernity and the city street. The tragedy is that this woman, about whom we know very little and never will, is so easily co-opted as a conspirator into her own sexual objectification, while her audience—both men and women—are taught about the exercise of sexual surveillance as power within the regime of the real.

2

THE FAIR VIEW

THE 1893 CHICAGO WORLD'S COLUMBIAN EXPOSITION

What a panorama of beauty to drink in and dream over and to carry home in general views and bits of detail, for the perpetual adornment of your mental picture-gallery . . . and the longer [you] stay, the oftener [you] . . . pitch . . . [your] mental camera on a new spot, the richer will be [your] . . . feeling of pleasure and self approval in after days of retrospection.

M. G. VAN RENSSELAER, "At the Fair," 1893

At the fairs the crowds were conditioned to the principle of advertisements: "Look, but don't touch," and taught to derive pleasure from spectacle alone.

WALTER BENJAMIN, *Das Passagen-Werk,* 1982

NO SINGLE EVENT heralded the onset of American modernity more than the 1893 Chicago World's Columbian Exposition. Occurring in the midst of a deep economic depression and widespread labor strife, the World's Columbian Exposition asserted a new American power of corporate capitalism and imperialism. Of course, the irony of such braggadocio was lost on most fairgoers who responded to the fair as though it was a tonic for the economic ailments of the current banking recession. Accounts of the fair from both official and unofficial sources avoid mentioning the partially completed edifices and empty buildings abandoned due to bankruptcies or the financial collapse of investors. Fair critics, journalists, and tourists similarly ignored the labor required to build the 633-acre city and the daily work required to keep it thriving. Instead, travelers' reports as well as more commercial accounts (e.g., souvenir albums, guidebooks, photographs) focus on the Exposition's rhetoric of display, which signified futuristic modernity. By serving as guides for how to understand the fair, Exposition commentaries proclaim the ways that the Exposition ushered in a modernist society.

Within this environment, "pre-cinema" was present as a new machine for seeing. Proto- or pre-cinema exhibits were on display in two places: a single peephole kinetoscope was at the Edison Manufacturing Company's phonograph exhibit in the Electricity Building and Eadweard Muybridge's lecture-demonstrations of animal motion studies occurred regularly at his specially built Zoopraxigraphical Hall on the Midway.[1] These exhibits seemingly contradict the ways they have been traditionally represented in film histories as the paired pre-cinematic apparati of science and commerce. Muybridge's projection of photographic animal motion studies with a Zoopraxiscope has historically represented cinema's origins in a purely scientific practice, and Edison's peephole kinetoscope for individually viewing stage acts has represented commercialized entertainment. In the standard accounts of cinema's origins, cinema sources in technology and industry are traced through a series of inventions back to the camera obscura; they construct a teleology of scientific progress expressed through industrial management.

At the Exposition, however, Muybridge's lecture-demonstrations were part of the entertainment arena at the Midway whereas Edison's kinetoscope was situated within the dominant scientific discourse of the Electricity Building. Edison's kinetoscope, a rapidly moving strip of photographs of the human body directly addressing the viewer, was initially meant to be viewed by an individual looking through a peephole while a phonograph record played. So little has been recorded about Edison's machine at the Electricity Building (indeed, there is some dispute over whether it actually appeared in the south corner of the building or for how long) that it is difficult to isolate its reception.

Muybridge's Zoopraxigraphical Hall lectures consisted of projected images of larger-than-life photographs of the phases of animals in motion—galloping horses, birds in flight—giving the appearance of motion through the projection. It is not really known whether he included the full range of photographic subjects that he elsewhere used in his lectures where the human bodies were naked or near naked to reveal the articulations of bodily movements. In these examples, the men usually engaged in athletic feats such as boxing, fencing, throwing a ball, or physical labor such as blacksmithing or brick laying. The women were naked or in translucent, diaphanous drapes that provided an erotic veiling while still making the contours of the body available for view. These women waltzed, curtsied, flirted, got in and out of beds and hammocks, and opened parasols.[2]

Muybridge's theater at the Exposition, however, did not do well. Given the paucity of specific detail about which motion studies Muybridge actually included in his lectures as well as claims that Muybridge's educational illustrated lectures could not compete with his neighbors (the Moorish Palace and the Street of Cairo) that featured sexually titillating female dancers, one might conclude that Muybridge showed only his animal motion studies. Whatever his program material, Muybridge responded to the commercial failure of his hall by selling his motion studies as souvenir engravings, plates, and phenakistascope disks mounted on handles as fans. Muybridge's solution was to turn a rather unpopular, didactically "educational," and technologically produced display into a market of commodities.

These localized instances of proto-cinema at the Exposition were not very important to those who produced the fair or to those who recorded their responses to the fair. One chronicler went so far as to reflect that the audiences for what he calls the "germ of the movies" were both "relatively small and indifferent."[3] The marginalization of such sites seems both curious and surprising to today's historians except that the meanings of such "pre-cinema" installations were produced in more complex ways than through an obvious or simple technological definition. The ways in which fairgoers learned about "the cinematic" at the Exposition had little to do with the emergent apparatus now associated with the origins of cinema. Fairgoers learned about a new modernist, cinematically situated spectatorship because it was part of the overall discursive formation of visual culture and the social practices acting upon the observer's construction of knowledge.

More than an archive for the technological origins of cinema, the Exposition was important because it became a ground for the practices that constituted modern spectatorship. The relevancy of gender is evident in the ways that mobile spectatorship functioned within the Exposition. If metropolitan Chicago was restrictive and even criminally threatening to the female tourist, then the Exposition attempted to counteract and expand upon feminine purpose for being "on the streets." An 1893 magazine exhorted: "The Fair will be a safe place, and there will be so many people in it that no one individual will be annoyingly observed. You need not fear to part from your wife for a time, or, on the other hand, to let your husband part from you. . . . The crowded galleries at the Fair will be like colossal shops with the counters for different wares sometimes a mile apart."[4] For white middle-class women, in particular, the Chicago Columbian Exposition promised to extend the freedom of the shopping zone and the boulevard promenade to the entire city.

Historians Neil Harris and James Gilbert have addressed the Exposition as a late nineteenth-century rationalized but heterogeneous public space, like the museum or department store, for the specular consumption of commercial commodities.[5] Along with historians Alan Trachtenberg, Robert Rydell, and John Kasson, they define the Exposition as a signal event representative of a shift or rupture in American society that characterized the origins of modern experience and particularly of experience rooted in a new mode of vision.[6] But they all ignore the centrality of gender in making up that vision. The Exposition constructed a socially sanctioned public space for women's participation, promising the possibility of mobile spectatorship in a safe urban environment, and this construction was integral to the definition of the modern. The Chicago Columbian Exposition promised to deliver to women the freedom of the flâneur's idealized city.

The 1893 Chicago World's Columbian Exposition was a fabricated environment, a world of consumer capitalism that contained an encyclopedia of objects and peoples. It housed dynamos, reapers, trolley cars, and commodities of manufacturing industries, agriculture, and commerce. Harris describes the object-filled displays that showed off the industrial and technological wealth of the western world: "[The interiors of] the fair buildings were little more than huge sheds, filled with bazaars, pavilions, tents, booths, heaping on their shelves and cabinets the latest products of art, science, and industry. Some of the pavilions were organized by nations or states; others, by corporations which were like small empires themselves."[7] These pavilions, imitation neo-classical and Renaissance palaces, were arranged in a carefully laid-out plan of axial boulevards, grand vistas, giant fountains, statuary, and lagoons.

Chief among these were the buildings around the Basin, the southern part of the grounds known as the Court of Honor. There stood a number of grand French Renaissance and neo-classical buildings, unified by continuous porticos and arcades around a lagoon 350 feet wide and 1,100 feet long. The Administration Building, Manufacturers and Liberal Arts Building (the largest of the palaces), the Agriculture Building, the Electricity Building, and Machinery Hall, all painted white, formed the majestic bulk of the Court of Honor. Animal statuary in front of the buildings and on bridges (also all white) as well as electric fountains with their curvilinear lines, organic shapes, and moving jets of water provided a neo-classical harmony to the buildings. At the far end of the Basin stood the tallest sculp-

8034. Mining, Electricity and Administration Building,
Columbian Exposition.

BENJAMIN WEST KILBURN, MINING, ELECTRICITY, AND ADMINISTRA-
TION BUILDINGS, CHICAGO WORLD'S COLUMBIAN EXPOSITION, 1893.
STEREOGRAPH VIEW OF THE COURT OF HONOR PHOTOGRAPHED FOR
SOUVENIR ALBUM.

ture at the Exposition, the 65-foot-high *Republic* by Daniel Chester French
(one of the most noted American sculptors of the 1890s and probably
best remembered today for the Abraham Lincoln statue in the Lincoln
Memorial in Washington, D.C.). Behind *Republic,* a double colonnade
with two identical pavilions (the Peristyle) at each end provided a gateway between the Exposition and Lake Michigan. The Grand Basin opened
up onto a North Canal and a South Canal, two water avenues that continued the style of the Court of Honor to the Stock Exhibits to the south
and to the Transportation Building, Horticulture Building, U.S. Government Building, Art Galleries, and smaller state and country pavilions to
the north.

The Court of Honor was the area most photographed for commercial
albums and guidebooks. These official views pictorially produced analo-
gies to the department store interior and even inscribed preferred vantage points from which to view both the great interiors and the grand
court.[8] Even when a visiting journalist like North Dakotan Marian Shaw
was "disappointed" at her first views of the Exposition because the entrance she used from the train station was behind several buildings and
in a service area, she knew enough to walk toward Lake Michigan to the
"broad, beautiful avenue" where she then emphasized her better view of
the grounds as the *real* one.[9] Shaw, like so many other journalists who
covered the fair, lapsed into metaphors of a heavenly afterlife to describe
the Court of Honor. This Court of Honor that became the focus of so many

travelers' descriptions was, as Harris says, "the Sunday clothes of the exposition where monumental planning received its consummation."[10]

Photographs of the fair encouraged a similarly singular reading of the fair experience centered on the Court of Honor as a celestial city of orderly open spaces, brilliantly reflected light on pools of water, and white buildings or as a ceremonial center for dark masses of crowds. They occasionally depicted a lone observer posed along a railing or sightline so as to extend a pictorial vantage point for panoramic viewing. Such a unified photographic vision was made possible because the Exposition's commissioners carefully regulated the taking of pictures on the grounds. They pictured the fair for souvenir albums, official records, and other types of discourse that promoted the Exposition within the codes of visualization for ceremonies, pageantry, and urban advertisements.[11]

The photographs reproduced the architecture as a monumental backdrop or set piece designed to be exploited for visual pleasure. While the whole of the fair's plan also had to function as an arrangement for people to move through and in which to live and work, it was primarily represented and promoted as a spectacle. Photographs repeatedly offer wide-angle views of empty or nearly empty spaces, heightening the atmospheric show of the buildings and sculptures. This effect is especially intensified in the number of photographs taken at night whose highly theatricalized drama depends on the contrasts of light and dark in dis-

➤ PERISTYLE, CHICAGO WORLD'S COLUMBIAN EXPOSITION, 1893.
WIDE-ANGLE STEREOGRAPH VIEW DEPICTING NEARLY EMPTY SPACE,
AN ATMOSPHERIC SHOW OF THE ARCHITECTURE.

CHARLES DUDLEY ARNOLD, "SOUTHEAST CORNER OF THE MANU-
FACTURES ROOF PROMENADE," CHICAGO WORLD'S COLUMBIAN EXPO-
SITION, 1893. PHOTOGRAPH OF A PICTORIAL VANTAGE POINT FOR
PANORAMIC VIEWING.

plays of both the electrical illuminations and fountain jets. This was a city portrayed as a functioning site not for commerce and industry but rather for visual consumerism and specifically for flânerie. For example, the moving sidewalk at the fair, touted as a new technology for urban pedestrians, was located as a promenade along the beach of Lake Michigan, intended not to improve circulation through the fair but to afford better panoramic views of the Court of Honor.[12] The dream city extended to the entirety of the city the notion of the arcade as an urban architectural space designed specifically for flânerie.

The sections of the fair beyond the Court of Honor maintained a unified sense of purpose and urban visuality. The Wooded Island, designed by Frederick Law Olmsted, at the tip of the North Canal was a romantic park in its imitation of the natural environment, a space for leisurely promenades. It housed the Ho-o-den Villa and teahouse sponsored by the Japanese government. It represented an urban "escape valve" to satisfy the need for solace in nature strolls. As described by Marian

Shaw: "No sound of traffic or labor disturbed the quietness of the scene. But for the crowd of pleasure-seekers wandering through the broad avenues, we could scarcely have realized that it was a city of the living."[13] The Wooded Island allowed for a bifurcated split of the utopian city by constructing nature (and simultaneously the Orient) itself in opposition to civilization and by contrasting silence as welcome relief from the sounds of city life.

Located along the western end of the Exposition grounds, the Midway Plaisance was a container for the elements of carnival and circus that always sprang up around international expositions as well as for those elements of racial and ethnic difference and sexual adventure that so thoroughly marked the new modern city. The Midway was a broad avenue that connected the Court of Honor with the tent cities and sideshows of commercial entertainment that camped outside the fairgrounds. The Midway Plaisance was organized in three distinct sections, although there were numerous restaurants, cafes, and small theaters in each section. The closest section to the White City included the German and Irish villages, Blarney Castle, a Colorado gold mine, a log cabin, the Japanese Bazaar, the Libby Glass Works, the International Congress of Beauties, the South Sea Islanders Village, the Javanese settlement, a panorama of the Swiss Alps, and the Hagenbeck Animal Show. The middle section included the Ferris Wheel, the Moorish Palace, the Street in Cairo, the East Indian Palace, the Algerian and Tunisian Villages as well as Eadweard Muybridge's Zoopraxigraphical Hall, and a scale-model of the Eiffel Tower. The farthest section included the Austrian Village of Old Vienna, the Chinese Village, the American Indian Village, Sitting Bull's log cabin,

>⌒ THE SOUTH CANAL (LEFT) AND THE MIDWAY PLAISANCE (RIGHT), *both from* The Columbian Gallery: A Portfolio of Photographs from the World's Fair, *1894.*

a panorama of the Volcano of Kilaueau, the Lapland Village, the Dahomey Village, the Bedouin Encampment, and an ostrich farm.

The exhibits and their juxtapositions defined exotic cultures as a combination of scientific visual anthropology, tourist concessions, and salacious sexual entertainment. For example, the Moorish Palace featured a series of "authentically" designed and decorated rooms along with a wax museum of popular figures, the guillotine that executed Marie Antoinette, and "the Persian Palace of Eros with a ground floor bazaar for trade and an upstairs 'trade for the bizarre.'"[14] The *Pictorial Album and History of the World's Fair and Midway* describes the spectatorial pleasures therein: "Old men and wicked youths haunted the little den called a theater and watched, in a bleary-eyed ecstasy, the Oriental athletes of the stage as they danced, toyed with the cigarette, and by their smiles gave a Persian-Parisian charm to the anomalous entertainment."[15] In her description of her single visit to the theater, the *Chicago Daily News* drama critic Mrs. Lillie Brown-Buck (who wrote under the pseudonym Amy Leslie) described the degree to which she understood such spaces as exclusively gendered: "A writhing Scheherezade [sic] in two shades of pink floated about the miniature stage by a series of muscular dislocations most alarming to a citizen of less sinuous education. I never beheld quite such an exhibition and I beheld this particular one about two minutes. . . . I am not up in the Sodom and Gomorrah of it but it has worried me a trifle."[16]

Although both Neil Harris and Robert Rydell have demonstrated that the Midway was a way of extolling exoticism and of incorporating racial difference by emphasizing a Social Darwinian geographical hierarchy of races, James Gilbert argues that the "coherence of the Midway [was] based upon "the unfamiliar . . . couched in familiar terms; what was foreign was made acceptable and commonplace. The tourist was reassured that what he or she viewed was authentic and, at the same time, fantasy."[17] Marian Shaw, the journalist from North Dakota, described it as a combination of "all peoples, tongues, nations and languages assembled for a summer holiday . . . [but] typical only to a certain extent. They represent some phases of foreign life, but it is life in its most whimsical aspect."[18] Amy Leslie said, "There is a spice of adventure, something rakish and modestly questionable about this legalized harlequinade of other people's habits. . . . Girls blush a little, not very much, and pellucid grangers . . . act devilish when mentioning a prospective tour through this licensed street of preferred iniquity."[19]

In this regard, the spaces of the Chicago World's Columbian Exposition provided a safe contrast to the city streets of Chicago proper. Even in the fictional literature about the World's Columbian Exposition, women were not-so-subtly warned that Chicago was dangerous. For example, in *The Adventures of Uncle Jeremiah and Family at the Great Fair,* the young Fanny leaves her downtown Chicago hotel and family to shop alone and to wander the city's streets only to be taken in by a "confidence man" who appears to be a gentleman. He suggests that they walk over to his mother's and sister's house so that she may meet them and get their advice on Chicago's best shopping. Fanny's younger brother Johnny, who has already met his own street danger in a gang of youthful thugs, espies Fanny but sees nothing wrong. It is only Johnny's friend, the street-wise Chicago lad Louis, who recognizes the confidence man and the house of their destination as an infamous brothel. He can read the semiotics of the Chicago street, and he warns Johnny. The two boys together rescue Fanny before she can enter the house.[20] The female tourist who is alone and strays from the confines of the department store takes the same risks as the woman adrift, and she narrowly escapes enslavement as a prostitute. The moral is quite clear: the city streets are not safe places. The gentleman in the crowd may be a procurer, and the house that sports an elegant facade may be a house of prostitution. The city poses sexual danger for the unaware or naive woman who misreads the signs.

Unlike their European counterparts, Chicago city streets posed a danger less specifically of classes co-mingling than of co-mingling foreign cultures. Fair guidebooks even pointed this out: "Standing on this thoroughfare [downtown State Street] one sees every nation represented and hears every civilized tongue spoken (and some uncivilized)."[21] One Wisconsin woman visitor wrote home in 1893: "I hardly know what to say of the city. It was worse than the confusion of tongues at the Tower of Babel. Humdrum noises and confusion existed all day and all night long."[22] The figure of Babel, of "polyglot" cultures, and of incomprehensibility permeate the literature. Chicago was, after all, a city of brutal labor strikes, of the 1886 Haymarket Square bombing, of corrupt politicians, of diverse foreign-speaking people, of increasing poverty and unsafe living conditions. To women journalists who wrote disparagingly of the noise, crime, and dirt of Chicago proper, the polyglotism of the Midway was by contrast unthreatening and even amusing, an example of the confusions of the city remade into spectatorial pleasures.

For example, the Street in Cairo featured replicas of Egyptian buildings, Egyptian mummies and other museum treasures as well as camel and donkey rides. The *Pictorial Album and History of the World's Fair and Midway* describes its reception:

➤ NOON HOUR ON STATE STREET, CHICAGO, LOOKING NORTH FROM
MADISON STREET. "STANDING ON THIS THOROUGHFARE ONE SEES EVERY
NATION REPRESENTED AND HEARS EVERY CIVILIZED TONGUE SPOKEN
(AND SOME UNCIVILIZED)." *Postcard.*

> People went wild with delight. They slipped into the Old World through a
> gate and reveled in the novelties of camel and donkey riding, of wedding
> marches in the air, of sword bouts, bazaars, and theaters. Flitting through
> the hurly-burly of strange creatures, one beheld veiled women, who saw but
> could not be seen. . . . People who had only read about the veiled women
> of the Orient here had an opportunity to study the reality of costume.[23]

The album suggests a heterogeneous space of spectatorial address unified
by the promise of sensory pleasures and the consumption of the unusual
and the fantastic.

But Shaw offers a perspective that begins to reassign mixed value to
the space according to visual and auditory markers codified according to
feminine social values. She remarks on the pleasures of mimesis and
models: "In the street of 'Old Cairo' may be seen a perfect representation
of the narrow roadway, and picturesque architecture of the old Egyptian

city. . . . Many curiosities and antiquities are offered for sale in the bazaar. In this street may be witnessed the curious ceremonies of an Egyptian wedding and a birthday festival."[24] But, she notes with displeasure the auditory sensations that she links to overtly racist typology: "[The donkeys are] driven by barefooted, yelling little Arabs, who, clad in long, dirty white garments resembling night gowns, scream and hoot and pummel the long-suffering beasts. . . . [The] little howling Cairo-street Arab can far surpass [the young American] . . . as regards variety and intensity of the shrill sounds that issue from his barbarous little throat."[25] Unpleasant sounds become attached or mapped onto bodies that are understood as primitive, unrefined, or, in her own words, "barbarous." Auditory experience supports the observer's visual reading of a hierarchy of races and especially of the unpleasurable social experience of their mingling in a crowd.

Even though it was like Chicago proper as a City of Babel, the Midway Plaisance could still be remade as a safe, coherent space through emphasizing its negotiation as a *visual* spectacle rather than as *auditory* sensations. For example, Theodore Dreiser wrote about women's experiences of the Midway when, as a journalist for the *St. Louis Republic,* he chaperoned twenty-four Missouri schoolteachers who had won a contest to go to the fair sponsored by his newspaper. Dreiser emphasized the ladies' safety even in exploring the more prurient parts of the Midway.[26] He implies that the Midway's polyglot avenue was safe for women visitors who were themselves remade into "harmless" objects of specular consumption as part of the experience.

Such written accounts more than the formal photographs reveal the importance of the fair thoroughfares, especially the Midway, as a new socially sanctioned urban space for ingratiating both men and women in the visual pleasure of their own participation in public spectacle. Amy Leslie observed this phenomenon, her insight due perhaps to her career as an actress and her sensitivity to social behavior in theaters: "A certain unusual configuration observable in the floating populace is in the main due to the celebrations involving cosmopolitan interests. The presence of spectacle in various stages of perfection and development, and a couple of burlesque troupes, together with assembling nations. Girls, girls, girls!"[27] Elsewhere, she more succinctly quoted a woman whom she overheard on the Midway Plaisance: "Let's go to the forestry and see nature. This is like a theater."[28] Journalists like Dreiser and Leslie suggest a particularly pronounced gender inflection to women's participation at the Exposition that made the space itself into a safe urban stage—a theatrically spatialized extension—of a newly available flânerie for women.

The hawkers, too, learned to follow new codes of visual spectacularization. Because fair authorities wanted to regulate and control a sound environment initially marked by auditory volume, excess, and confusion, they outlawed the oral selling of wares. The author of a souvenir photograph album describes the situation,

> A special feature of the Midway was its noise, the volume and variety of which first astonished and then pleased the visitor. The street was a Babel without a tower. Vendors of common and unique wares, criers for places of amusement, uncouth music on uncouth instruments, merchants in the hot kabab (sausage) trade, and traders in Oriental wares, commingled their voices and their trumpets continuously. . . . There was a breeziness and spiciness that enticed the pleasure-seeking public. . . . The Fair authorities did not appreciate the situation. . . . They issued an edict for silence.[29]

The author went on to suggest that the auditory experience, which may have meant confusion or danger to some, also resembled the pleasures associated with flânerie:

> The looker-on enjoyed these vocal contests. There was a breeziness and spiciness that enticed the pleasure-seeking public. Thousands stopped, listened, laughed and "caught on to" for repetition, the sententious "Ot! Ot!" of the Selabia waffle man, the winning speech of the Ottoman with his "here here! Turkish girls—pretty girls—up-stairs," and the veracious assertions of the ostrich man that "they're all alive! they're all alive!" There were hundreds of such special pleaders. . . . Without them the Midway would have been lonesome.[30]

If the Midway initially mimicked the din associated with city streets, Exposition officials remade it into an auditory space that would be less offensive to women like the lady from Wisconsin or North Dakotan Marian Shaw. As a response to the Exposition's edict of silence, Midway concessionaires hired pantomimists who continued to "hawk" entertainments and objects to crowds who now gathered around to watch these silent demonstrations.

The same souvenir album that provides such detailed, lengthy descriptions of the Midway's auditory environment, however, does not use printed language to interpret the revised setting. Instead, it portrays the remade Midway through two photographs of pantomiming hawkers.[31] In both cases, hawkers appear in front of signs advertising foreign dancing girls ("Persian Palace Dancing Girls," "Dark-eyed Bedouin girls dancing") and perform before gathered crowds. The highly specialized, autonomous visual experience of the photograph focalizes the visual experience, mimicking the remaking of the fairgoer into one wholly given over to visual knowledge.

There was another function for the Midway's spatial arrangement and assortment, exemplified in the Javanese and Dahomey villages. These human showcases had no entertainments, theaters, or restaurants associated with them; they existed ostensibly for "pure" anthropological purposes. First shown on a midway at the Chicago Exposition, the same groups of Dahomeyans and Javanese had formerly been displayed at European expositions at national exhibits promoting the benefits of colonialism and the superiority of European ways of life.[32] Their placement outside the exhibition halls proper in Chicago, however, mitigated "any atmosphere of learning into a fairground side-show."[33] Fair historians agree that "the humiliating racism [of the Dahomey exhibit], apart from fulfilling a propaganda role for co-operating foreign nations, had a distinct purpose for reactionary elements within American society."[34]

The Dahomeyans were part of the fair organizers' and Congress's efforts to keep African Americans and Native Americans from any role in the organization and representation of the fair. Black American exclusion from the Exposition is well documented in Rydell's, Gilbert's, and Greenhalgh's histories of the fair.[35] Even while the fair was still going on in 1893, Ida B. Wells-Barnett and Frederick Douglass published and distributed a pamphlet entitled *The Reason Why the Colored American Is Not in the World's Columbian Exposition*.[36] Douglass called the fair "a whited sepulchre" for black Americans and explicitly identified the Dahomeys, who "as if to shame the Negro . . . are also here to exhibit the Negro as a repulsive savage."[37] Numerous guidebooks corroborate this purpose, describing the Dahomey as "barbaric" and "repulsive": "[T]hey eat like animals and have all the characteristics of the very lowest order of the human family."[38] The *Chicago Daily News* reporter said, "[The] Dahomey, of course, carried everything savage before it with a vehemence of physical exertion and spiritual ecstasy overwhelming in diabolism."[39] The Dahomeyans in Chicago provided a visual illustration of the essentialist racial inferiority of African Americans.

By including on the Midway such racist spectacle presented as scientific anthropology, the Columbian Exposition dramatized in its most theatricalized public spaces an important social disparity between the audience as civilized and nonwhites as objects for entertainment. The fair mediated the dialectical tension that characterized nineteenth-century urban life: it masked and obviated the social dangers of mixing classes, races, and ethnic groups through its highly controlled and regulated urban environment while it simultaneously celebrated the newness and excitement of modern urban life. It was an attempt "to enclose reality in manageable forms, to contain it within a theatrical space, an enclosed exposition or recreational space. . . . If the world outside the frame was beyond control, the world inside of it could at least offer the illusion of mastery and comprehension."[40] The Columbian Exposition asserted itself as a safe cultural environment that disguised and distanced itself from the effects of the city marketplace, from the chaos and dangers of the congested street. Indeed, one of the most popular visual representations of the fair provided just this effect: the imaginary bird's-eye point of view, reproduced in everything from maps and tourist guides to ceramic souvenirs and fans, displayed the Exposition as a distant panorama, emphasizing "the carefully ordered planning of the Exposition as an environment free of the grime and hurly-burly of everyday life."[41]

Women's novels about the fair corroborate this perceptual pleasure in a safe, clean city by regularly adopting a distant voyeuristic view as a preferred way to contemplate the fair. In Clara Louise Burnham's *Sweet Clover, a Romance of the White City,* the novel's main characters regularly seek out-of-the-way places for seated observation of the fairgrounds without their being seen.[42] In addition to viewing the Fair from on top of the Ferris Wheel, two characters contemplate the Street of Cairo as a spectacle of human performances from the "romantic eyrie" of a hidden window-seat in an Egyptian house.[43] Other sweethearts watch a drill parade and survey the crowds below them while they are shielded by a curtain on the second-floor balcony of the New York State Building.[44] The climax of the novel—an admission of love by a headstrong, independently minded young woman—occurs while the couple watches the "enchanting vision of early evening in the White City" from the rooftop tower of the Brazil Building.[45] These scenes allow intervals of intimate tête-à-têtes and romantic courtship through dialogue that were important for plot development in the romance genre. At the same time, they support lengthy descriptions of the Exposition perceived as theatrically framed spectacle.

Century Magazine likewise promoted the panoramic view as the way to make sense of the fair. One writer advised: "Take a day to get your bearings. . . . Go all over the Fair grounds, and to the top of at least one of the big domes or towers. See the Fair, as a Fair, from its various centers, and from different parts of its circumference, especially from the lake."[46] Such a directive for proper sightseeing seems to have been taken to heart by Sarah Jane Kimball, a fifty-five-year-old farm woman from Iowa, when she visited the fair. For the first four days of her week long trip to the Exposition, she alternated her daily time between the interiors of a small cluster of buildings (with their countless inventories) and contemplation of the fair grounds from vantage points that offered panoramic views—the Ferris Wheel, the Movable Sidewalk, the Wooded Island, and the Lagoon facing the Electric Fountain.[47]

The effects of the fair's presentation as a safe cultural environment may be best illustrated, however, in artists' ink drawings of the fair. These drawings embrace the White City not only through distant, detached panoramas but through depictions of pedestrians who co-mingled with each other. Sketches drawn by ambulatory journalists whose newspapers were barred from bringing in cameras offered representations of people caught in the act of walking and seeing that depict the point of view of the flâneur.[48] These drawings showed what the Exposition's more formal commercial portraits of the architecture and grounds could not—female observers caught in a triangle of looking relations. The women simultaneously gaze at exhibits and at passing men while other men look at the women. The Exposition's official emphasis on photographic formality and monumentality precluded and even disallowed the representation of the observer caught in the act of looking. When photographs did include a discernible human figure, the observer was located and posed for viewing the scene as panorama, thereby suggesting to the photograph's audience the preferred vantage point for placing oneself in the picture. The presence of individual bodies acts as support for the vantage point of the larger panoramic displays. The sketches represent instead the pictorial tradition of placing women as the object of the male gaze through a triangle of looking relations within which women also actively look at men.

For example, F. Robertson's drawing along the canal features a woman sitting in a gondola half visible in the left side of the frame.[49] Her arm is extended in a gesture of welcome or beckoning, her face turned toward another woman standing on a canal bridge at the right side of the frame. This simple "hello" is doubly complicated by the presence of another man and woman whose figures loom large in the foreground. First, the man and woman function as inscribed spectator-tourists who observe this salutatory spectacle while the woman in the boat is unaware of being watched. Second, the woman who watches is made available in profile to the implied viewer while the man to her right holds her hand and watches her.

F. ROBERTSON, UNTITLED SKETCH OF TOURISTS AT THE CHICAGO WORLD'S COLUMBIAN EXPOSITION, 1893. *From Lillie Brown-Buck,* Amy Leslie at the Fair, *1893.*

Charles Graham's "On Cairo Street" offers a vantage point from slightly above street level so that the entire alleyway and its Egyptian-styled spires are visible.[50] In the center foreground, a group of three fairgoers— two women and a man—observe the street around them. In the cluster of three, the woman to the left looks left; the man to the right looks right. The woman in the center looks ahead. They seem to be the exemplary group of tourists, an intimate social group by virtue of their physical closeness to each other while their eyeline gazes extend outward to the

CHARLES GRAHAM, "ON CAIRO STREET" (LEFT) AND "IN THE ELEC-
TRICITY BUILDING" (RIGHT), CHICAGO WORLD'S COLUMBIAN EXPOSI-
TION, 1893. *From* Chicago Tribune Art Supplements in Two Parts: World's Columbian
Exposition.

street sights of the other inhabitants and the architecture. Yet, once again,
such a seemingly straightforward representation of tourism is complicated by another viewing subject. Here, formally foregrounded by location, color, and arrangement, a man in Arab dress to the left of the group
stares openly at the woman who, unaware of his look, gazes off into the
left foreground. Other sketches by Graham as well as those by artist Art
Young similarly feature men in foreign dress watching women who are
unaware of their gaze while they look at other men (in such places for
authorized looking as the art building, the horticulture displays, and the
Wooded Island).[51]

In these images, there is a hint that even the model community for
women's urban freedom was still riddled with tensions. Dreiser supports
this tension in one of his descriptions of the schoolteachers at the fair:

> Another thing that has caused considerable comment among the young
> ladies has been the manner in which the inhabitants of the Orient and East-

ern Europe travel about the streets of the city. . . . These Turks, Arabs, Hindoos, Japs, Egyptians and others fix themselves up as fantastically as possible for no other reason than to attract attention. . . . As ugly as many of them are, they will smirk and grin upon observing the slightest glance cast in their direction.[52]

Such scenes repeatedly encode foreign, nonwhite men as both the object of women's glances and as the open (often leering) spectators of white female observers.

In a study of the Dahomey at the 1895 Paris Exposition Ethnographie de L'Afrique Occidentale, Fatimah Tobing Rony notes a similar tension in the public spaces where visitors and Dahomeyans mixed. In public restaurants, Paris Exposition visitors encountered Dahomeyans who looked back at them; they discovered that "the performers had eyes and voices too."[53] In these interactions, Tobing Rony sees the public playing in fascination with the very boundaries that the fairs helped to set up:

> Even as the exposition strived to construct and address clear subjectivities . . . there were marginal spaces at the fair where one could "straddle the fence" . . . and the very act of voyeurism [endemic to the ethnographic displays] was undermined. . . . White visitors could view at the fair all that was forbidden, flirting with the boundaries of Self and Ethnographic Other, while at the same time maintaining a distance.[54]

➤ "AMID THE PALM AND CYPRESS, HORTICULTURE BUILDING" (LEFT), "FRENCH DEPARTMENT, LIBERAL ARTS BUILDING" (CENTER), "AROUND THE FISHERIES ARCADE" (RIGHT). *From* The Columbian Gallery: A Portfolio of Photographs from the World's Fair.

Tobing Rony concludes cinema became in the twentieth century the rational consequence of the exhibiting of "native villages" since it "eliminates this potentially threatening return-gaze of the performer, offering a more perfect scientific voyeurism."[55] It advances the modern anthropological spectacle because, through cinema, the Other can be unthreateningly imagined whereas the utopian Exposition space—in all its play—can only evoke racist tensions.

While such relationships of seeing and being seen were played out daily on the city streets and at the Exposition, the drawings are notable for the ways that they construct a *triangulated* rather than reciprocal relationship of women seeing and being seen. Women may look at both white and nonwhite men, but they do so only while they simultaneously are held as the unaware objects of other men's gazes, both passersby as well as the sketch artist. The frequency of this pictorial triangle suggests two possibilities: first, that the fantastically theatricalized space itself and its spectacular displays of consumption were themselves complicit in this extension of a *sexualized* gaze to passersby made over into spectacle and, second, that the wandering sketch artists implicitly used such representational conventions because they understood the fair as an excuse for and containment of that kind of authorized voyeurism. Whereas the photos promote and localize an autonomy of vision that expresses the purpose of seeing the fair as a spectacle of commodities, the sketches made by journalists depict human figures as the subjects and the objects of each other's gazes. The journalists dramatize the way that surveillance overlapped with spectacle.

What happened at the 1893 Chicago Columbian Exposition two years before the "invention" of cinema was the cue for what would make cinema a popular commercial entertainment. Seven years later, when cinema itself was exhibited at the Paris Universal Exposition, it still could not compete commercially with panoramas or theatrical spectacles except in those cases where cinema was incorporated into such spectacular displays.[56] People responded enthusiastically not to cinema per se but to cinema in the service of a spectacle. For cinema to succeed, it required more than the technology necessary to produce it and the serial images of film.

Within a study of the origins of modern spectatorship, pre-cinema installations at the 1893 Chicago World's Columbian Exposition should not be taken, then, as the "origins" of cinema as defined through their apparati. Rather, they are part of a larger accommodation of new technologies to available processes of vision and to subjects normalized through their places in relation to sight. Spectatorship at the fair (and its concomitant modes of presentation) served a process of ongoing mediation between Chicago's two distinct urban cities, the metropolis and the Exposition grounds. In this division of public spaces, the lines were drawn between the controlled display of commodities and attractions and the historically growing, expanding spaces of the American city as a place of habitation and work. Both spaces, in turn, were organized around ethnic and racial differences, and both regulated access differently, with the Midway at the Exposition facilitating a playful reenactment of the pleasures and perils of urban living. The display of foreign cultures and women's safe immersion in them on the Midway promoted an understanding of the Other and provided a model through which one could assess the more unpredictable mixing and conflict of cultures in the city proper. The Exposition emerged as important, then, as a substitute public sphere for women—a place that provided the kind of urbanism that women especially found lacking in the American city and where a very different kind of walking was available to women.

Thus the real significance of spectatorship at the Exposition resided in its inscription and organization around new forms of visuality that cinema would adapt to and build upon. At the end of the nineteenth century, cinema emerged not just as an invention tied to the Renaissance notion of perspective but as a distinctly modern machine responding to new cultural issues. For cinema to succeed, it had to be articulated as a masculinist form of address even while it also became necessary to incorporate a space for the female as consumer. The disposition of the Exposition and eventually the movie house as new commercial social centers for observing subjects had less to do with the evolution of the camera obscura and the progressive chain of representational or picturing technologies than with the social importance of involving men and women in the same locale for the purposes of seeing and being seen.

3

E V E   I N   T H E
G A R D E N   O F
D E S I R E

THE DEPARTMENT STORE AND
THE WOMAN WHO LOOKS

The crowd was the veil from behind which the familiar city as phantasmagoria beckoned to the flâneur. In it the city was now landscape, now a
room. And both of these went into the construction of the department
store, which made use of flânerie itself in order to sell goods. The department store was the flâneur's final coup.

WALTER BENJAMIN, "Paris—Capital of the Nineteenth Century," 1935

Buying and selling, serving and being served—women. On every floor, in
every aisle, at every counter, women. . . . Behind most of the counters, on
all the floors . . . women. At every cashier's desk, at the wrappers' desks,
running back and forth with parcels and change, short-skirted women. Fill-
ing the aisles, passing and repassing, a constantly arriving and departing
throng of shoppers, women. Simply a moving, seeking, hurrying, mass of
femininity.

C. E. CAKE, "Arranging Goods to Make the Shoppers Buy," 1910

IN THE LATTER HALF of the nineteenth century, the department
store became one of the most prominent new institutions in the industrial urban landscape. By combining the legacy of the rural or small-town
general store that carried a little bit of everything and the urban shop that

specialized in a narrow line of merchandise, the metropolitan department store overran the functions of both and transcended all prior notions of selling. Because many items that had traditionally been made at home—such as clothing, canned and preserved foods, and household furnishings—were increasingly manufactured outside the home after 1850, women of all classes more often purchased household necessities using cash or credit. By 1890, the department store catered to these consumers by offering them ready-to-wear clothing, prepared foods, and an array of household utensils and furniture in grand visual displays offset by majestic architecture and elegant facades. As historian Susan Porter Benson has remarked, "The palace of consumption elevated prosaic goods and touched them with the aura of elegance while fostering a taste for luxury and encouraging the sale of finer goods."[1] These new palaces were based on an enticing principle of free entry: one could entertain the right to look without having to make a purchase. These department stores—in cities such as Paris, London, New York, Philadelphia, and Chicago—presented themselves primarily to female shoppers as democratic domains for *looking,* which would make the changing downtowns new places of excitement. The department store promised a new kind of flânerie to women and, in the process, conquered the potential flâneuse by making her into the modern consumer.

Chicago's department stores, strung out one after another in a six-block row on State Street, offered women at the turn-of-the-century a socially acceptable, visually exciting zone for walking and looking. The biggest and most prestigious, Marshall Field & Company (begun in 1865), was easily a rival in style, elegance, and size to such other grand emporiums as Au Bon Marché in Paris, Macy's in New York City, and Wanamaker's in Philadelphia.[2] In 1893, when the store was enlarged for the Chicago World's Columbian Exposition, advertisements proclaimed, "Marshall Field's is an exposition in itself."[3] The store was enlarged again in 1902 and, in 1907, the original building was demolished for the current building on the same site—a twelve-story structure that includes thirty-five acres of selling space and a 6,000-square-foot Tiffany glass dome that covers a six-story interior court.

Others that may never have entirely rivaled Marshall Field's in opulence were important competitors and contributed to the creation of a downtown pedestrian zone of visual excitement and pleasure. The Mandel Brothers grew steadily as a large department store and expanded several times until it rebuilt an entirely new State Street store in 1912.[4] The Big Store covered the entire block between Congress and Van Buren.[5]

⊁ STATE STREET, CHICAGO, LOOKING NORTH FROM VAN BUREN
STREET. A SOCIALLY ACCEPTABLE, VISUALLY EXCITING ZONE FOR WALK-
ING AND LOOKING. *Postcard.*

A. M. Rothschild and Company faced the Big Store across State Street;
"We know no dull days," its advertisements declared.[6] The Fair, which occupied a full city block on State, Adams, and Dearborn streets, featured
cheap jewelry, notions, crockery, kitchen utensils, and hardware at low
prices that even the poorest of the working class could afford.[7] Schlesinger
and Mayer's, one block south from the Marshall Field's store and across
from the Boston Store, also based its sales appeal on cheap prices (its ads
declared that it had "popular prices").[8] In 1904, architect Louis Sullivan
designed for Schlesinger and Mayer a twelve-story steel building that featured an elegant art nouveau entrance of distinctive iron grillwork.[9] Sullivan's architecture became a model for numerous other department stores
in America and Europe.

The typical interior arrangement of most department stores was:
linens, toiletries, and items for leisure on the first floor to encourage im-
pulse buying; clothing, hats, and undergarments on the next floors; sports

equipment and toys housed on the floors above that; furniture and food floors located near the top. The uppermost floors were for storage and business operations. The basement contained bargain counters as well as cheap household goods and crockery. In addition, the stores featured such amenities as restaurants and cafes, banks, post offices, doctors' and dentists' offices, barber shops, beauty salons, pharmacies, and nurseries.

Both the sheer quantity of commodities and the collective visual opulence of the stores tantalized the eyes of the beholders.[10] According to historian Elizabeth Abelson, shopping zones like State Street were "an environment dedicated to sensory stimulation and unfettered abundance."[11] For example, Marshall Field's State Street store was painted a gleaming white throughout, its brilliance heightened by the number of glass windows and a central light well that allowed in sunlight. A central rotunda had floor-to-ceiling columns, fancy railings, and cornices.[12] The 1902 addition added red marble floors, Tiffany glass chandeliers, polished mahogany and French glass counters.[13] Merchandise was displayed in low standing glass cabinets so that the passersby would have visual accessibility not only to the goods in the cabinets but to the sweep of the floor as a whole. The overall effect of light-reflecting surfaces—glass, mirrors,

MARSHALL FIELD & COMPANY'S RETAIL STORE. THE 1907 BUILDING ON STATE STREET AND WASHINGTON STREET. *Postcard.*

MARSHALL FIELD & CO.'S RETAIL STORE, CHICAGO

MANDEL BROTHERS' AND SCHLESINGER AND MAYER'S DEPARTMENT STORES, CORNER STATE AND MADISON STREETS. SCHLESINGER AND MAYER'S STORE (RIGHT) WAS DESIGNED BY LOUIS SULLIVAN IN 1904. *Postcard.*

bright colors, white walls, highly polished woods and brass—in the open, illuminated spaces was one of eye-dazzling extravagance.

Theodore Dreiser's *Sister Carrie* portrays this effect in Carrie's first Chicago downtown shopping trip in 1889. Dreiser describes The Fair's beguiling charm: "Each separate counter was a showplace of dazzling interest and attraction. She [Carrie] could not help feeling the claim of each trinket and valuable upon her personally. . . . She realized in a dim way how much the city held—wealth, fashion, ease—every adornment for women, and she longed for dress and beauty with a whole heart."[14] In *Carrie,* Dreiser introduces the important idea that free admission and visual opulence had a purpose—one of instilling desire. Abelson aptly describes this calculated arousal of desire: "Shopping had transcended functionalism, and . . . shoppers were expected to want, if not to purchase what was visibly arrayed all around them."[15] Anne Friedberg expands upon the same phenomenon: "The 'paradise' of the department store relied on the relation between *looking* and *buying,* and the indirect

➤ MARSHALL FIELD'S INTERIOR. FIRST FLOOR, MAIN AISLE. MERCHAN-
DISE WAS DISPLAYED IN LOW STANDING GLASS CABINETS SO THAT THE
PASSERSBY WOULD HAVE VISUAL ACCESSIBILITY NOT ONLY TO THE
GOODS IN THE CABINETS BUT TO THE SWEEP OF THE FLOOR AS A
WHOLE. *Postcard.*

desire to possess and incorporate through the eye."[16] For Friedberg, the department store environment authorized a flâneuse only in a paradoxical sense—flânerie was available to her but only in ways that played upon deeply rooted conceptions of gender roles.

Thus, the empowerment of a female flânerie that the department store represents for Friedberg is not necessarily a form of liberation. The definition of the flâneur upon which it trades—a wandering subject who pleasurably absorbs a succession of visual impressions—needs to be transformed into one who *buys* the commodities offered in the store as a substitute for the fleeting visual possession of the spectacle as a whole. In this way, the department store offers consumer goods as fetishistic substitutes for the style and grandeur associated with the store.

Of course, there is an aspiration to class and gentility in such commodity desire. As Porter Benson recognizes, "[In the department store,] the humblest daughter of the working class could rub shoulders with the city's wealthiest grande dame."[17] But it was also a woman's observation of wealthier women shoppers who were part of the spectacle that helped to stir a woman's desire to buy. Hilda Satt, a Polish-Jewish immigrant, describes just such a Chicago shopping experience in the late 1890s:

> All of a sudden I was in front of the Marshall Field store. I walked in. To my surprise no one paid any attention to me. No one asked me what I wanted. I wandered about and no one objected. I walked down the aisles, admiring the displays and wondering how many people had the money to buy all those things.
>
> I found myself in front of an elevator and heard the words "Going up." So I went up. When I heard the operator call "Third floor, waiting room," I stepped out and walked to the famous Marshall Field waiting room.
>
> I sank into a luxurious chair and just sat there watching the well-dressed people.
>
> How many times have I thought of that day?[18]

Even in fiction, the same thing happens. In Dreiser's novel, Carrie

> noticed too, with a touch at the heart, the fine ladies who elbowed and ignored her, brushing past in utter disregard of her presence, themselves eagerly enlisted in the materials which the store contained. . . . Their clothes were neat, in many instances fine, and wherever she encountered the eye of one it was only to recognize in it a keen analysis of her own position— her individual shortcomings of dress and that shadow of manner which she

MARSHALL FIELD'S THIRD-FLOOR WAITING ROOM. "I SANK INTO A
LUXURIOUS CHAIR AND JUST SAT THERE WATCHING THE WELL-DRESSED
PEOPLE." *Postcard.*

thought must hang about her and make clear to all who and what she was.
A flame of envy lighted in her heart.[19]

The floors of the department store may have provided a democratic
sphere for women of different classes to co-mingle, but they were hardly
there to serve egalitarian purposes.

The equality shared among women through their looking in the department store may well have been undercut by their inequality in buying and, what is more important, by the ways that both department store
clerks and the increasing systemization of the department store exploited
those very inequalities. Carrie's and immigrant Hilda Satt's invisibility
both to other women shoppers, as well as to the clerks, could just as easily have contributed to producing a sense of social hierarchy as a sense
of democracy. As Porter Benson says, "Both [the poor and the wealthy]

would of course not be equally courted by managers. . . . They certainly could not buy equally, the former very likely not at all."[20] The female clerks, also working class girls, sought out paying customers who would be more likely to contribute to their sales commissions. Department store employees thus assumed a hierarchy dependent upon women's physical appearances and manners.

Department store managers were likewise sensitive to the differences among the women who visited. They noted that bourgeois women—the ones in whom they were most interested—did not really like mingling in a crowd with working class women. In 1902, a national magazine aimed at retailers (*Dry Goods Economist*) offered the following advice:

> People of culture and refinement dislike crowds and crushes in stores. Your true "swell" likes to trade at a store where there is plenty of room and an abundance of air, with surroundings of an elegant, not to say esthetic, character. Shawl-crowned people wearing market baskets on their tawny arms are not the sort that frequent such stores, and it is their company to which elegance and refinement are especially adverse.[21]

Store managers responded by adding new departments expressly for the lower class—turning the basement into bargain counters with sale goods and lower priced items that would draw the working class away from the main and upper floors. In this way, department stores attempted almost immediately to sort out the crowd by class and to produce a hierarchy through the economics of store organization and customer circulation that would result in the renewed importance of women's class-identified appearances. Even though the stores promised to be a new democratic space organized through looking, the working class woman's very presence in that space undermined the appeals to bourgeois manners, styles, and pretensions that undergirded the store's real purpose.

The department store's logic of fantasy—its imaginary realm of wealth and opulence, its rhetoric of accessibility, and its production of desire—was key to building a culture of mass consumption. In an environment in which buying was mixed with leisure entertainment, customers' imagined freedom to look always meant more than the liberty of indulging in dreams of upward mobility and material pleasure. By encouraging customers to identify with and to invest themselves in things, the new stores tried to ensure that all customers would buy *sometime*. In the department store, as Rosalind Williams has argued, "Consumers are an audience to be entertained by commodities, where . . . arousal of free-floating desire is as important as immediate purchase of particular items."[22] The cultural significance of the production of such desire, as several critics have persuasively shown, is that women of all classes learned to become increasingly alienated from the production of goods as the essence of the work process and to compensate for that alienation with consumption itself as an amusing recreation—even when the act of consumption shored up traditional lines of class and gender.[23]

In following this line of reasoning, however, it would be wrong to think of women's shopping only as a leisure activity. Shopping became important work and part of the daily routine for urban middle-class women. As Abelson notes, "By the closing decades of the century traditional female skills based in home production were replaced by the skills required to purchase factory-produced goods. . . . Women had to walk a tightrope between real needs, defined by practical use, and stimulated wants created by a suggestive ambiance, lavish display, and, often, manipulated prices."[24] It may be difficult to consider women *shopping* as women *working* because they were also enjoying themselves. But women's purchases of commodities outside the home became an essential part of their work routine for the household, and even here the pleasure of shopping could easily have been undercut by a woman's financial *inability* to purchase what she needed. Many women had to learn how "to make ends meet." Mass consumerism may instill anxiety and frustration as much as it does pleasure.

These shopping women who ambled alone, were accompanied by men, or walked in groups were ersatz flâneuses. Their flânerie was ersatz because it was not purposeless; it was dramatically contained in cordoned-off spaces of restricted mobility; it was an act of gazing circumscribed by models for consumption, by regulated and standardized modes of circulation through department store spaces, and by reassertions of class hierarchy. Ambulation alternated with periods of stillness, standing, waiting, and pausing to consider the goods on display. As Abelson observes, "The store was a sanitized, safe environment that catered both to their [women's] needs and to their fantasies and provided them with a quasi career in the form of shopping."[25] It was hardly a model for flânerie.

There is a single element of department store shopping, however, more frequently associated with the rise of a female flânerie—one that has provided film critics with an analogy for cinema spectatorship.[26] It is the matter of women peering into the store windows along the streets. As one rural woman visiting Detroit in the 1880s described the experience: "The windows are full of such beautiful things. . . . You can imagine me standing in front of the windows . . . until I take everything in and then I go in and stand and look and look and then when I come home try to remember all I saw."[27] Indeed, as early as 1895, one journalist even used the same Shakespearean formulation to describe shop windows that would later become commonplace to characterize the cinema: "[Store windows] furnish the stuff that dreams are made of."[28]

Beginning in the 1890s, the department stores arranged their windows as artistic, colorful displays so that women who were parading up and down the street would be drawn to the stores' facades. At Marshall Field's beginning in the late 1890s, Arthur Fraser created theme windows. One department store trade magazine compared the unveiling of a new Fraser window at Marshall Field's to "an opening of a new show."[29] Abelson calls these windows "a miniature theater fronting on the public sidewalk."[30] Fraser's dramas behind glass were so imposing that when he decorated all six store windows completely in red in 1897, he launched a fashion vogue known as the "red epidemic."[31] Another pioneer window dresser in Chicago in the late 1890s was L. Frank Baum, the author of *The Wizard of Oz* (1900). Baum became the editor of *The Show Window* from 1897 to 1902 and was a leading national authority on what he called the "arts of decoration and display."[32] He advocated turning windows into tableaux in which entire outfits would be shown in artistically pleasing settings or fully decorated rooms. He promoted the idea of an "illusion window," where a live female model wearing store outfits would pose. He even recommended spectacular moving electrical displays of revolving stars and wheels, mechanical butterflies, and lighted globes. Baum urged store managers to get the customers to "watch the window! [Make the windows] come alive. . . . People will always stop to examine anything that moves."[33] In Chicago, Fraser and Baum extended the stimulation of visual desire from the store interiors to the street outside the department stores.

Inasmuch as Baum's words elicit the germ of cinematic thinking, his and Fraser's techniques also borrowed a great deal from other popular visual media of the day. The use of full-figure mannequins in store windows adapted a display technique from the dime museum, and the panorama was a model for the window display's effects of color, sensational and theatrical arrangements, motion and implied motion, and tableau orientation. It seems curious then that feminist film critics have relied so exclusively upon the store window as the grand urban precursor to a female cinema spectatorship. Anne Friedberg's explanation is the most detailed: "From the middle of the nineteenth century, as if in a historical relay of looks, the shop window succeeded the mirror as a site of identity construction, and then—gradually—the shop window was displaced and incorporated by the cinema screen."[34] In the 1890s, Chicago had as other models for ambulatory meditation its numerous dime museums and three grand panoramas located near the State Street shopping district. Among Chicago's dime museums, the most famous was the Eden Musée (built in 1889), renamed The Casino by 1893. The Eden Musée often featured such sensational wax dummy exhibits as a chamber of horrors labeled "The Inquisition." Chicago's panoramas were enormous murals in circular rooms—the Battle of Gettysburg, the Niagara Panorama, and the Cyclorama of the Chicago Fire. All of these commercial entertainments available to the masses encouraged the kind of distant, visual contemplation combined with the thrill of theatrical display generally associated with the store window and later with cinema.

But what separates window shopping from these other available forms of visual spectatorship in the 1890s was that female shoppers could study their own reflections and those of passersby in the glass and in carefully placed mirrors as well as examine the goods and the frozen mannequins through the glass partitions. Glass that serves as a transparent partition separating the viewer from access to the goods may also reflect back and serve as a mirror for the viewer to behold herself and others. Just as women at the Exposition studied things and other fairgoers while they themselves were the objects of masculine attention, female window shoppers likewise participated in acts of looking that united commodities, people in motion, and their own self-images. Glass reflections alerted women shoppers and those watching the shoppers alike to a relationship between motion and immobility and to the interchangeability between persons and things. In this regard, a "window shopper's" attraction to the frozen or living mannequin in the glassed-in display is always an incomplete explanation of the female viewer's relationship to the scene since the woman also had equal access to her own reflection and those of other men and women. Seen in this light, cinema spectatorship represents a psychic transformation from these processes of spectatorship at the department store. Enclosed glass displays did allow, however, for consumer contemplation that would provide a powerful model for eliciting desire that the cinema eventually drew upon to address its female spectators.

The cinema extended the legitimate public space for women to look, and it expanded their possibilities of a mobilized wandering gaze from the restrictive zone of the street window and department store to new virtual territories. As Giuliana Bruno has written, "Mobilizing the gaze—the 'panoramic' feature of cinematic language—implied the appropriation of territories and the freedom of 'streetwalking.' In its embodiment of fantasy, female spectatorship maps out the spaces of the gaze as sites to traverse and trespass." [35] This allows one to make an important distinction between the shop window and the cinema since it is only through the cinema that women were able to acquire the 'peripatetic' gaze of the flâneur. [36] Cinema is analogous to the department store window only insofar as it may well have provided women with an equally pleasurable source of urban looking. But, more importantly, where nighttime flânerie had previously been denied to women, the cinema legitimized women's viewing in a darkened public place and associated desire with the location itself. [37]

The cinema did more than welcome women as moviegoers to a new spot; it depicted women looking in socially sanctioned spaces. Most scholars have considered only how early cinema put into place an earlier version of Laura Mulvey's famous argument about the Hollywood cinema—men look and women are to-be-looked-at. [38] Both Judith Mayne and Mary Ann Doane have argued that early cinematic representational practices were steeped in an increasing narrativization of women's bodies as the objects of spectacle and surveillance by male spectators. [39] Yet, even here, there are classic examples where a male spectator's sexual gaze results in a punitive ending. In such films as *The Animated Poster* (Edison Manufacturing Company, 1903) and *The Poster Girls* (American Mutoscope & Biograph, 1899), women as the objects-looked-at punish the men for their acts of sexualized looking. *The Animated Poster* shows a bill poster pasting up a poster advertising a burlesque show on the wall of a house. The poster features a full-length portrait of an actress in tights. He has placed the poster so that when the shutters of the house are opened, the woman who sticks her head out the window appears to assume the head of the figure on the poster. A male passerby laughs at the effect, and the shutters are closed. The shutters open again, and the woman throws a pail of water on the bill poster, who falls into his paste bucket. In *Poster Girls,* another bill poster posts a sign for a burlesque show featuring a similarly designed full-length portrait of an actress. When a male passerby stops to contemplate the bill, the poster girl comes to life and kicks him in the pants. These comic displays suggest that the presentation of sexual difference and looking relations was not nearly so linear or monolithic as Mayne and Doane think.

When Mayne does examine how early cinema constructed a female subject, she argues that it put her forth only as a "primitive narrator," a figure whose inscription still "depend[ed] upon and [relied] on the classical polarities of (male) subject and (female) object." [40] She offers three categories: first, the earliest films in which women self-consciously exhibit

>>> THE ANIMATED POSTER *(Edison Manufacturing Company, 1903).*

themselves for the camera (e.g., *Annabelle Butterfly Dance,* Edison Manufacturing Company, 1895); second, women who display themselves but
within a structure marked by the separation of a male viewing subject
and the woman as the object of his gaze (described earlier in discussions
of such films as *Trapeze Disrobing Act, A Subject for the Rogue's Gallery*
[American Mutoscope & Biograph, 1904], and *What Happened on Twenty-
third Street, New York City*); third, actual female voyeurs, women whose
gazes provide rudimentary points of identification for the viewer. But such
female voyeur films in the period before 1909 largely serve Mayne's overall argument to show how films between 1909 and 1913 channeled the
woman's look "into the conclusion of marriage which would become the
classical form of resolution *par excellence.*"[41]

Thus, while Mayne acknowledges that there was a handful of exceptional films that do portray women looking, she is able to account neither for their frank admission of women's desire nor for the fact that there
were more than just a handful of isolated, anomalous examples. The few
instances that depict what Mayne calls "a desire that would have no place
in the emerging codes of narrative cinema" she sees merely as the ex-
ceptions that prove the rule of the ascendancy of women's narrative objectification.[42] When, however, one examines a wider array of early films
than previous feminist film scholars have considered, one learns that such
films as *A Search for the Evidence* (American Mutoscope & Biograph,
1903) and *The Story the Biograph Told* (American Mutoscope & Biograph,
1904) are not exceptional. Early cinema routinely portrayed women either
in possession of a visual gaze or overturning the male mastery of the gaze.

Early cinema thus offered up the possibility of an alternative formulation of cinematic desire through the inscription of the woman who looks.

Perhaps the best known example of a female spectator represented in early cinema is the wife in *The Story of the Biograph Told* who, visiting the cinema with her husband, sees a film made earlier that day of him flirting with his female secretary at the office. Charles Keil suggests how this example coordinates a female's look and power:

> What differentiates this scenario from Laura Mulvey's description of visual pleasure is that the cinematic image in *Biograph* is neither centered on the female as object, nor is it empowering. The male viewer looks on, sees himself, and is rendered helpless. The husband's appearance in the film-in-the-film marks him as guilty in the eyes of his wife. She becomes possessor of the controlling gaze, a condition emphasized by her subsequent action in the movie theatre (she beats her husband) and the office (she hires a new secretary and sends the previous one away). In this way, the wife comes to control the film's mise-en-scène, entering into the husband's work world and orchestrating changes of her own desire.[43]

Once the male has been made the spectacle, his spectacularization enables the woman to assume a position of mastery. Yet this kind of socially sanctioned mastery available to women—to enact moral indignation and righteous outrage—is itself even compromised or dulled by first offering up the humiliation of the woman equally as a spectacle as she bears witness to her husband's infidelity.

Another example of this type of scenario is *A Search for the Evidence*. This film is a "through-the-keyhole movie," a type that emerged between 1901 and 1906 and showed a subject (usually a man, but sometimes a woman) looking through a keyhole followed by the image of what he (or she) is seeing (e.g., *The Boarding House Bathroom* [American Mutoscope & Biograph, 1905]; *Through the Key-Hole in the Door* [American Mutoscope & Biograph, 1903]).[44] Most through-the-keyhole films are inspired by a man's curiosity and end with the discovery and subsequent punishment of the voyeur for his looking. Sometimes these films alternate views of the voyeur with what the voyeur sees, and sometimes they do not.

Tom Gunning has noted that the inscription of such point-of-view shots makes the genre an important transition between the earliest exhibitionist cinema and the development of a narrative cinema, and many film scholars regularly cite *A Search for the Evidence* as the peak of the through-the-keyhole genre.[45] Elena Dagrada elaborates on Gunning's ob-

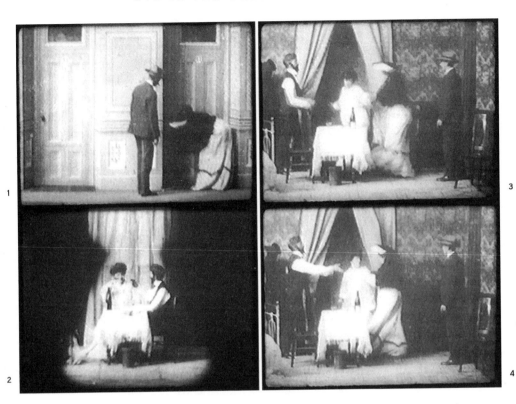

A SEARCH FOR THE EVIDENCE *(American Mutoscope & Biograph, 1903).*

servation with the caveat that these are not literally point-of-view shots since the views do not exactly correspond to what one would really see from that position or distance. She argues that these would more accurately be called shots *mediated* by a character's look: "They are there for an audience filled with wonder and excitement before the artifice of moving and magnified images, just like the characters on the screen who exhibit wonder and excitement before each of the observed views."[46] Gunning amplifies this difference from the point-of-view shot as it later emerged in classical cinema: "Rather than providing narratively significant information, or indications of character knowledge or psychology, these glimpses deliver bits of scopic pleasure, spectacle rather than narrative."[47]

A Search for the Evidence is unlike other through-the-keyhole films that begin with a man's curiosity and conclude with his detection and castigation. *A Search for the Evidence* is motivated by a woman searching for her adulterous husband in a hotel. With a detective at her side, the wife peers into one keyhole after another, and the film depicts a new scene each time framed by a keyhole mask. Noël Burch describes the end: "The last room is the 'right' one, and the point-of-view shot is linked—in a way quite unusual for the period—to a shot showing the same set from a different angle (the wife and the detective burst in on the right to catch the husband *in flagrante delicto*."[48] For Burch, the film is especially important because the final shot from the reverse angle of the keyhole views provides an alternating structure for narration that is more cinematic than previous films. Mayne argues, despite this summary, that once they discover the husband with his paramour, the *detective alone* rushes into the room, and it is his ability to "penetrate the room" and to cross the "threshold dividing subject and object of the look" that grants him the most important narrative power.[49] For Mayne, his look and movement motivate the finale of the film, and he stands in for the kind of narrative movement that will eventually be taken over by the movement of the camera itself.[50] But Mayne is incorrect: while the detective's look—as an impetus for his effort to pry open the door—is important for the development of cinema's narrational syntax, the wife still enters the room with him.[51] In fact, the wife drags the "other woman" from behind a curtain where she is hiding and throws her against the bed. The wife raises a wine bottle as if to strike the woman, but the detective takes the bottle from her. The husband and wife each bury their heads in their hands.

While the film is important for an emerging specifically cinematic specific vocabulary, no one has recognized that *A Search for the Evidence* was also a remake of a Biograph film released only a month earlier and retells a story in a more economical albeit increasingly cinematic fashion. The prior version, *The Divorce,* featured three separate views: 1. *Detected* showed the husband, wife, and baby at home. The husband "bids his wife an affectionate good-bye but drops a compromising letter which the wife picks up and reads."[52] 2. In *On the Trail,* the wife appears at a detective agency, states her case, and is assigned an operative. 3. *The Evidence Secured* more closely resembles *A Search for the Evidence.* In a hotel corridor, the detective approaches and looks into a keyhole. Seeing the husband and his paramour, he beckons the wife, and they burst in and confront the couple. *A Search for the Evidence*'s shift then to a female Peeping Tom is all the more telling. It is not merely a consequence of "edits" or abbreviations made from the previous story of *The Divorce* that presumably would have been familiar to its audiences. It shifts to the wife as both narrative and cinematic subject. The wife possesses the authority not only to penetrate the room and to perpetrate the punishment but also to act as a consequence of her own voyeuristic search for optical truth. Yet, however much the film's proto-narrative organization depends on a woman's gaze, the wife's actions are still authorized by a chaperone, the detective who serves as a representative of the Law. A woman may be a voyeur in some circumstances, and she may even control looking, but only and always within carefully circumscribed situations.

In this regard, Miriam Hansen argues, the Peeping Toms may also be understood as figurations of early film-viewer relations in that they "articulate the precarious nature of cinematic space, its peculiar interpenetration of public and private realms"; they ultimately stage a psychosexual ambivalence since they "engage in a collective ritual of seeing and being seen in the tradition of the theatrical public sphere."[53] The Peeping Tom who looks through the keyhole into a private realm is himself the spectacle in the theater space of the cinema. Thus, the Peeping Tom keyhole view may be seen as a step toward a more cinematic analogue for the act of spectatorship.

Although Hansen does not recognize it, the views of the room interiors in *A Search for the Evidence* are an especially good example of this even though they are configured in relationship to a female Peeping Tom. First, they literally offer up standard cinematic views—the melodrama of a young husband walking the floor with a sick baby, the comedy of a country rube trying to light the electric light with a match, the spectacle of the old maid, and a card game in progress. Second, the female Peeping Tom keyhole view may be seen as a cinematic analogue to the act of gazing into the department store window—women contemplating a spectacle usually presented as a domestic interior, a representation of the private, while they serve as the objects of the public spectacle on the street.

There are numerous other instances of women looking. Another exceptional film that both Mayne and Hansen single out is *What Happened in the Tunnel* (Edison Manufacturing Company, 1903), a film in which a gentleman tries to steal a kiss from a white female railway passenger just as the train enters a tunnel. The screen goes to black, and when the train emerges and the image returns, the male passenger is kissing the woman's black maid. The two women laugh uproariously, and the maid looks at the camera as she laughs. Mayne describes the racist joke on which the film depends: "The man looks and wants to possess what he sees, but he kisses the 'wrong' woman, the inappropriate object of spectacle. The two women . . . are objects of the male look, but they *return the look,* by laughing at the man" [emphasis mine].[54] Hansen even adds that the maid's

WHAT HAPPENED IN THE TUNNEL *(Edison Manufacturing Company, 1903)*.

glance at the camera may indicate that she "was not merely a prop but that she, rather than her mistress, might have authorized the substitution."[55]

What both Mayne and Hansen neglect to say about *What Happened in the Tunnel* is how conventional was this depiction of male loss of visual mastery. What is important is how widespread and exemplary is this syntactical employment of gendered, classed, and racial elements for the empowerment, not of a generalized but of a highly particular kind of female gaze. There are numerous contemporary variants of *What Happened in the Tunnel*. For example, in *The Mis-Directed Kiss* (American Mutoscope & Biograph, 1904), another white lady and her maid (played by an actor in blackface) are visited by an elderly gentleman carrying a bouquet of flowers. The maid takes the caller's hat and cane, and the man almost trips over a chair. He then takes out a magnifying glass to see what is in front of his eyes. He gives the lady a box with a diamond ring in it. He kisses her hand and, as she steps aside to allow the maid to take away the flowers, he takes up the maid's hand and kisses it. He discovers his error when he looks at her hand with his magnifying glass, and he follows the glass up the path of her arm to her face, whereupon both she and her employer laugh. *A Kiss in the Dark* (American Mutoscope & Biograph, 1904) opens with a white woman sitting in the center window of the front of a house. A young man reaches up to try to kiss her. She indicates "no" by several shakes of her head. Then she gets up from the window, and the man tries to look into the room. As he turns to face front, a black mammy (an actor in blackface) covers his eyes with her hands. She vigorously kisses him and smiles at the camera. The first woman watches from the next window. Upon his release, the man stretches out his arms out and grins. But when he looks back into the window and discovers the substitution, his facial expression changes, and he rushes out of the frame while both women laugh. Such films routinely turn the male's specular power against him through a racist joke while they also allow his loss of visual mastery to become the source of humorous pleasure for the two women. In all these films, it is the loss of the man's vision that prompts the mistaken identity, and the women's laughter may be seen as their resistance to the authority of the male gaze even if the women are themselves locked into a racist hierarchy of femininity.

One of the most delightful and unfortunately obscure examples of a female spectator who prompts the overturning of male visual mastery for the fulfillment her own sexual desire is *Girl at the Window* (American Mutoscope & Biograph, 1903). In this film, a woman at a window is smiling and looking through a pair of binoculars into the foreground. She

A KISS IN THE DARK *(American Mutoscope & Biograph, 1904).*

1

2

3

4

smiles repeatedly and even seems to speak or, rather, to chatter in an animated fashion to the camera. Then something catches her eye, and she looks through the binoculars at it. She indicates that she sees something, smiles broadly, and uses two fingers to whistle and to wave at someone offscreen. A man enters, and she hands him the binoculars. As he looks through the glasses, she grabs him and kisses him on the mouth. Then she leans back and laughs. She talks to him as he attempts a second time to look through the binoculars, and she again grabs him and kisses him. This is a bold depiction of a female subject whose visual agency is not only the subject of the film but exists in service to her sexual pleasure.[56]

Girl at the Window exists alongside a number of early films that depend upon a character looking through an optical instrument like a telescope or microscope. In all these instances, the technological mediation makes things visible and, as a kind of prosthetic, allows the character to exceed the normal limits of vision. In general, critics have understood these films as historically significant only for the way they make an instrument of seeing analogous to the cinema.[57] The visual mastery that the character achieves with an optical device is a mise-en-abyme for the spectator's own viewing position at the cinema. It is important then that most of these films (e.g., *As Seen Through a Telescope* [Smith, 1900], *Grandma's Reading Glass* [Smith, 1900], *Grandpa's Reading Glass* [American Mutoscope & Biograph, 1902], *Un Drame dans les airs* [*A Drama in the Air,* Pathé-Frères, 1904] *Le Déjeuner du Savant* [*The Scholar's Breakfast,* Pathé-Frères, 1905]) reveal what is made visible and observed by the character.[58] *Girl at the Window* offers no view as-seen-through-the-binoculars. If it did, it would prompt a kind of role reversal of gendered looking. It would fix the sweetheart as the specular object of the woman's desiring gaze, a position then also being offered to the viewer in the theater. Her gaze may fix on a man so long as she remains the object of the spectacle for the viewer. Once, however, the male has been made the object of her gaze, she is empowered to control the drama. The irony here is that, although she hands him the binoculars so that he, too, can achieve the position of visual mastery that the binoculars afforded her, his looking is undercut because it is the cause for his *not seeing her* as she grabs him for a quick kiss. The comedy of the film depends not specifically on a gendered reversal of subject-object looking relations but on a gendered reversal of visual control and sexual power, on an ambivalence about the power and truth of optically aided sight.

Perhaps this extraordinary film was made because of its well-known theatrical star, Kathryn Osterman. Osterman, who is also the paramour in

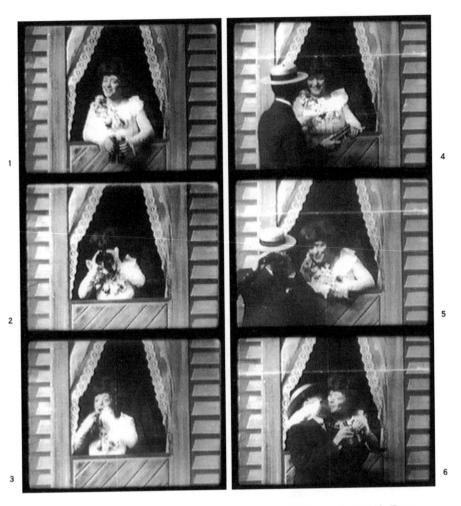

☛ GIRL AT THE WINDOW *(American Mutoscope & Biograph, 1903).* THE
BOLD DEPICTION OF A FEMALE SUBJECT WHOSE VISUAL AGENCY IS NOT
ONLY THE SUBJECT OF THE FILM BUT EXISTS IN SERVICE TO HER SEXUAL
PLEASURE.

A Search for the Evidence, made a series of films for Biograph (including
Girl at the Window) in the summer of 1903, each of which features her
in an off-the-shoulder gown in waist-up shots doing some ordinary activity: putting on makeup before a mirror, cuddling a kitten, holding a
rose, pulling petals off a daisy and mouthing "he loves me, he loves me
not," eating candy, and preparing Welsh rarebit.[59] In all of these films, she
talks animatedly to the camera. As a famous actress, her celebrity may

have motivated and authorized her visual agency since the films may be as much about granting the audience some measure of "optical truth" about Osterman as about the highly feminized activity set out in each film.

The most improbable example of a woman looking occurs in *On the Window Shades* (American Mutoscope & Biograph, 1904). This film is best approached as a corollary to *Pull Down the Curtains, Suzie* (American Mutoscope & Biograph, 1903), a one-shot film frequently heralded for inscribing an onscreen male spectator who voyeuristically watches a woman undress in a window.[60] Made a few weeks later (photographed on January 16, four days after the release of *Pull Down the Curtains, Suzie*) on the same set with a similar scenario, *On the Window Shades* opens with two side-by-side windows that are backlighted and the silhouettes of a woman *dressing* (in a reverse of the former film) in each window. When they finish dressing, they each lower their window shade. One of the women enters the street from a door on the right of the painted backdrop. As she passes in front of the windows, the remaining woman pulls up the window shade and watches her as she walks by.

This woman's appropriation of the gaze to watch another woman for her own pleasure seems to be quite singular in early cinema. In general, feminist film criticism has considered women looking as dependent on the psychic dynamics of sexual difference.[61] The limitation of thinking of the act of looking only according to the dictates of such scopic pleasure becomes quite apparent in *On the Window Shades,* when the difference that produces one woman's curiosity and interest in looking is not sexual difference. One might construe this woman's look at the other fully

ON THE WINDOW SHADES *(American Mutoscope & Biograph, 1904).*

clothed woman, just after we have witnessed both of them dressing, as part of the process of her identity construction. That is to say, as does Jackie Stacey when she considers one woman looking at another in Hollywood cinema, that her desire is "partly a desire to become more like her, but also a desire to know her, and to solve the riddle of her femininity."[62] In this instance, the woman's look then encompasses an assessment of the other's material adornments of femininity for comparative purposes. She looks at the other figure as one constructed to be feminine through dress, hair, jewelry. In this way, her looking would be no different from that of the women who watched other women shoppers in the department stores. Her gaze could be about how to align herself to the feminine image offered to her; this gaze would also be a consumerist one.

The film itself, however, complicates and even compromises such a radical interpretation. Of the two silhouetted women, the one on the right is stuffing her corset and adding a wig in order to achieve feminine contours whereas the woman on the left is more "naturally endowed." The catalogue description of the film further reinforces how this element undercuts any unparalleled depiction of female identificatory processes and desire: "One is a young and pretty girl and the other an old maid who uses a wig and other artificial means to achieve beauty."[63] Just as the "misdirected kiss" films compromise the women's achievement of visual mastery through a turn of a racist joke that neatly divides the women into categories of appropriate and inappropriate femininity, so *On the Window Shades* also subverts its process of female viewing for pleasure through a similar comic splintering. The result, in both cases, allows one to interpret these films as effective renderings of female specular power while they are also contained by overlaying a gendered visual power with other classifications that make the films also about the denial of sexual potency to women.

Beyond a simple collapse of this film into a justification for female identification, the women in *On the Window Shades* are both divided by and joining subject and object, spectator and image. The beginning of the scenario places them as objects on display for the cinema spectator's voyeuristic pleasure. Through the lighting, what is private or intimate in their boudoirs is rendered public and visible to the street. As the internal diegetic scene of their "exhibition," the public thoroughfare is first penetrated by the woman who enters into it and then controlled by the gaze of the woman who looks at the first woman. The desire expressed by the second woman's gaze, the possible expression of her sheer pleasure in looking at another woman, seems to fall outside the conventions of early cinema, and it was certainly repressed in the cinematic vocabulary that developed in the years that followed. While both women's presentations relegate them to being images for the spectators' consumption in the theatrical space of the movie house, they are ambivalently presented as shifting between the statuses of object and subject, between looking and being-looked-at. They are figures who both resist and give support to the representation of female agency and female desire. Inasmuch as early cinema thus represented women's active processes of looking as bound up in tensions between power and containment, it gave expression to the ideological dilemma of the newly important female spectator in the public sphere and extended the site of expression of her visual agency from the store window to the cinema.

The film that best represented the culmination of this tension in the gendered economy of vision is *The Teddy Bears* (Edison Manufacturing Company, 1907). A hybrid fairy tale, trick film, through-the-keyhole film, and chase film that also depends upon viewer familiarity with contemporary actuality films, *The Teddy Bears* complicates the seemingly simple story of Goldilocks and the Three Bears. It is a depiction of female spectatorship at the threshold of institutional change—at the moment when the inscription of female desire became both contained within the emerging vocabulary of classical cinema and reduced to a consumerist mode. It is, as Hansen summarizes, the encapsulation of the paradox "between the [movie] industry's increased catering to female audiences and the structural masculinization of the spectator position attributed to classical cinema."[64] The film generally depends on the familiar children's fairy tale but shifts from studio backdrops to outdoor locations when Goldilocks is discovered by the bears at the conclusion of the originating fairy tale. At this point, the film turns into a chase comedy as the bears pursue Goldilocks through a series of snow-covered landscapes. When Goldilocks runs into a hunter, the film takes a completely unexpected turn by playing off President Theodore Roosevelt's much publicized hunting expedition. Effecting a narratively unmotivated grim mood, the hunter shoots the mama and papa bears and, then, as Roosevelt did in a famous incident, spares the cub.

There is a scene midway into the film—after the highly domesticated family of the three bears has left its home and Goldilocks has intruded—when Goldilocks peeps through a knothole in a door, and as in a through-the-keyhole film, we are shown a suggestive point-of-view shot of a chorus line of animated teddy bears who perform a charming set of gymnastic turns. After looking and expressing her delight by clapping her

➤ THE TEDDY BEARS *(Edison Manufacturing Company, 1907).* GOLDI-
LOCKS PEEPS THROUGH A KNOTHOLE AT ANIMATED TEDDY BEARS WHO
PERFORM A CHARMING SET OF GYMNASTIC TURNS.

hands, Goldilocks tries unsuccessfully to get behind the door, to break
into the space inhabited by the objects of her gaze. But she cannot.

This seemingly innocent diversion that plays upon the contemporary
vogue for teddy bears is important for the film's conclusion. (Edison
Manufacturing Company advertisements called the film "A Laughable Satire on the Popular [Teddy Bear] Craze.")[65] After the hunter and Goldilocks
have spared the cub's life, they lead him by a halter and leash back to the
cabin. With the bear in tow, they go inside and reemerge with armfuls of
the teddy bears. The young Goldilocks, who is not yet fully a woman, re-
ceives the reward for the desire that was earlier frustrated. As Hansen
says, "She is female consumer enough to accept him [Baby Bear] as her
new toy, along with the stuffed bears she gets to pillage from the deserted
cabin. Her desiring look at the dancing bears suggests her collusion,
retroactively, with the hunter's acts of violence and domestication."[66] The
young Goldilocks has been trained to see, to link desire with sight, and
to fulfill her desire in the same way that female shoppers were educated
at the department store.

Whereas *The Teddy Bears* links sight and shopping only allegorically,
a small number of films depicted the desire of female subjects within the
spaces of the department store itself. *Bargain Day* (American Mutoscope
& Biograph, 1903), *Bargain Day, 14th Street, New York* (American Mutoscope & Biograph, 1905), and *Bargain Fiend, or Shopping à la Mode* (Vitagraph, 1907) all portrayed that desire as excessive in comedies about the
pandemonium of overeager female shoppers at store sales. It might seem

surprising, however, that there were apparently few films on women's looking in department stores since there were many early films devoted to places of visual kineticism and the act of seeing—especially films about amusement parks. But filmmakers, particularly Edison Manufacturing Company, had an economic stake in advertising the amusement parks' vast electrical displays of illumination, whereas they appear to have had little economic incentive to feature the sumptuous visual displays of department stores. More practically, early film companies did not yet have the cameras, film, or portable lights that would enable them to photograph in the interiors of department stores, while filming at amusement parks and expositions could be accomplished out of doors. Thus, the only films set in department stores were produced using painted backdrops on studio sets.

One example that interestingly manifests the ambivalence with which women were figured in early cinema is *A Busy Day for the Corset Models* (American Mutoscope & Biograph, 1904). Set in the interior of a fashionable department store, the film depicts a model dressed in a peignoir who sits on an overstuffed couch on the left while a female salesclerk works at a table on the right alongside a second model who is shaking out corsets. A well-dressed woman enters, and the salesclerk seats her on the couch. The first model climbs onto a pedestal, and the salesclerk turns her around and shows off a snugly fitting corset over the model's underslip (a loose fitting nightgown). The model goes off to the right, and the other model takes off her robe as she gets on the pedestal, models a corset, and then gets off. Meanwhile, the first model removes her corset and puts on another one. She returns to the pedestal and is turned around

▷ **A BUSY DAY FOR THE CORSET MODELS** *(American Mutoscope & Biograph, 1904).*

by the saleswoman. She gets off, and the other model, who is wearing another corset, gets on the pedestal. She is turned, and the customer appears to be making admiring gestures. If this is merely a contrived conceit for exhibiting women's bodies, it also includes a female spectator who watches the models because she is the customer, the woman who has been invited to look at other women and commodities in the department store. She is diegetically authorized to look because she is going to buy, not the women, but the commodities they model.

Other films (e.g., *The Way to Sell Corsets* [American Mutoscope & Biograph, 1904], *The Shocking Stockings* [American Mutoscope & Biograph, 1904], and *Four Beautiful Pairs* [American Mutoscope & Biograph, 1904]) set in a department store space recast ambiguities about the status of woman as the object of desire in variations of the "animated poster" film. *The Way to Sell Corsets*—shot the same day on the same set as *A Busy Day for the Corset Models*—depicts a male salesclerk unfolding corsets at a store display. When a man in a hat and carrying a suitcase (a tourist?) enters and shakes hands with the salesclerk, a woman outfitted in a black corset enters and stands on the pedestal behind the customer. He turns, stares at her, and then sits down. The salesclerk turns to the corset model and lifts off her head, revealing that she is now a mannequin. The customer, the inscribed spectator, reacts in surprise as the salesman continues to work on the model, handing the corset to the surprised man, undoing her chemise, and finally revealing that the mannequin is a mere wire dummy. The joke may well be about the instigation of male sexual desire only for it, too, to service capitalism. But the film accomplishes its humor through the trickery of woman's cinematic interchangeability between liveness and objecthood, between her appearance and disappearance.[67]

The Shocking Stockings features a frontal view of a store counter, where two pairs of shapely legs are displayed in front of the counter. Behind the counter, two salesgirls act busy while they stand in front of the pairs of display legs. In this manner, each salesgirl supplies the "missing torso" for each pair of legs and thus presents to the spectator a "complete" body of a woman. When an old woman (played by a man in a dress) and her fat husband arrive, the husband spies the trick and stares at the women behind the counter. His wife notices his sexual reverie, throws up her hands, and blocks his view by standing in front of the counter and lifting her own skirts to reveal her bloomered ankles. *Four Beautiful Pairs,* shot the same day on the same set as *The Shocking Stockings,* varies the joke only slightly. In this twist on the same film, there are four pairs of legs displayed in front of the same counter, four salesgirls, and the same husband-wife customers. The actions are identical except that when the wife discovers her husband's sexualized looking, she hauls him away. These films ostensibly authorize the interchangeability of the salesgirls with the lifeless forms of mannequins, making women in the department store space equally the object of male sexual surveillance. But by simultaneously marking the inscribed spectator as another naive, astonished rube whose own partner is so clearly a parody of femininity (and an inappropriate sexual object of desire), the film slyly offers up a clever "wink" that replaces the punitive ending of the "animated poster" films.

The Corset Model (American Mutoscope & Biograph, 1903) begins with a "woman" modeling a corset. But the model is the combination of a mannequin and a saleswoman who stands behind the headless mannequin so that her head substitutes for the one that is missing. The film marks her initially not as the subject of the film but as the object-to-be-looked-at. She steps out from behind the figure and removes the mannequin's legs. The film reveals, in this humorous gesture, that the "complete" woman who poses as an object solely for the viewer is an illusion. It fractures the illusion of the whole and available female body as it reveals the desirable object to be merely a visual trick rather than the attainable corporeal body naively imagined by the rube in *Four Beautiful Pairs* and *The Shocking Stockings*. In fact, all these films, just like the "animated poster" movies, posit a sexualized female object while simultaneously frustrating or mocking desire for that fetishistic object. They do so through a set of instantaneous reversals of: complete/dissembled, perfection of the whole/ the violence of dismemberment, objecthood/liveness, visual truth/optical trickery. The department store thus easily figures as a new urban arena where desires (both masculine and feminine) that are visually triggered may be rendered ambivalently.

However, *The Corset Model* does not end with the usual punishment or mockery of looking. Instead, the salesclerk moves to the side of the frame to allow a live model to enter. The new woman puts on a corset. Two female customers enter, look the corset model up and down while the saleswoman exclaims, talks to them, and shows off the corset on the model. In a highly interesting move, the film rechannels the "animated poster" mode associated with the comic revelation of Woman as a fetishistic object and with punishment for the sexualized gaze to a mode of socially sanctioned female looking in the consumer gaze and the displacement of the possession of femininity onto the purchase of a prosthetic, in this case, a corset. *The Corset Model* may begin with a familiar mode of address but reverses and even undercuts that address with its shift to inscribed female viewers who reproduce the same looking process as in *A Busy Day for the Corset Models* or *On the Window Shades,* an inscribed gaze of female desire for the acquisition of femininity, which is fundamental to the female shopper's role in capitalism.

More interesting, perhaps, are two films that link female desire and looking in department store spaces to the gendered shopping disorder that emerged from encouraging such desire—kleptomania. By the time that both *Arrest of a Shoplifter* (American Mutoscope & Biograph, 1903) and *The Kleptomaniac* (Edison Manufacturing Company, 1905) were produced, the kleptomaniac had become a popular stereotype. Kleptomania was the new name given to thievery that occurred in the department stores and was perpetrated not by pickpockets and lower-class female thieves but by middle-class women. As Abelson succinctly describes kleptomania in her book about shoplifting at the turn of the century, "As a concept about gender and female sexuality, it was a social construct. Women 'suffered from' or were 'victims of' kleptomania because they were female."[68] It was a disease that only women could have and a disease that was inherent in their very beings. The labeling of such thievery as a physiological disorder may be seen as pathologizing the female body—an explanation rooted in the woman's body for her desire run amuck in the store—and as a medical-scientific justification that blames her for the *dysfunction* of her desire. If the store was ordered by a circuit that connected looking, the production of desire, and buying, it also sometimes short-circuited into a relationship among looking, the production of desire, and *taking.*

The popularization of the kleptomaniac as a type and as a disorder depended upon making visible her secret—upon showing her in the act of shoplifting. The activity of detection became a built-in part of store practices through an elaborate system of surveillance. Thus, the very reflective surfaces—especially glass and mirrors—that enhanced the visual opulence of the stores and reflected the woman shopper back to herself also reflected her image to those in authority who were constantly watching her. Part of the salesclerk's job was to watch the customers, not only for possible sales, but for possible thievery. Floor walkers and male department managers watched both the salesclerks and the female clientele (in this regard, salesclerks were not held above the customers in the stores' suspicions about who might steal), and some stores even hired professional detectives, guards, or police to watch from a distance or to mingle with the crowd by impersonating shoppers. The unobstructed views enjoyed by the ladies were equally important for providing unobstructed views *of* the ladies.

As with most surveillance systems and especially with the contemporary model of panoptic surveillance that was then being popularized, the objects of such watching did not always need to see the authorities who watched them to learn the lessons of self-restraint and to be disciplined in behaving properly in the stores. In fact, the invisibility of the watchers, broken by their untimed appearances, prompted the success of the panoptic gaze for surveillance as it caused the object of that gaze to assume she was always being watched. Thus, the very space of spectacle—the department store that promised a flânerie for women—was equally a space for surveillance. In this latter guise, the department store emerged as a bogus sphere of flâneuserie. The Eden may well have *appeared* Adamless to its Eves, as declared by Boston department store owner Edward A. Filene.[69] But the women were all trained to know that "patriarchal gods" were watching and monitoring their behavior.

Two films especially articulate this lesson: *Arrest of a Shoplifter* and *The Kleptomaniac*. *Arrest of a Shoplifter* opens in front of a department store display laden with material goods. Signs in the background are labeled "Reductions in Corsets" and "Bargains in Hosiery." Women pass back and forth in front of the display and signs. A well-dressed woman in a skirt, blouse, and hat stops in the center to look at the merchandise. She puts an item into her bag. Her act of thievery occurs in the center of the frame; it is available to the spectator as a view unobstructed by passing traffic within the diegesis. One of the salesclerks, a man standing on the left side of the screen, has seen the woman's action, and he seizes her. While he

➤ ARREST OF A SHOPLIFTER *(American Mutoscope & Biograph, 1903).* THE UNOBSTRUCTED VIEWS ENJOYED BY THE LADIES WERE EQUALLY IMPORTANT FOR PROVIDING UNOBSTRUCTED VIEWS OF THE LADIES.

does this, another clerk goes offscreen. The first clerk opens the woman's bag despite her protestations and pulls out some garments. A policeman and the other salesclerk enter, and women shoppers gather around the shoplifter. The policeman takes the woman away as she cries into her handkerchief. The crowd of women shoppers and the salesclerk (still holding the evidence) follow.

The Kleptomaniac enlarges upon this simple narrative act, turning it into a multiple-shot moral tale. A well-dressed, wealthy woman is shown leaving her home by carriage as she heads for the department store. She arrives outside the store and enters a display space that offers a richer depiction of the department store than the simple table and painted backdrop of *Arrest of a Shoplifter*. Multiple counters frame the studio space, and the painted backdrop depicts a significant amount of detail in drawered cabinets, hosiery that hangs on the wall, and shelves filled with bolts of dry goods. Customers, clerks, and cash girls (young children who were hired to run the money between central cash registers and the salesclerks) occupy the area. All of this contributes to a representation of space in greater depth.

Female clerks show their wares to stylishly dressed customers. A male floor walker with a white flower in his lapel walks to and fro giving orders to the female salesclerks, and the cash girls flit among the customers. Sales transactions are made, orders are written, and goods are wrapped up. The extended length of this scene and the circulation of so many individuals in this space mask the activities of the wealthy woman. She

THE KLEPTOMANIAC *(Edison Manufacturing Company, 1905).*

becomes interchangeable and indistinguishable from the other women. The motions of all the characters within the mise-en-scène allow one to lose sight not only of which one she is but of where the shoplifting is occurring.[70] Charles Musser has reflected on the film, noting that many more specifics that could help direct the spectator's eye as well as fill in missing information were likely supplied in a showman's lecture accompanying each film screening.[71] For this particular scene, Musser notes how a lecturer would have linked the problem of spectators' detection of shoplifting—making visible the thievery—to the same problem in actual department stores.[72] In this way, the film invited an identification between the cinema spectator and the surveying authorities in the department store.

Musser also suggests that lecturers could have based their narrations on the catalogue description, which offers greater detail and more contextual information than does the film. For example, the catalogue description identifies the address of the department store as Macy's, a denotation that would have added an element of realism that the mise-en-scène alone is unable to support. It also spells out the chronology of the woman's shoplifting: "Mrs. Banker quickly conceals a pair of hose in her muff and then passes on to the glove counter. In the meantime, her actions have excited the suspicion of a female detective, who now shadows her from counter to counter. . . . She seizes the opportunity to take a silver flask from the counter and secret it in her muff."[73] The Edison catalogue description reinforces how exhibition would have strengthened the purpose of training moviegoers to the relationship between surveillance and spectacle.

As the customers empty out of the space, a gentleman shopper (the catalogue identifies him as the store detective) and a woman dressed like the other female shoppers (the lady detective) politely approach the kleptomaniac. They speak to her, and she leaves with them to the next scene in the store superintendent's office. There, the lady detective takes several store items from the wealthy woman's fur muff and displays them for the superintendent. The woman customer drops into a chair and sobs, and the superintendent's female stenographer watches with interest. The kleptomaniac, sobbing all the while, is led away by the male detective to her carriage waiting in front of the store. At this point, the narrative shifts to the concurrent story of a poor woman whose children are hungry and without food. The poor mother tries to steal a loaf of bread and gets caught. The two women's arrivals at the local police station are contrasted with each other: the kleptomaniac's carriage comes up the street, and she (still sobbing into her handkerchief) alights from the carriage while she is assisted by the detective and a man in a cape, whereas the poor woman arrives in a paddy wagon, and she is more forcibly led into the station by a uniformed constable.[74]

In the ensuing courtroom scene, a magistrate hears the cases of a line of accused criminals on the left, their lawyers on the right. A bailiff escorts the wealthy woman (still sobbing) away from the other prisoners to sit on the right. Then there is a parade of criminals. A short man who fits the stereotype of a street thug holds his cap, gesticulates in front of the judge, and is ushered off (the catalogue says he is found guilty of vagrancy). A woman sallies forth from the line at the left. She is well dressed, holds her head high, and half turns to smile at those seated on the right and at the camera as her lawyer speaks to the judge. At the conclusion of their discussion, she turns, nods to the judge, smiles, and simultaneously salutes him and executes a can-can kick before she is ushered off to the right. The next two criminals follow quickly as they appear before the judge and then are pulled off to the right—an unshaven man in tattered rags and a man in a straw hat who slouches and acts in an easygoing manner. Then the poor mother is brought before the judge. While a bearded lawyer pleads her case, she begs for mercy. She even brings in her child and hugs her before she, too, is ushered away. Then it is the kleptomaniac's turn. The lady detective lays out the case while the wealthy woman continues to cry. The judge pounds his gavel, and over the lady detective's protestations, the kleptomaniac smiles in relief and hugs her husband. The film ends on a tableau shot of Lady Justice, her blindfold askew, as she holds her scales tipped in favor of the scale holding a bag of gold over the one holding a loaf of bread.

More than an ironic commentary on the system of social justice, *The Kleptomaniac* embraces dispositions about women, their visual agency, and spectacle. The film makes the act of detection of shoplifting in the store space a spectacle in and of itself. An accompanying narration could not only help the spectator to select important characters and actions from the general hubbub onscreen but also further direct the spectator to identify through the process of looking with the store detective who watches female customers. It aligns the surveillance in the department store space with the act of voyeurism in the theater.

Second, the courtroom scene juxtaposes three types of women, putting the bourgeois kleptomaniac into sharp relief through a comparison with two other types: the self-sacrificing mother and the selfish whore. If there is any doubt about the identity of the prostitute based on her physical manner, since this is the only appearance she makes in the film, the catalogue supplies the additional description: "A flashily dressed woman appears and tries to flirt with the judge. She is quickly given an extra sentence 'on the island' for her impertinence, and as she is led away by the officer she raises her foot and dress and waves ta-ta to the judge."[75] In this constellation of femininity, the prostitute is the only character who looks at the camera, although her transgressive look has already been channeled back into the morality play of the film. It is still interesting, however, that she retains the ambivalent status of a subject who is both spectacle and looker. She is differentiated in this way from the other penitent women who may serve only as the object of the spectacle.

Both the department store and the cinema addressed female movement and visual perception in the city in an entirely new way. There had previously been no female equivalent of male wandering since female mobility was possible only within a division of sexual realms that restricted female movement to private space unless she was chaperoned by a gentleman. Outside those confines, a wandering female connoted social ostracism and danger. But as women gained greater and even unlimited access to public space, the heretofore denied possibility of their *public* pleasure in leisure time was overturned. By linking public urban female movement to consumerism, there would be no female flâneuse since it was a permissible form of movement and looking in zones specifically designed and contained for such purposes. Of course, the actual dynamic of this process was that capitalism required women to undertake the work of consumption—shopping—and so social forms of acceptable female movement and looking had to be devised so that this economic activity could take place. These new social forms—and their concomitant representations in such new forms as cinema—created a range of cultural anxieties while the boundaries of acceptable female conduct shifted.

The department store thus taught women new ways of seeing that they then put to use in the cinema. As did the department store, the cinema encouraged the consumerist mode of contemplation by inscribing women looking in similar ways. Early cinema certainly gave her a place of importance as it continuously shifted her status between subject and object—holding her up as both the manifestation of male desire and the agent of her own desire. In all these films, perhaps most literally in *The Kleptomaniac,* the cinema played upon cultural tensions about women's new public role as a mobile spectator, reinterpreting the paradox surrounding her appearance and visual agency in the department store as a woman-oriented space by treating the woman looking as an ambivalent figure.

Movies and Their Places of Amusement

DANGERS OF THE HOUSE OF DREAMS

If your daughter in the future is to make her living in the big city, prepare her for the temptations that will beset her. . . . Teach her that it is the place of amusement that seems innocent, the drinking of pleasant drinks, the association with characterless men.

ROBERT O. HARLAND, *The Vice Bondage of a Great City; or, The Wickedest City in the World,* 1912

"Going to the show" for thousands of young people in every industrial city is the only possible road to the realms of mystery and romance; the theater is the only place where they can satisfy the craving for a conception of life higher than that which the actual world offers them. . . . The theater becomes to them a "veritable house of dreams" infinitely more real than the noisy streets and crowded factories. . . . And yet the whole apparatus for supplying pleasure is wretchedly inadequate and full of danger to whomsoever may approach it.

JANE ADDAMS, *The Spirit of Youth and City Streets,* 1910

BETWEEN 1906 AND 1909, nickel movie theaters—with their cheap prices and easy accessibility—became widely popular, especially with immigrants and the working class. The same theaters also attracted the unwelcome attention of members of the middle class and particularly of reformers, who detested and denounced them. The nickel theaters' appeals to sexual pleasures (both in what showed onscreen and in what took place in the space of the theater itself) upset Chicago's civic-minded reformers who saw the theaters in the same light as other urban institutions of commercialized vice—dance halls and saloons. The nickel theaters, cheap theaters, nickelodeons, or nickel dumps (as they were called) represented, on the one hand, stolen moments of pleasure and fantasy, escape from indecent living and working conditions, neighborhood social centers, and opportunities for sexual expression and adventure. On the other hand, they represented for the reformers a new licentiousness and harbors for young, out-of-control immigrant and working class women. Richard Maltby summarizes the reformers' attitude toward the nickel theaters: "[The reformers] constructed a vision of a hidden city of concealed, unlimited, unlicensed sexuality, while to their despair, they succeeded in seeing depravity where they looked, even in the darkest of places."[1] These theaters and the class conflict that they aroused led to one of the first controversies over the limits to women's sexual freedom in the city.

Chicago's attempt in 1907 to regulate its motion picture theaters, the first effort to do so in the country, was an important part of the city's broader political responses to the new visibility of women and the spread of heterosocial environments. By identifying the nickel theater as a repository for a newly ambiguous commercial relationship between the sexes, the city produced a more manageable target for control. By localizing the threat, civic leaders and reformers reduced the complexities of urban social and moral disorder. Yet, in the process of determining what form regulation would take, the movies themselves became publicly defined as an important cultural institution. For movie audiences, for civic leaders, and for film industry entrepreneurs, basic notions about cinema became instituted through arguments about the moral regulation of the nickel theaters and women's roles therein.

By 1907, the movies had been in Chicago for eleven years.[2] On July 5, 1896, John D. Hopkins Theater (on State Street near Harrison) first introduced Chicago audiences to Thomas Edison's Vitascope and to projected motion pictures. The event drew the praise of the local press: "The vitascope is a combination of electrical forces reproducing scenes from life with a distinctness and accuracy of detail that is almost startling, bringing out on the canvas screen on the stage not only the outlines but the details of color, motion, changeable expression."[3] Throughout the summer of 1896, Hopkins's patrons watched scenes supplied by Edison during both matinee and evening vaudeville programs. Some were views that W.K.L. Dickson and his assistant William Heise had filmed at Edison's

Black Maria studio in 1894: *Annabelle Butterfly Dance; Annabelle Serpentine Dance;* an "umbrella dance" by the Leigh Sisters; a scene and a dance from the musical comedy *A Milk White Flag;* Madame Edna Bertoldi, the contortionist; and *Bucking Broncho,* with members of Buffalo Bill's Wild West Show. Other subjects included the now-famous May Irwin–John Rice kiss (*The ["Widow Jones"] Kiss,* Edison Manufacturing Company, 1896); *Herald Square, New York City* (Edison Manufacturing Company, 1896); *Rough Sea at Dover* (Paul, 1896); *Falls of Niagara* (Edison Manufacturing Company, 1896); *Elevated Railway, 23rd Street, New York* (Edison Manufacturing Company, 1896); *Fire Rescue* (Edison Manufacturing Company, 1894); *Shooting the Chutes* (Edison Manufacturing Company, 1896); and *Jim Corbett vs. Peter Courtney* (Edison Manufacturing Company, 1894).[4] It was a mixed bill of fare with actualities—scenes from everyday life—combined with theatrical acts, the male world of prize fighting, and the sexual titillation of dancing female bodies being exhibited for the camera. In this regard, the bill provided a model for what followed over the next decade. The Hopkins's Vitascope showing was a hit, playing to standing-room-only crowds and drawing new audiences who had not previously attended vaudeville.[5] It became the headliner on the theater's vaudeville bill for the next twenty consecutive weeks.

But by November of 1896, other downtown vaudeville theaters (including the Great Northern Roof Garden and the Schiller Theater) had introduced cinema when competing projection machines had become available. The pictures shown at these theaters were from several English, French, and American producers as well as from Edison (*The Burning Stable,* 1896; *Feeding the Doves,* 1896; *Morning Bath,* 1896; surf scenes from Atlantic City; and more Annabelle dances).[6] For example, the Columbia Theater featured the American Biograph in between acts and displayed eleven short films made by American Mutoscope & Biograph, including *Rip's Toast* (1896) from the current popular play *Rip Van Winkle; Major McKinley at Home, Canton, Ohio* (1896), which showed the President-elect outside his residence receiving congratulatory telegrams; *Empire State Express* (1896); and *Fire Department, N.Y. City, 1st and 2nd Alarms* (1896).[7] By 1897, a variety of machines were flooding the market, and vaudeville theaters regularly began to feature such movie showings as part of their bills.[8]

This glut on the market might have led to movies' dismissal as only a passing fancy or fad had it not been for the outbreak of the Spanish-American War in 1898. In Chicago, Hopkins Theater had stopped advertising its Vitascope feature in the fall of 1897. No other theater appeared to be showing movies either, and the situation was the same in Boston, New York, and Philadelphia.[9] Then the Hopkins replaced the Vitascope with the Biograph and began showing movies again on Monday, February 7, just one week before the USS *Maine* blew up in Spanish-colonial Cuba, signaling the beginning of the Spanish-American War.[10] With the outbreak of war, Biograph filmed a number of war- and nationalist-related subjects, and the Hopkins featured Biograph's *Battleships "Maine" and "Iowa"* (1898).[11] A local reporter described the reception: "A howl of enthusiasm went up at Hopkins' Theater at the initial appearance in this city in the evening of the biograph picture of the battleship Maine which, was sunk in the Havana harbor. . . . Many of the patrons rose to their feet. There was a yell of three cheers for the United States navy. Men whistled and yelled. There was a stampeding of feet, and women waved their handkerchiefs."[12] In April, the Hopkins added Biograph's *The Wreck of the "Maine"* (1898), *General Lee at Havana* (1898), and other war-related subjects.[13] Many of these views seemed to illustrate the front-page stories in William Randolph Hearst's chain of newspapers ardently covering the war.

War-related motion pictures multiplied in Chicago. Local newspapers reported that "the cinematographs, kinetoscopes, vitascopes, and biographs are almost clogged with war pictures."[14] In May and June, the Schiller Theater showed films depicting military camp life at Camp Tanner in Springfield, Illinois, and "a realistic representation" of General Dewey's victory at Manila.[15] The Clark Street Museum added a magniscope to its bill and showed views of the battleship *Maine* and Havana harbor throughout the summer while the Hopkins periodically added new war-related movies.[16] In addition, many local vaudeville houses featured naval dramas (e.g., *The Ensign,* about the adventures of an American officer in Cuba; *The White Squadron, Under the Dome,* and *Held by the Enemy*), military songs, and illustrated song slides of war-related subjects and of nationalistic icons.[17] The Clark Street Museum even headlined the quartermaster from the battleship *Maine* who had survived the blast.[18] The theaters' programs offered varying combinations of materials that included documentary movies and photographs, mock battles, war-inspired dramas and comedies, and nationalistic symbols. Their cumulative effects were more than that of simply acting as visual newspapers. In their combination of journalism and patriotism, they extended an ideological force. They spectacularized war and the concept of U.S. imperialism as had never before been accomplished.

By 1900, Chicago movie exhibition had stabilized although it did not initially grow at the same pace as on the East Coast. A few theaters periodically showed movies as part of their vaudeville bills; however, there were often weeks when no movies at all were shown. The principal local producers who emerged during this period were William Selig and George Spoor, both of whom had found enough success selling war-related motion picture services that they continued to market their projecting machines after the war as the Polyscope (Selig) and the Kinodrome (Spoor) built by Don J. Bell, who later became part of Bell & Howell.[19] Spoor supplied Edison films and foreign trick films to vaudeville houses.[20] However, the average number of advertised exhibitions from 1899 to mid-1901 in Chicago—most of which were either Polyscope or Kinodrome showings—was still less than two sites a week.[21] Georges Méliès's *Cinderella* [date unknown] did, however, have a steady run at Chicago vaudeville houses for three months in early 1900.[22] When William Selig's Polyscope Company began producing its own pictures of local interest, it found a regular outlet at the Hopkins Theater from August 1900 until January 1901.[23] Selig offered a number of views of local fire fighting (likely to be of particular interest in Chicago where the 1871 Chicago Fire was still a vivid public memory), scenes of the Union Stock Yards, panoramic views of State Street and Lake Michigan, local parades and other public ceremonies. Throughout 1901, Polyscope or Kinodrome showings occurred at Chicago's vaudeville theaters and, by 1902, motion pictures became a permanent fixture on local vaudeville house bills. In 1903, vaudeville houses increased the number of story films over the number of actualities and views offered to their customers. In 1906, various entrepreneurs began to convert downtown storefronts into nickel theaters exclusively for showing motion pictures.[24] Proprietors reported that among the most popular films were such sensationalist narratives as *Escape from Sing Sing* (American Mutoscope & Biograph, 1903), *The Great Train Robbery* (Edison Manufacturing Company, 1903), *Voyage dans la Lune* [*A Trip to the Moon*] (Georges Méliès Star Film Co., 1903), and Pathé-Frères's comic street chases.[25] Cinema was no longer a novelty but a full-fledged commercial industry. It had weathered its first business crisis, flourished in vaudeville houses, and begun to proliferate in storefront motion picture theaters. It had undergone a transition from being a mechanical headliner on the vaudeville bill to becoming a sensationalistic storytelling show. By April 1906, even the *Chicago Tribune* had taken notice of the new phenomenon; it reported that "nickels count."[26]

Indeed, immigrant Milwaukee clothing store owner Carl Laemmle took this advice to heart when he visited Chicago in 1906. He had planned to invest in a chain of five-and-ten-cent stores. But the Jones, Linick & Schaefer nickel theater at State and Polk streets just a few doors away from his hotel captivated him. He described his reaction to the novelty: "Not only was every seat occupied, but the right and left sides were jammed with standing patrons. The rear was also filled and after waiting ten minutes, the duration of the performance, at which time people trickled out, I was finally able to secure a seat."[27] He reported that he was "so pleased with it, and with the idea of a quick turn over of money to be made in this new business" that he visited it and the nearby Nickelodeon on Halsted and Van Buren streets several times.[28] One month later, he opened his first Chicago nickelodeon, the 214-seat White Front Theater on Milwaukee Avenue.

The number of five-cent theaters or nickelodeons rose quickly and steadily. Within a short time, there were nickel storefront theaters along State Street in the center of the city's retail district; along State Street to the south (the vice district known as "Whiskey Row") and strung out on Halsted to the west in neighborhoods that were filled with storefront brothels, burlesque shows, penny arcades, dime museums, winerooms and saloons; on North Clark Street to the north of the Loop; and along the main thoroughfares of immigrant and working class neighborhoods. The *Chicago Tribune* reported that "there hardly is a section of the city that is without this class of show houses."[29] By all accounts, there were at least 158 nickel theaters in operation by early 1907 and over 300 by 1908; in addition, approximately 20 vaudeville theaters had films on the bill.[30] According to one report, there were 405 nickel theaters in 1909 with a seating capacity of 93,000.[31] A social worker estimated that Chicago's daily nickelodeon attendance was 200,000.[32] Nationally, it was reported that there were three to five thousand nickelodeons operating by the end of 1907 with a daily overall attendance of two million.[33]

The quick success of the nickel theaters may be linked to the massive influx of new immigrants into Chicago as well as into other major U.S. cities. Immigration reached all-time highs in the United States in 1907; immigration rose from approximately three hundred thousand annually in the 1890s to nearly one million in 1907, and Chicago was one important destination for new arrivals. By 1910, Chicago's population of 2,185,283 included 781,217 immigrants, roughly 35.9 percent of the city's population.[34] They contributed disproportionately to Chicago's overall growth in numbers; Chicago's population increased 54.4 percent between 1890 and 1900 and 28.7 percent between 1900 and 1910.[35]

Along the main thoroughfares of those Chicago working class neighborhoods that were daily receiving new immigrants, new storefront theaters especially drew recent arrivals who spoke no or little English and who had little money for other forms of entertainment.[36] As the head of the Immigrants' Protective League of Chicago recognized, "As soon as her relatives have bought her [the newly arrived immigrant girl] some American clothes, they take her to the nickel-show. It is almost the only amusement they know to offer."[37] Although lower State Street in the heart of the downtown cheap amusement district was one important site for new storefront theaters, the nickelodeons that dotted Milwaukee Avenue, Clark Street, and South Halsted—those streets that were the centers for the Polish, Slavic, and Jewish neighborhoods—were just as important for the success of motion pictures.

The populations who patronized these theaters came from southern and eastern Europe, rather than from northern Europe, raising local discussions about whether or not they would be assimilated into American culture and values or whether their foreign and strange ways would overwhelm the traditional character of American cities like Chicago. Charity workers (who were renaming themselves social workers) were disturbed by the effects of immigration on class conflict and social unrest.[38] Rather than attempt social reform, they worked for social control, focusing on the spread of public commercial cultures in immigrant neighborhoods. They were interested in remaking the Europeanized, lower-class slum neighborhoods as ideal communities where "American" and moral values (which they associated with traditional small towns) would prevail. As a district agent for the Charity Organization Society wrote in a charity workers' magazine in 1902, "With a united front, the forces of righteousness and intelligence need not fear that these thousands [of immigrants] who are falling upon us will mar and hurt us; they can take heart that the hordes will be recreated and made a helpful part of us."[39] The nickelodeons, identified by charity workers as popular immigrant neighborhood centers, were important in the burgeoning immigrant landscape of Chicago.[40] As Musser notes, "Nickelodeon managers were often immigrants, often Jewish, and often from out of town. Established community leaders didn't know what to think about the change except to know that they did not control it."[41] From its outset, the nickelodeon was at the center of interest in modern mass culture as an ideological force in American society.[42]

A nickelodeon had two important architectural public spaces: its interior and its exterior. The interior was usually a plain dark room with a stage, a muslin-covered wall at one end, and seats for anywhere from fewer than 200 to more than 500 people. A theater seating under 300 was required to take out a license that cost $200 annually. A theater seating more than 300 was considered a different class of amusement and was regulated by different city codes and carried more expensive licensing foreground and to the washed plane of wall that occupies most of the painting's upper half. The "movie" itself provides an interesting focal point, a representation of exactly the kind of public sexual liaison the reformers were fighting.

The audience that occupies fully half of the frame is bathed in the shadows, and many are only visible from behind. Their preoccupation with the screen reproduces the conventional portrayal of moviegoing depicted in contemporary illustrations and photographs. Yet, among this sea of humanity, four individuals stand out. At the far right, one of the few spectators depicted in profile is a woman with a very dark complexion, a marker of her nonnative ethnicity that is thrown into sharper relief by its contrast to her white blouse. Slightly above her head, a man in worker's clothes and a woman in a large plumed hat stand, either because

JOHN SLOAN, MOVIES, FIVE CENTS, *1907. Private collection, New York City.*

they are arriving or leaving. Within the frame of the theater, they act as symmetrical doubles for the couple on the screen.

In the very center of the painting, a woman seated in one of the rows is turned directly to the viewer and stares outward as though she is aware of being watched. Her direct stare or return gaze is an arresting feature in an otherwise amiable atmosphere of commercial leisure candidly and surreptitiously observed. It throws the comfortability of the observer's voyeurism into doubt. Rather than subscribe to the conventional representation where everyone looks *at* the screen, this outward-looking woman centers the painting on the relay of *looking relations,* both between the audience and the viewer and between the audience and the movie screen. In this way, Sloan's approach departs from contemporary practices and demonstrates that he may well have been satirizing the dynamics of the nickelodeon that were currently controversial and a source of class conflict.

The theaters set up daily continuous programs that usually lasted approximately a half hour to an hour. This bill of fare, according to the *Chicago Tribune* was "the continuous performance . . . of cheap songs, tawdry singers, and suggestive pictures."[49] To put on the show, a theater also employed a piano player and a lecturer. Some theaters hired singers who entertained the patrons between films and sang along with the illustrated song slides that accompanied the movie bill. Song slides, stereopticon views, or magic lantern slides might also fill in the time in between reel changes and rewindings. The camera projector and the projectionist were sectioned off from this room in a cubbyhole (sometimes insulated to keep the highly inflammable film, should it catch fire, from spreading to the room that held the audience).

The outside facade and the area in front of the theater were equally important, as they had to attract the customers in from off the street, and they defined the boundaries of a sociable zone for those who waited, often resulting in spontaneous sexual flirtations or at least promising the possibility of romance and courtship in a semi-public heterosocial environment. Another prominent Chicago reformer and a friend of Addams, Louise de Koven Bowen, noted as much: "The boys and men in such crowds often speak to the girls and invite them to see the show and there is an unwritten code that such courtesy shall be paid for later by the girls."[50] The *Chicago Tribune* went even further: "The suggestive and vulgar take the place of entertainment. They prove the drawing cards. The show itself is made subordinate to the evil designs of men who seek to mislead the youth of this city."[51] They reiterated Addams's concern that it was the venues themselves that were dangerous because they promoted a set of exchanges centered on sex.

Most theaters relied upon extensive electrical illumination to identify the theater's name and to call attention to the site. The advent of architecture supply houses that could now inexpensively mass-produce ornamental ·pieces that imitated architectural elements of high culture also allowed nickel theaters to become increasingly ornate, with molded cornices, columns, and sculptural reliefs. The decorations' imitation of baroque and classical architecture styles attempted to associate the elements of luxury and material wealth with the movies.

Billboards held boldly printed posters that advertised the current fare, and most theaters employed barkers to stand on the sidewalk, announce the bill, and cajole potential customers while phonographs cranked out popular music to attract further attention. One reporter lamented, "The approach to the 'theatorium' always finds a crowd of gaping children of all sizes standing in front of the rasping phonograph, standing in awe of the hidden splendors within and in envy of those more fortunate ones who walk to the window and deposit the pennies clutched tightly in damp little hands."[52] An investigating reporter from another local newspaper also disapproved: "The theaters were found to be patronized almost exclusively by boys and girls, who clustered around the gaudy portals until a late hour, spending their petty savings and earnings with an insatiable appetite for the crude sensations that are experienced within."[53] A social worker even objected that "many of the lithographs on the billboard are immorally suggestive, and put robbery, and murder, and crime in glowing colors in the eyes of children."[54] The *Chicago Tribune* further complained about the theaters' "tawdry galvanized iron facades and discordant graphophone attachments, screaming mechanical ragtime into the streets."[55] Another social worker described the atmosphere as "blaring and glaring with trumpeting phonographs."[56] Sometimes as many as half a dozen of these similarly outfitted theaters could be clustered on one city block.[57]

If one turns again to John Sloan's New York paintings, he has conveniently portrayed this very setting. But Sloan's *Movies* (1913, Toledo Museum of Art) does not moralize in the tone taken by the reformers and journalists. He instead asserts a warmly attractive street scene. In Sloan's painting, the bright illuminations, large posters, groups of gaping children, loitering men, and fashionably dressed women are all there. Indeed, the very center of the painting contains a poster strung across the nickelodeon facade that reads, "A Romance of the Harem," promoting exactly the kind of sexually allusive fare to which the reformers objected. But, as in Sloan's other nighttime street scenes (e.g., *The Haymarket*), the yellow light dramatically bathes the street in front of the nickelodeon, making it an inviting oasis from the dark night of the city around it. The colors used to unify this space—yellows, whites, ochres, and golden orange-yellows—are all warm hues. They sharply contrast with the flatly toned black night and black-brown buildings that frame the scene.

The social dynamics within this setting duplicate those that the reporters and reformers observed. Children, including a toddler, study a poster in the foreground while to their right two women in profile look off to two men in the right-hand corner of the painting. Meanwhile, a man unobserved by the two women stares at them. On the left side of the

JOHN SLOAN, MOVIES, *1913. The Toledo Museum of Art, Museum Purchase Fund, Accession Number 1940.16. Courtesy of The Toldeo Museum of Art.*

painting, a man and woman arm-in-arm appear to be stepping into the bright circle of light. Another couple stands together in front of the ticket window. All the figures are somewhat sketchily detailed, due to a loose and even occasionally thick brushstroking. The technique both unifies the circle of attendees and differentiates them from the flat planes of black and brown that represent the street facade. Sloan's painterly attitude toward the nickelodeon opposes that of the reformers and expresses an excitement about the urban landscape and its energy.

The reformers, reporters, and Sloan all appear to have agreed, however, upon one element, that women and children were a substantial part of the nickelodeon audience. Social historian Kathy Peiss has noted that immigrant parents were more willing to let their daughters attend nickel theaters than other commercial entertainments.[58] Even married working class women could integrate going to the movies into daily routines that included constant domestic responsibilities and were not so neatly bifurcated between work and evening leisure as were the days of their factory worker daughters. In response, many nickel theaters hired older children to look after baby carriages while the mothers were inside the theaters, and there are numerous reports of movie patrons with babies in their arms.

The makeup of the nickel theater audience could shift, then, depending on the time of the day. Afternoons were given over to matrons and especially to children in the after-school hours. There was a turnover in the early evening as the audience became composed more of working girls and, as the evening wore on, of both men and women. A Chicago reporter who spent a day at nickel theaters noticed,

> After 4 o'clock the audiences were composed largely of schoolgirls, who came in with books or music rolls under their arms. . . . They remained sometimes for two or three views of the pictures. . . . Around 6 o'clock or just before that hour the character of the audiences in lower State Street shifted again. This time they were composed largely of girls from the big department stores, who came in with bundles under their arms. These are the heaviest patronage of the 5 cent theaters at that hour. They remain in them as late as 7 o'clock with the excuse that they have no other recreation and that the street cars are uncomfortably crowded at that time of day.[59]

For women and girls of the working class, in particular, the cinema was a significant public place to which they had access.

What is important throughout here is how the cheap theater itself was just as significant as what was represented on its screen. The nickel

theaters provided immigrant and working class women with an important alternative to traditional forms of ethnic, working class, and gender-
specific culture at a moment when these women were excluded from
dominant forms of public culture. It was not just the relationships that the
women developed to the movies themselves but their social participation
in the theater space that made the experience a crucial reorganization
of woman-oriented urban culture. Miriam Hansen summarizes how this
worked:

> The variety format not only inhibited any prolonged absorption into the
> fictional world on screen, but the alternation of films and nonfilmic acts
> preserved a perceptual continuum between fictional space and theater
> space. . . . Such exhibition practices lent the show the immediacy and sin-
> gularity of a one-time performance, as opposed to an event that was re-
> peated in more or less the same fashion everywhere and whenever the
> films were shown. Hence the meanings transacted were contingent upon
> *local* conditions and constellations, leaving reception at the mercy of rela-
> tively *unpredictable,* aleatory processes.[60]

Women's pleasures in the moviegoing experience were always twofold:
first, they enjoyed the activities and figures on the screen. Second, they
could experience a local collectivity through sing-alongs and amateur
nights as well as through particularized sound effects, live music, lectures,
and audience interaction that might well capitalize upon and emphasize
neighborhood, ethnic, class, or racial ties and connections. For example,
a West Side nickel show in a Jewish neighborhood would include Yiddish
jokes and songs, American popular music as well as motion pictures.[61]
A social worker even reported in 1909, "Certain houses have become
genuine social centers where neighborhood groups may be found any
evening of the week; where the 'regulars' stroll up and down the aisles
between the acts and visit friends."[62]

This combination of spatial, perceptual, and programmatic organization made moviegoing both social interaction and sensory stimulation. It
produced a psychological involvement that might aptly be called a "sensory fascination" to differentiate it from the model of "distraction" as the
dominant mode of spectatorship for classical cinema. Whereas distraction
means a rapt attention and absorption in the events on the screen, sensory fascination allows for perceptual attentiveness to the sensations on
screen without sacrificing one's self-awareness of the theater space. Notions of distraction as a model of film viewing posit moviegoing as an ex-

perience of alienated, atomistic, isolated individuals who were each offered ideal vantage points from which they could witness the story as voyeuristic individuals. When moviegoing was experienced as sensory fascination, arousals of the female moviegoer came from a variety of sources both in the theater space (live) and from the phantasmagoria of the screen, and they overlapped and mixed with each other. Hansen recognizes this: "This arena consisted not merely of the theater's physical space and the social environment it assimilated, but crucially involved the phantasmagoric space on the screen, and the multiple and dynamic transactions between these spaces."[63] Hansen concludes that since it is difficult to recover female viewers' interpretations of this experience, it is impossible to generalize a female spectator produced by this setting.

However, since moviegoing as a sensory fascination preserved the *experience* of being in a certain physical setting, it did not produce the modernist female spectator otherwise asserted as emerging in early cinema. This modernist female spectator has frequently been cathected to cinema's onset and, according to Mary Ann Doane, embodied an effective psychic solution to the shocks of modernism "through the progressive despatialization and disembodiment of the spectatorial position. The spectator is increasingly detached and dissociated from the space of perception."[64] There is no historical evidence to indicate that early audiences necessarily understood movies in this way nor is there any substantiation that they understood *movies* as a unique experience separately from the social interactions, the live performances, the music and sound-filled envelope. In fairness to Doane, she does not specifically date the origins of her modernist distracted spectator but implies that movies and moviegoing, from the outset, offered a gradual progression toward accomplishing this spectator and finally did so fully in the 1930s.

The nickelodeon between 1906 and 1909 occupied a kind of urban liminal space that resisted dominant culture, something in between the middle-class varieties of theater and the mass entertainment the cinema would become. It was both variable with each performance and immediate in its perceptual insistence on the here-and-now rather than on the far-away of what was depicted on the screen. The cinema offered, as Hansen says, "an horizon that made it possible to negotiate the historical experience of displacement [as a result of immigration or migration] in a new social form."[65] As a social activity, it could promote ethnic collectivity, heterosocial frenzy, or an unruly self-expressiveness.

Urban commercial entertainment provided an important alternative cultural space for African American women, particularly those who had recently migrated to the cities of the North. At the end of the first decade of the twentieth century, black women were just starting to become visible in cities like Chicago in greater numbers. Chicago's African American population was 30,150 in 1900; it reached 44,103 by 1910.[66] Hazel V. Carby persuasively argues that African American women were understood differently than were sexually independent white women.[67] The public appearances of greater numbers of black women who were migrating from the rural South produced a different kind of moral panic because these women were understood less as victims and more as pathological repositories of carnal desire, as women without "any moral fiber or will of their own."[68] Therefore, both black and white local agencies and reform organizations were more concerned with policing and disciplining the urban behavior of black women than with "saving" them. In addition, Carby maintains that black urban life itself became associated with commercialized vice because "black communities were forced to live in or adjacent to areas previously established as red-light districts in which prostitution and gambling had been contained."[69]

In Chicago, the South Side emerged as one such black community near the infamous Levee, a red-light district to the south of the Loop that included the city's largest concentration of brothels, saloons, pawnshops, peep shows, and streets filled with thieves and pickpockets.[70] Since African American women were systematically excluded from dominant cultural formations and since their employment chiefly as domestics or laundresses allowed them to participate in cultural production in only the most menial jobs, the commercial entertainments close to their neighborhoods offered an important alternative to these employments.[71] The figure of the cabaret singer, dance hall hostess, and, by extension, the woman who participated in nickel theater productions as either a singer or in the amateur shows promoted a powerful sexual expression of a black woman's desire in a culture that was attempting to repress that expression.

Descriptions of the neighborhood nickelodeon amateur show illustrate that the theaters were far more than "spectatoriums" for mass-reproduced images. According to Jane Addams, the nickel theaters offered a sense of community as well as potential employment possibilities:

> The young people attend the five-cent theaters in groups, with something of the "gang" instinct, boasting of the films and stunts in "our theater." They find a certain advantage in attending one theater regularly, for the habitués are often invited to come upon the stage on "amateur nights," which occur at least once a week in all the theaters. This is, of course, a most exciting

experience. If the "stunt" does not meet with the approval of the audience, the performer is greeted with jeers and a long hook pulls him off the stage; if, on the other hand, he succeeds in pleasing the audience, he may be paid for his performance and later register with a booking agency, the address of which is supplied by the obliging manager, and thus he fancies that a lucrative and exciting career is opening before him.[72]

De Koven Bowen also attributed a gendered component to the shows: "Girls in their craving for excitement are only too anxious to appear in public. They give the little stunts which they have learned and, if they please the audience, are sometimes rewarded by pennies which are thrown to them."[73] Addams enlarged upon this element: "For the success of a song in these theaters depends not so much upon its musical rendition as upon the vulgarity of its appeal. In a song which held the stage of a cheap theater in Chicago for weeks, the young singer was helped out by a bit of mirror from which she threw a flash of light into the faces of successive boys whom she selected from the audience as she sang the refrain, 'You are my Affinity.'"[74] A *Chicago Tribune* reporter described another nickelodeon show:

> When the lights went out and all was hushed in expectation, a girl sang a song about "Mary Dear." Mary was one of that clinging variety of maidens who caress pictures of departed lovers and lean against chairs on the porch on moonlight nights expressing great anguish of spirit. There is some character of this sort to introduce all the shows. The lover always comes home after he is reported dead and there is much kissing and weeping.[75]

Much of the scorn heaped upon the illustrated songs by reformers and reporters more accurately targeted the sentimental strains of the genre for its excesses of emotional empathy. Through the amateur shows and the illustrated songs that nickelodeon critics labeled cheap, tawdry, and vulgar, local women were both part of the audience and the performance.

These descriptions of amateur shows and illustrated song performances also illustrate the ambivalent ways in which women could lay claims to the spaces of the nickel theaters. While the theaters may be understood as an alternative spot for accommodating working class, nonwhite, and immigrant women's desires and for resisting dominant culture, they also helped to legitimize a woman's role as sexual spectacle and to connect a sexual economy of monetary rewards to woman's position as the object of male desire. One may denigrate the concern of middle-class social reformers and charity workers because it stemmed from their desire to impose their values on an unruly underclass and ultimately to control new urban populations. But their reform efforts also raised important objections to the fact that the theaters taught women their position was as an exchange commodity in modern industrial culture.

Chicago reformers began to investigate the activities of nickel theaters soon after they became widespread in 1906. The first expression of their dismay was published in January of 1907 by the Chicago Relief and Aid Society.[76] This report limited its attack on nickel theaters and penny arcades to their unwholesomeness for children, and the report was part of an effort by Chicago's organized charities to build more playgrounds in the city's slums.

At around the same time, Chicago's City Club also launched an investigation into the nickel theaters. As historian Kathleen D. McCarthy has pointed out, these two investigations were undertaken not as solitary efforts but rather as part of a phalanx that also included the Juvenile Protective Association (headed by prominent socialite Louise de Koven Bowen), the Juvenile Jewish Protective League, the Anti-Crime League, the Chicago Women's Club, Hull-House (headed by Jane Addams), Chicago Commons Settlement House, the Young Men's Christian Association (YMCA), the Northwestern University Settlement House, and the city's vice commission.[77] Some of Chicago's best-known leaders were involved in these investigations and in the subsequent campaign against the nickel theaters: Addams and de Koven Bowen were joined by Juvenile Court Judge Julian Mack, two university professors, and business tycoon and philanthropist Julius Rosenwald who was head of Sears, Roebuck. Unlike early censorship campaigns that followed in other cities where attacks on nickel theaters came from a single organization, Chicago's crusade was led by a coalition of diverse groups. Their heterogeneous mix helped to lend public credibility to their concerns.

In April 1907, as the City Club committee finished its report on the nickel theaters, the *Chicago Tribune* voiced its support for the reform organizations and began a daily attack on the nickel theaters. It expressed an even harsher opinion of the cheap theaters than had the reformers and charity organizations: "Most of them [five-cent theaters] are evil in their nature, without a single redeeming feature to warrant their existence. . . . Its influence is wholly vicious. It belongs with the lowest kind of dance hall, where the enjoyment of a popular form of recreation is made subservient to the pandering to the basest passions of wicked men and women."[78] Whereas the reform groups initially publicized their concern that the theaters were inappropriate for children, the *Chicago Tribune* forged in a different direction on its crusade against the theaters.

For the entire month of April, the *Chicago Tribune* daily kept its anti-nickelodeon campaign before its readers in editorials, news reports, and letters to the editor. It quoted at length from local ministers' sermons that denounced the nickel theaters.[79] It editorialized that the five-cent theaters "are worse than the cheap fiction which has long been a power for evil, by so much more as moving scenes in real life are stimulating to the imagination than printed words."[80] The newspaper even sent reporters to nickelodeons, and they wrote detailed reports of their visits, including the more sensationalist movies that were showing and at which theaters.[81]

Ironically, the reporters from the *Tribune* and other local newspapers provided the only guide available to these entertainments since most of the theaters they visited did not advertise, and these reporters may have inadvertently functioned as the first journalists who were also movie critics. They provided plot summaries, addresses to the theaters where the films were showing, and they also reported on the makeup of the audience and the other activities going on in the theater—from song and dance acts to socializing to outright pandering. For example, one newspaper story related,

> Probably the most objectionable one [nickel theater] is at 993 Milwaukee Ave. . . . Girls under 15 years of age and boys formed the larger part of the audience. First a 'comedian' told several suggestive jokes and sang a risque parody. . . . After his retirement the lights were switched off and a moving picture sketch, entitled 'The Moonshiners,' was shown. Exciting revolver fights, much blood, and many dead moonshiners threw the audience into raptures of delight. When the revenue officer finally was killed the cheers of the audience could be heard a block away.[82]

In another instance, a reporter recounted,

> There were a number of little girls who . . . got in the habit of going to George Brown's place on Halsted Street, near Madison. George made the acquaintance of the girls. They were none of them over 14 years old. George told them he knew some young men who could give them a better time than the Frenchman gave his "lady friends" in the picture show, and then for a small consideration from each of the young men mentioned, he introduced them to the foolish girls. The next step, after a few more visits, was a hotel a few doors down the street, where the girls began going with the young men.[83]

The report accomplishes both moral outrage and sexual titillation: it is the standard sex adventure narrative of the girl who eagerly seeks pleasure but is really the victim while it also serves up the sexual pleasures available in the city.

But the campaign that the *Chicago Tribune* waged was not so unified around the argument that the theaters were merely spots for commercialized vice. The newspaper denounced the nickelodeons as well for a range of other reasons. It voiced regular concern that the nickel theaters were causing children to steal money for admission and that the dark, poorly ventilated theaters were unsafe and liable to catch fire or to spread disease through airborne germs. But the chief consternation expressed by the *Tribune* was the movies themselves. The *Chicago Tribune* argued that the cinematic realism of a new breed of fiction films, through their sheer verisimilitude, suggested to both women and children (who were culturally understood to be mentally and emotionally impressionable and immature) criminal and sexual behavior that they could mimic.

The films that the *Tribune* singled out in its campaign cut across a variety of domestic and foreign manufacturers—Vitagraph Company of America, Sigmund Lubin, Selig Polyscope Co., Gaumont, Pathé-Frères, and even Georges Méliès's Star Film Co. But the preponderance of the films that the newspaper denounced were of French manufacture, and of these, most were made by Pathé-Frères. This is not surprising given that Pathé had captured more than one-third of the American market by 1907.[84]

Pathé's dramas represented the emergence of an increasingly narrativized cinema. They were based more in mimetic storytelling than in the "showing" that is the hallmark of "the cinema of attractions" of 1895–1904. In his study of Pathé films from 1904 to 1907, Richard Abel enumerates how conceptions of space and time were evolving into a coherent filmic system through which the movie makes its meaning intelligible: "The autonomous tableau gave way to a synthetic space no longer bound to a pro-filmic event or scene but constructed out of interrelated, discrete shots. . . . The significance of a shot became increasingly dependent on those that preceded and followed it and, ultimately, on even larger patterns of organization."[85] As Musser puts it, the crucial question facing filmmakers at this moment was how to create succession, simultaneity, and internally generated causality.[86]

Practically all the films that the *Tribune* found objectionable were fictional dramas or melodramas that related their stories through multiple settings, a sequence of linear causality, and a new sense of time duration and ellipses. For example, *Retribution* (Vitagraph, 1907) was about a man who first ax-murders his robbery victim in snow-filled woods and then later dreams he is tried and convicted. *Billboard* reviewed the plot in detail, praised the film's realism, and called the film one of the best of the year:

> An inn-keeper entertains a guest who displays much gold. The sight of the gold incites the inn-keeper to murder. He follows the departing guest, way-lays him on a lonely road and murders him. The gold is taken and the body thrown into a lime-kiln.
>
> Upon returning home to gloat over the proceeds of his crime, the inn-keeper is discovered and denounced by his wife. Remorse overtakes him and in the pangs thereof he seems to see the victim as he peers through the window. Here the dissolving view shows his vision, the sight of which causes the guilty man to fall fainting to the floor. He is carried to his room and put to bed, where he dreams that he is tried, convicted and hung. The view dissolves and shows his dream. He awakes as the halter is being put about his neck, staggers from his bed, falls to the floor and dies.[87]

The depiction of objective and subjective states, the details of the graphic actions, and the sensitivity to the temporal unfolding of cause and effect were all novel features that contributed to a heightened sense of realism as well as the reformers' alarm.

Bad Son (Gaumont, 1907) was the tale of a wayward boy who first smokes a cigar in his parents' house, then steals a wad of bills, and finally sneaks out at night to gamble away the stolen money. After he considers committing suicide over his shame, he instead joins the French navy, where he sails the high seas, participates in a mutiny, and enjoys a Turkish harem complete with an opium den. (The *Chicago Tribune* reporter duly noted that "the girls [in the Turkish harem] are dressed in a careless fashion, displaying an alluring assortment of arms and ankles.")[88] Under the influence, the bad son dreams of home and summarily returns to his mother, begs for her forgiveness, and has a happy reunion.

By way of contrast, another movie to which the *Chicago Tribune* objected, *Raffles, the Amateur Cracksman* (Vitagraph, 1905), was more typical of the style associated with the years immediately preceding the influx of Pathé films. The plot's intelligibility depended upon viewer familiarity with the popular play and short stories about Raffles, a high-society gentleman who leads a secret life as a criminal. In a series of tableaus that maintained a distant, frontal relationship to the action centered within the frame, the film depicted Raffles's criminal activities, which go unpunished since he was never caught. Musser observes: "Such portrayals might have been acceptable in books or plays directed at the middle class, but when they were presented to working-class audiences in nickelodeons, many community leaders soon voiced their opposition."[89] Jane Addams claimed that she knew of "thirteen young lads [who] were brought into the Municipal Court in Chicago during the first week that 'Raffles, the Amateur Cracksman' played and who each admitted that the gentlemanly burglar . . . had suggested to him a career of similar adventure."[90] A *Tribune* reporter expressed alarm over the number of murders, hangings, madhouse scenes, and burglaries being shown to "the families of foreign laborers [who] . . . formed the early stage of that dangerous second generation which is finding such a place in the criminals of the city."[91] Thus, it was never entirely the new realism with which "immoral" subjects were being treated that attracted the ire of reformers but, rather, the ideological force of cinema on working class and immigrant audiences whom the reformers were trying to "Americanize" to middle-class morals and norms.

Several Pathé films in circulation in Chicago in 1907 that survive today were among those singled out as morally insidious. The *Chicago Tribune* labeled the film *The Lawyer Enjoys Himself* (Pathé-Frères, 1907) as of a "decidedly suggestive nature."[92] The film depicts a gentleman leaving his wife for his day at the office. He goes around the corner to his office and is joined there by "a young girl in a 'sporty hat.'"[93] She perches on his lap; they hug and kiss "at a great rate," according to the *Tribune* critic.[94] When the wife telephones and thinks she hears some unusual noise in the background of her husband's office, she "puts on her wraps and prances over to the office. The irate wife pulls the girl's hair and beats her husband with an umbrella."[95]

From Jealousy to Madness [*Jalousie et folie*] (Pathé-Frères, 1907) "attracted a large number of women, who came many of them with babies in their arms," reported the *Chicago Tribune*.[96] This French peasant drama is about a wife who meets a lover in the woods. Her husband, who has followed her, becomes mad when he spies on her infidelity. The Pathé-Frères catalogue emphasized the performance of the man's deteriorating mental state and likened his downward trajectory to something from the stories of Edgar Allan Poe or Arthur Conan Doyle.[97] The *Tribune* chose rather to stress the sensationalistic aspects of the rest of the plot: "His wife has him taken to an asylum and comes there with her lover to mock him. He is shown in the horrors of a dungeon, plucking rats out of his face. He is shown in a padded cell, raving. Finally he escapes, goes home, and finds his wife and the man together. He strangles his wife, shoots an officer who tries to arrest him, and is in turn killed himself."[98]

Modern Brigandage [*Le Brigandage moderne*] (Pathé-Frères, 1905) is a good example of the narrative sophistication of the French product and of its ambiguous treatment of the law. On a country road, a highwayman riding a motorcycle stops an automobile. Armed with two revolvers, he robs its three wealthy passengers of all their jewels and valuables, and he takes off. A second automobile rescues the hapless victims. The subsequent pursuit of the bandit across several settings that uses both bicycles and automobiles is similar to many chase films of the period but advances the sense of spectacular illusionism. The characters traverse the same extremes of depth that occur in the opening as pursuers and the pursued repeatedly move from deep background to foreground in similarly matched entrances and exits. Burch applauds the film:

> French directors used characters to show that none of the space visibly represented is on a painted backdrop, that it can all be entered and touched, is "haptic," to use the technical term psychologists of perception have derived from the Greek word for touch and juncture. Pathé's fine film *Le Brigandage moderne* is entirely constructed on this principle: the "victims's" automobiles, the policemen's bicycles and the brigand's motorbike come and go in all directions, and at one point a policeman climbs a telephone pole. There is a particularly significant shot in which the police tie a rope across the street to capture the motorised brigand and hide from him by hiding from us—they leave the screen. This sort of exploitation of off-screen space . . . serves to emphasize the circumscribed geometrical nature of the perspective box. This method of staging is *a three-dimensional version of the autarchy of the primitive tableau*.[99]

The developing cinematic vocabulary that achieves both prolonged suspense and spatial depth makes the bandit (the modern brigand) pleasurably heroic in his efforts to elude the police.

Scenes of Convict Life [*Au bagne*] (Pathé-Frères, 1905) also combines use of three dimensional space and camera movement to produce an enhanced sense of realism. It depicts a series of nine scenes of prison life, including a revolt, escape, capture, and execution by firing squad. Although quite unlike *Raffles* in film style, it, too, asks the spectator to sympathize with the criminal rather than with the authorities. The Pathé catalogue made this quite explicit: "Spectators will be pleased to recognize types of social rebels who, in spite of the terrible repressions which the law exercises against them, never stop fighting, even in the face of death."[100] But what was for one culture a populist cinema was for American reformers the dangerous encouragement of the loosening of social controls and class order.

The Unwritten Law: A Thrilling Drama Based on the Thaw-White Tragedy (Lubin, 1907) especially came under attack. A re-creation of the events surrounding the murder of famed architect Stanford White by millionaire Harry K. Thaw, the film capitalized upon the crime that was the sensation of the season. In 1906, Thaw shot and killed White at the Madison Square Roof Garden because Thaw's chorus girl wife Evelyn Nesbitt was once White's mistress. In the most celebrated trial in America, Thaw was tried for murder but found insane. Although Lubin was not the only film manufacturer who exploited public interest in the trial (e.g., *Thaw-White Tragedy* [American Mutoscope & Biograph, 1906], *In the Tombs* [American Mutoscope & Biograph, 1906]), his film was unlike Biograph's entries. Biograph's were brief, single-shot tableaus. *Thaw-White Tragedy* showed Thaw entering into a restaurant, pulling out a pistol, and killing White. *In the Tombs* depicted Thaw in prison being visited first by his grieving mother and second by a weeping Evelyn. *The Unwritten Law* was both more complex in its narration and more explicitly sexual. This film alone featured Evelyn's visit to White's mirrored bedroom, where White drugged her wine and raped her.[101] Musser summarizes the film's effect: "The film's integration of sex and violence, its revelation of decadence and corruption among the rich, fascinated many and scandalized others. It was banned in Houston, Texas, and many other locales, but in others it was the biggest hit of the year."[102] In Chicago, it played in downtown theaters during the height of the *Tribune's* campaign.[103] *The Unwritten Law* conformed to the continuing concern that the representation of sexual behavior outside of marriage, even more than the depiction of social rebelliousness, would unduly influence working class women and result in the spread of immoralities.

It is interesting that the Chicago newspapers that catered more to the working class dismissed the *Tribune's* charges regarding the films themselves. At the height of the *Chicago Tribune's* campaign against nickelodeons, a *Chicago Daily News* editorial rebutted: "Fully one-half, possibly three-fourths, of all the sets of pictures are instructive. They afford healthy stimulation to the imagination of people whose lives are monotonous."[104] The *Chicago Inter-Ocean* poked fun at the police force investigation of the five-center theaters in a satire about two policemen who visit several nickelodeons looking for immoralities.[105] The *Daily News* repeatedly countered the *Tribune's* charges: "There are 5-cent shows where moving pictures are presented which give a pleasing and unobjectionable enter-tainment. One may travel in a foreign country, take a ride to the summit of a mountain, see people in their native costumes, or have some laugh-able scene reproduced."[106] They even commented on the theater space as potential employment for the working class: "The new places offer a welcome opening to many amateurs, among whom are some who show the possessions of talent."[107]

Letters to the editor regularly echoed the editors' sentiment and de-fended the theaters as important *familial* spaces of affordable recreation for the working and immigrant class. One reader wrote: "The writer has visited many of the 5-cent theaters in our business district and not once has he seen any picture that was immoral or objectionable. . . . To these places of amusement the patrons can bring their whole family and make themselves as comfortable as they like."[108] Another letter echoed and built upon this attitude:

> Far from being detrimental to the character of the young American, these 5-cent theaters are one of the best institutions of learning and character molding we have in the city. . . . The sensational pictures displayed in so many of these theaters, while portraying crime in all its details, also portray the finish giving the punishment of those who are guilty of wrong-doing. . . . In the thickly populated sections around Milwaukee Avenue foreigners predominate and as a rule, these people are extremely saving and at the same time they keenly enjoy a trip to the theater, which is usually a 5-cent theater.[109]

Testimonials based upon personal experience peppered the "Letters to the Editor" column: "I believe that the moving-picture shows are doing a great deal of good by providing wholesome amusement for the toiling masses. Ever since the 5-cent theaters came into existence I have been a weekly patron of them, and I have yet to find anything indecent or bad about them. I find great entertainment in attending moving-picture shows."[110] It is worth noting, however, that the authors of such letters at least appeared to be fluent in English, frequently had German surnames, and might logically have been at least first- or second-generation Chicago-ans; they were not the immigrants or toiling masses who were the object of the controversy.

Inasmuch as the *Daily News* contradicted the moral dangers of cinema itself and forwarded the theaters' legitimate service to the community, it still concurred that the explicit danger of the theaters was as a social space for female sexual independence, "Such resorts may become foci for the spread of moral degradation. There young girls particularly are in danger of forming associations that are ruinous."[111] The paramount issue for concern underlying the debates about the social values of cinema and the nickelodeon was always the control and regulation of female sexual behavior outside family governance.

Both George Kleine and Carl Laemmle, important film distributors in Chicago and suppliers of many of the films that the *Tribune* found objectionable, forwarded many of the same points as the *Daily News* had. As chief distributors of a large number of foreign films, they had become visible as industry leaders at just the moment when the Chicago campaign against the nickelodeons emerged. Kleine wrote to the editor of the *Tribune* (although there is no evidence that the letter was ever published in the paper) and sent copies of the letter to motion picture business trade papers, where it did appear.[112] Like the *Daily News,* Kleine asserted that sensationalistic subjects made up "but a small percentage . . . forming not five percent of the total output" of available films and, instead, singled out *La Vie du Christ* [*The Passion Play*] by the French manufacturer Gaumont (1906), scenic views accompanied by Burton Holmes's lectures, and the story of Cinderella as current uplifting films.[113] He also defended the so-called objectionable films as "on a par with the melodrama ordinarily shown in the cheap class of the regular theaters" and claimed that no American manufacturer made truly indecent, obscure, or vulgar films and that distributors rejected such pictures outright when they arrived from Europe.[114]

Laemmle—a chief distributor of Pathé-Frères films—launched an even more defensive campaign. Like Kleine, he, too, wrote to the *Tribune* (his letter was never published) and sent the same kind of letter as Kleine's to the motion picture trade papers.[115] Laemmle also took out a sizable advertisement in *The Billboard* in which he alerted moving picture businesspeople around the country to the *Chicago Tribune*'s campaign, exhorted nickelodeon managers to use "good, clean, wholesome, entertaining, and interesting films," and to advertise that they do so.[116] Laemmle defended his product and encouraged his potential customers to take him up on a promise for free "catchy" and "educational" illustrated newspaper advertisements because his ads would "create a stronger desire in the people's minds for moving picture shows."[117] For Laemmle and Kleine, the stakes were very high considering that, by their own estimates, movies played in Chicago nickelodeons to a daily attendance of 100,000.[118]

Both of them sounded within the industry the fundamentals of the argument regarding regulation of motion pictures that would prevail for many years. They focused their discussion solely on the films and their content whereas the *Tribune* and Chicago reform groups had expressed equal concern over the venues, too. They defended the wholesome image of the film industry and its product, defining the industry itself as primarily centered around production and distribution. They encouraged businesspeople within the film industry to promise that they would exert their own censorship; in short, that they would provide self-regulation *of the films* as a solution to any problems. In this regard, they forwarded a definition of the moviegoing experience as made up only of immersion in the phantasmagoria of cinema and omitted the more troublesome, less manageable association of a moviegoing public sphere with expressions of female sexual identity.

On May 2, 1907, the reform committee held a meeting at the Chicago City Club to read the results of the investigative reports on the nickel theaters and to debate what further actions should be taken. One of the chief items for discussion was a proposed ordinance prohibiting the attendance of children unaccompanied by an adult at the nickel theaters. Indeed, Jane Addams spoke against restricting the theaters: "We already have too many ordinances that are not enforced. What is needed is regulation of the theaters. They are useful in providing a place of amusement for those who cannot go to the regular theaters and can be made instructive." [119] Several others agreed with Addams and argued against age restrictions because, as the head of the Visitation and Aid Society stated, "The 5 cent theaters are not the worst evil that we have. More young girls are ruined through acquaintances they form at the small parks than through any other agency." [120] (It is interesting that this charity worker singled out the one other prominent site where movies were also shown—the amusement park—as the most dangerous place for female independence.) It is worth remembering here that "anti-saloon" groups especially favored nickelodeons as an affordable working class entertainment because it was alcohol-free, despite the number of theaters that were adjacent to or had doors leading to saloons.

The 1907 Chicago reform coalition then was bound together by a rhetoric neither of repression nor elimination. Their deliberations at the May meeting focused more on how to regulate and monitor a new social sphere of leisure for women and children. As film historian Moya Luckett has observed,

> Progressives did not try to prevent women and children from participating in public leisure activities, but they did not allow them total freedom. . . .

> The sights, sounds, and events of the city were considered a potential
> threat to femininity, while women's arrival in public life was frequently as-
> sociated with the rise in vice. This led many reformers to claim that female
> behavior should be monitored . . . and stimulated demands that the spaces
> they attended be strictly and constantly regulated.[121]

The campaign for censorship of motion pictures passed into discussions
about controls and management of the films and the theaters although the
ensuing controversies emphasized *either* films or theaters as the chief target for control, but rarely both.

In the next twelve months, the burgeoning film industry more than the
reformers took up the campaign of controlling the films' content. By focusing on the films themselves as the single component requiring greater
supervision, they posed both a definition of movies and a system for management that they could control. Trade papers regularly interviewed film
manufacturers who made statements like that of Essanay's George Spoor:
"I venture to assert that of all the dramatic moving picture films on the
market at the present time there is less than 1 per cent that do not point
a good and wholesome moral."[122] The industry papers even quoted a
Chicago minister's allegation that the five-cent theater was "a sink hole of
vice" in order to call upon "the power of the manufacturers to avoid such
undesirable comment."[123] The theme and tone were consistent:

> [The picture show business] is the poor man's grand opera and this was rec-
> ognized by Miss Jane Addams of Hull House. . . . There will be no more
> immoral or criminal pictures put out and an effort will be made to push as
> vigorously as possible such pictures as are elevating and instructive as well
> as amusing. Geographical, classical, pure comedy and similar lines will be
> followed with a touch of mystery and spectacular as well. It is a matter of
> record that the only failures of consequence in the business are the result
> of such subjects as the Thaw trial and the French creations.[124]

By the beginning of 1909, the *Moving Picture World* proposed that manufacturers bar depictions of "the inside of prisons, convicts, and police
stations, considered to be too morbid; contemporary sensational crime;
anything to offend any religion; lingering over murders and executions;
piling horrors on horrors, comedies that depended on the degradation of
people or their defects."[125] Capitalizing on Addams's renown as well as
the reform discourse, manufacturers repetitively promised a self-regulated
and unified *American* industry as the means for controlling the morality

of cinema, albeit cinema understood as entirely defined by the film products themselves.

Reformers, however, kept returning to how to regulate the spaces of the theaters themselves since it was the associations formed in them, that is to say, the loosening of sexual controls over women in heterosocial environments, that they wanted to address. Representatives of the film industry sidestepped this issue entirely and presented the problem as purely of content control: "[The film manufacturer] surely must exercise responsibility for film morality expressly not with the exhibitor but with the producer. . . . He cannot say that the sale of the film ends his responsibility. . . . His responsibility goes with the film to the exhibition." [126] So long as manufacturers could redefine the morality of cinema through product supply, they could then provide a problem to which they contained the solution, a solution that enhanced their role in the system at the moment when distributors were becoming the linchpin in the industry.

Two short-term solutions emerged as a result of the May 2 Chicago City Club meeting: Jane Addams proposed to run a model nickelodeon at Hull-House, and movie industry distributors (the film exchanges) shifted the content of their lists, especially resulting in a revival of the scenic accompanied by a travel lecturer and the outbreak of the chase film as the first truly popular film genre. The response of offering more lecturers and scenics was an early attempt to uplift the nickelodeon's status by bringing middle-class forms of culture to the working class. The illustrated travel lecture was already familiar to middle-class audiences.[127]

Chase films, produced in the United States since late 1903 as a response to popular British imports, used a literal chase as a central narrative element. In such films as *The Lost Child* (American Mutoscope & Biograph, 1904), a woman fears her child has been kidnapped and, when she spies a male passerby carrying a large basket, she chases after him. *The Lost Child*'s chase picks up momentum as neighborhood denizens join the pursuit—including a policeman, several neighbors, a woman with a baby carriage, a one-legged man on crutches, and an old man in a wheelchair. They chase the hapless man with the basket across a series of suburban terrains—along sidewalks and streets, across a meadow, and down a steep hill. At the film's conclusion, the man shows that he is carrying a guinea pig, and "the lost child" is revealed to be merely hiding in the family doghouse. Musser cites the film's effect for gently spoofing suburban society's insecurity and paranoia regarding the criminal element.[128] But a greater spectacular appeal lies in the film's diverse chasing pack and their display of the human body in motion. Thus, if chase films were important, as they have been commonly described, for their linking of several actions in disparate spaces, for their exploration of three-dimensional spaces, and for their introduction of continuity editing, they remained equally rooted in their appeal to the visual display of the moving body as itself a spectacle.[129] Hansen calls on this latter aspect of the chase film, suggesting that the narrative seems little more than a pretext for "a relentless display of awkward positions" when she observes the number of chase films that set up a lone man pursued by a pack of women.[130] *Personal* (American Mutoscope & Biograph, 1904), *Meet Me at the Fountain* (Lubin, 1904), and *How a French Nobleman Got a Wife Through the New York Herald "Personal" Column* (Edison Manufacturing Company, 1904) are all variations on the same bachelor hunt and afford similar displays of women's ankles, calves, and petticoats during the chase. All the major U.S. manufacturers made chase films, and Pathé-Frères was especially adept and prolific at them, too (e.g., *Modern Brigandage*). The industry's response of offering a greater number of chase films, what would now be commonly known as duplicating their success through a genre or cycle of films, introduced product differentiation as the solution.

Addams's solution was an attempt to regulate the social space of the theater and to manipulate it into a more middle class behavioral milieu — to govern female behavior and identity formation by controlling her environment. Jane Addams's Hull-House nickelodeon thus represents a transition between the nickelodeons as a liminal space for the unruly underclass and the incorporation of movie theaters into middle-class society. The Hull-House nickelodeon opened in June of 1907 as an experiment for the summer and ran on weekday evenings from six to eleven and all day on weekends. It seated three hundred, and it even included a barker and an electric sign. Under the guidance of Hull-House administrator Gertrude Howe Britton, the nickelodeon featured literary adaptations like *Uncle Tom's Cabin* (Edison Manufacturing Company, 1903), scenics like *Picturesque Japan* [*Japon pittoresque*] (Pathé-Frères, 1907), fairy tales including *Cinderella* (Pathé-Frères, 1907), and religious films with the goal of also including short, educational lectures as well. Carl Laemmle supplied the films at no cost.

By all accounts, the Hull-House nickelodeon was a short-lived failure. A reporter polled some of the youths on their way out of the Hull-House nickelodeon and offered their responses in his own version of their streetwise lingo: "'Oh, it's a good show, all right, but it ain't lively enough.' 'Dat Cinderella show was swell, but it's too slow to make a go of it on dis street. . . . Things has got ter have some hustle.'"[131] At one weekend showing, only thirty-seven people attended a Hull-House program while neighboring nickelodeons on Halsted Street drew crowds for such sensationalistic films as *The Pirates [Les Forbans]* (Pathé-Frères, 1907), *The Defrauding Banker* [unknown], *The Adventures of an American Cowboy* [probably *Cow-Boys et Peaux Rouges*] (Pathé-Frères, 1907), *An Attack on the Agent* [unknown], and *The Car Man's Danger* (Pathé-Frères, 1907).[132] The irony is that it is likely that Laemmle was also the distributor for many of Hull-House's more nefarious competitors.[133]

The Hull-House nickelodeon, although it quickly and quietly folded, led to important consequences. Addams and other reformers more vociferously championed legal censorship as a means of control. According to Kathleen D. McCarthy, Addams decided that the nickelodeon failed for two reasons: the "popular taste" of the working class was not refined enough and competitors would only contribute to uplifting taste and behavior when legally required to do so.[134] Their renewed efforts met with success when, on November 4, 1907, the city passed an ordinance that required every film shown locally to obtain a police permit. Such permits were issued by the general superintendent of police after a ten-man police board had reviewed the film for immoral or obscene content. Films shown by religious organizations, schools, libraries, museums, or private societies did not require permits.

However, the sheer numbers and rapid expansion of nickel theaters made the ordinance unenforceable and the board ineffective. By 1909, de Koven Bowen reported frequent abuses of the ordinance; she discovered many films playing that had not been inspected by the board. Her organization, the Juvenile Protective Association, would report such violations, and the chief of police would remove the film, but it would soon turn up in another part of town.[135] The city met that problem with a token gesture: it passed a second ordinance that enlarged the censorship board and added civic leaders to it.

Addams's failure further taught distributors and exhibitors what they were already learning: they could successfully satisfy their critics and fend off oppressive city intervention by incorporating wholesome comedies and travelogues, films which were deemed by the middle class as socially harmless, even uplifting and, therefore, more wholesome in nature. Publicity about the Hull-House nickelodeon confirmed this practice when Howe Britton acknowledged that the only way to draw in crowds without resorting to "vulgar" material was to "inject more humor" into the pictures. She said, "Of course, Alexander won't get his revolvers and bandit scenes in our films, so we'll have to do the next best thing to his mind and get funny ones." [136] She echoes rather than prognosticates the current trend among exhibitors who were already shoring up their lists with more scenics and chase films.

It was, however, the reformers who had initially brought to public discussion the conviction that an independent, even aggressive female sexuality was being expressed at the nickelodeons as a result of a relationship with *both* the theater space and the screen simultaneously. Their relinquishment of attempts to control the nickelodeons and their capitulation to both civic pressures for movie censorship and industry exhortations that they would self-censor their products marked a reversal of the definition of the moviegoing experience. Increasingly, moviegoing experience was defined as ruled by identification with screen figures and absorption in the screen space itself. Thus, the authorities constructed an experience to which they could offer a manageable outcome by regulating what was depicted on screen.

But the way that female identity was formed at the cinema always embraced a sensory fascination with movies that incorporated a sense of the here-and-now; it was not purely a process of identification with what was happening on the screen. The cinema established itself as a public place for forming cultural collectivity through social participation. What is important here is how a public culture (albeit an alternative to other public forms) became defined through its incorporation of gendered differences and active female subjectivity. In their campaigns to regulate these theaters, Chicago reformers explicitly addressed this process of female identity formation. It was a process that was dependent on the manifold regimes of activity offered at the nickelodeons even if that process was written out of history once the public discussions became dominated by the film industry's own self-regulatory discourse.

THROUGH THE
PEEPHOLE

CINEMA AT THE AMUSEMENT PARK

People found themselves in an "Erector" world . . . remarkable for [its] visual accessibility. . . . An onlooker has immediate access to the construction, to the design decisions of the engineers and architects. Open to view, so obviously *designed,* the world of girders and gears invites the onlooker to see its internal workings, its component parts. . . . Gears go round, bearings roll, pistons push, girders support. The foremost traits of this world are its visuality and its kinetics.

CECELIA TICHI, *Shifting Gears: Technology, Literature,*
Culture in Modernist America, 1987

To be gulled, to know you are gulled, and to know that the people who gull you know you know they're gulling you—ah! the bliss! Here at the park a mimic railway carriage, with biograph pictures at its farther end, takes you spinning along the funicular "up Mt. Vesuvius."

ROLLIN LYNDE HARTT, "The Amusement Park," 1907

More young girls are ruined through acquaintances they form at the small parks than through any other agency.

SHERMAN C. KINGSLEY, *Chicago Tribune,* 1907

NOTHING WAS A BETTER SYMBOL of the new American urban landscape than the turn-of-the-century amusement park located on the outskirts of the city. The amusement park brought together various

strands of American culture at the moment when the country was becoming a more thoroughly urbanized industrial nation, an international
empire—the moment often elided with the onset of American modernity
and the beginning of consumer culture. It was the best amalgamation of
the new metropolitan society of commercialized leisure and of its limits.
It was an Erector-set world of mechanical thrill rides, shows of human
and animal oddities, saloons and swimming pools, beer gardens and ball-
rooms, restaurants and roller skating rinks. It was characterized by its dy-
namism—its brash colors, constant noise, and the continual movement
of people and machinery. It was a place for city-dwellers to counter modern mass alienation, to encounter new technologies, and to learn with
their bodies. The amusement park foregrounded the importance of the
range of sensory experiences in relationship to visual perception.

Cinema was especially important at the amusement park because it condensed the park's discourses while it simultaneously converted women
from private individuals into their new status as both consumer and commodity in a mass culture. Movies, available inside the parks at penny
arcades, tent or wooden vaudeville theaters, and at specially outfitted railroad cars, offered up novelty, informal peer relations, and sexual excitement consistent with what was available elsewhere throughout the park.
Movies and other park attractions may have liberated young women,
newly arrived in the city and cast adrift from their families, from familial
supervision and Victorian sexual restraints. But they also exercised a new
kind of cultural authorization of sexual objectification and of women's
roles as consumer and consumed. The amusement park invited women to
find sensual pleasure in their own bodies as it simultaneously transformed
them into spectacles. The questions of women's identities in moviegoing
activities at the amusement parks are related, then, to the ways that the
sites functioned for integrating regimes of pleasure.

Every municipality of any size at the turn of the century had at least
one amusement park on its outskirts. Of course, the best known was
Brooklyn's Coney Island. But New Yorkers also frequented Palisades Park
on the Jersey shore just opposite 130th Street and Paradise Park at the
end of the Third Avenue trolley line in Fort George. By the end of the
century, Cincinnati boasted its own Coney Island, and Luna Parks (named
after Coney Island's successful Luna) were constructed in Cleveland, Indianapolis, Scranton, Pittsburgh, Washington, D.C., and Chicago. There
were White City amusement parks (named after the 1893 Exposition) in
New Haven, Cleveland, Portland, Indianapolis, Louisville, Worcester, Fort
Worth, Denver, and Chicago. There were parks that intimated they were

romantic settings in nature: Wildwood (St. Paul), Forest Park Highlands (St. Louis), Elitch's Pleasure Garden (Denver), Willow Grove (Philadelphia), Highland Park (Houston), and Riverview (Chicago). There were parks simply named after their geographic locations: Euclid Beach (Cleveland), Kennywood (Pittsburgh), Chester Park (Cincinnati), and West End Park (New Orleans). There were parks even more generically designated "Electric Park" in Kansas City; Niagara Falls, New York; Albany, New York; Baltimore; Detroit; Oshkosh, Wisconsin; and Montgomery, Alabama. But there were also more fancifully named parks whose names conjured up a fantasy space: Wonderland Parks in Boston, San Diego, and Minneapolis; Dream City in Pittsburgh; Dreamland Park in San Francisco; Fairyland Parks in Memphis and Little Rock; Chicago's San Souci or "without a care." In fact, there were over fifteen hundred amusement parks in the United States by the year 1906.[1] What they all had in common was that they were easily accessible by public transportation, physically enclosed, architecturally whimsical, affordable to their patrons, and exciting.

The amusement park brought together the legacy of a number of nineteenth-century institutions. It was an outgrowth of the country fair, the circus, and the dime museum. It was the distinctive heir to the Midway and indeed to all the Chicago Columbian Exposition. It also incorporated the practices of two nineteenth-century institutions that attempted to educate the growing middle class to the pleasures of visual spectacle—the museum and the department store. Their purposes may have been radically different since the museum was steeped in educational aspirations and the department store in economic ones, but they both participated in a growing insistence on visual spectacle and commodity consumption as the order of pleasure in modern life. The amusement park synthesized the techniques and values of all these high and low cultural orders into one commercial enterprise that was aimed at everyone: it offered the new concept of a commercialized *mass* culture.

Chicago, throughout this period, had no fewer than five major parks. It was estimated that on an average summer weekend in 1907 or 1908, approximately a half million Chicagoans (or almost one quarter of the city's population) visited area amusement parks.[2] The oldest was Chutes Park (1894–95 at Sixty-first Street and Drexel Boulevard, 1896–1907 at Jackson and Kedzie avenues), a west side park organized around the featured attraction of a Shoot-the-Chutes mechanical water slide. Sans Souci (1899–1929), at Sixtieth Street and Cottage Grove Avenue on Chicago's south side, appeared for the same reason as numerous parks did in other cities: the traction company City Railway constructed it at the end of a

streetcar line in order to encourage business. Like other traction companies that owned amusement parks, City Railway Company was content
to break even on the park so long as it encouraged streetcar revenues
and ridership.[3] White City (1905–1934) was the preeminent south side
park just south of the original Midway at Jackson Park and Sixty-third
Street (and very close to Sans Souci). The short-lived Luna Park (c. 1907–
1911) was at Fiftieth and Halsted streets, near the Union Stockyards. Forest Park (1908–1923) was farther out past Chicago's west side in the sub-
urb of Forest Park. But the biggest and most enduring area park was
Riverview (1904–1967).

On the north side along the Chicago River at Western and Belmont
avenues, Riverview Park was the country's biggest amusement park and
among the most successful at encompassing a range of ethnic and class
groups for one mass entertainment. It drew heavily from Polish, Irish,
Italian, Bohemian, Scandinavian, and Jewish immigrant neighborhoods
as well as from the surrounding prosperous ones. Three and a half million people visited the fifty-acre site in 1906; and the following year,

WHITE CITY AMUSEMENT PARK, JACKSON PARK AND SIXTY-THIRD
STREET, C. 1909. *Postcard.*

White City Amusement Park, Chicago.

 RIVERVIEW PARK, WESTERN AND BELMONT AVENUES, VIEW FROM
THE TOP OF THE CHUTES, C. 1909. *Postcard.*

Riverview claimed its Sunday attendance alone as greater than two hundred thousand each week.[4]

Like most parks, Riverview was geographically secluded yet close to the urban center of town. Its general accessibility depended on the 1907 extension of one elevated railway line that opened a station outside Riverview as well as on free streetcar service from the terminus of the other elevated railway. The park also had a landing for the public ferryboat that came from downtown Chicago. Riverview promoted the trip to the park itself as a summertime pleasure—whether by boat or streetcar—for the working class consumer without capital or extended leisure time. As one advertisement proclaimed, "Riverview is as good a tonic as a visit to a summer resort and many of its visitors have decreed that it is an excellent place to spend one's vacation."[5] Its promise of isolation from the city perpetuated cultural patterns that identified leisure with spatial representations of nature and with tourist travel as opposed to urban civilization.

Riverview was also different from Coney Island in that it did not develop out of a commercial environment of taboo pleasures linked to female immorality (e.g., "girlie" shows, exotic dancers, prostitution). Unlike Coney Island's identification as a vice-ridden "Sodom by the Sea," Riverview was the subject of publicity, programs, trade, and daily newspaper reviews that reiterated the park's beginnings as a private picnic grove and shooting range for the families of successful German businessmen. Men of German descent were the heads of Chicago's industrial, political, and commercial institutions and dominated the controls over civic life.[6] Emphasizing that Riverview's owner, George Schmidt, had also been the president of the German Sharp Shooters Club, Riverview Park publicity claimed the park was founded when Schmidt installed a merry-go-round for club members' wives and children—an advertising tactic that served as a constant reminder that the park would uphold standards of family respectability and maintain the appropriate sexual divisions of leisure.

Inside the park entrance, the landscape, architecture and spatial organization were a combination and confusion of boldly lettered signs, incandescent lights, eclectic and exotic architectural styles, and exposed architectural skeletons. The extravagance and scale of the architecture, the mix of different architectural styles and details, the bright colors, and the mechanical structures that dominated the visual environment addressed the visitor's eye through their visual excess and velocity of parts-in-motion: "The color scheme of white and green predominates and broad promenades all lead to the various buildings and features all through the grounds. At every turn something of a clever and inviting sort is offered and a number of sensational outdoor exhibitions are included in the general programme."[7] Frederic Thompson, entrepreneur and planner of Coney Island, likewise emphasized the importance of inviting the spectator's physical involvement through processes of vision and initiation of desire, "The very architecture must be in keeping with the spirit of carnival. It must be active, mobile, free, graceful, and attractive. It must be arranged so that visitors will say 'What is this?' and 'Why is that?'"[8] The new cultural authority of the urban landscape was its invitation to knowledge through visual display, rapid movement, and sensory involvement.

Riverview's mechanized thrill rides best exemplify how the amusement park inscribed this process. The Hell Gate, Figure Eight, and Velvet Coaster were all roller coasters with steep inclines, dips, and the element of speed. The Water Chutes (generally called Shoot-the-Chutes at other parks) were passenger cars mechanically swept down an inclined track onto the surface of a pool of water. The Circle Swing was a high steel tower whose radial arms each suspended a passenger carriage so that when the whole device was rotated at increasingly higher speeds, the seats swung out in a wide circle. The Haunted Swing was actually an illusion ride in which a large swing, suspended from a bar in a room, allowed seated passengers to feel odd sensations of oscillation when the closed room itself shifted back and forth as the swing remaining stationary.

These rides all offered pleasure by reversing the usual relations between the body and machinery in which the person controls and masters the machine. The person surrendered to the machine which, in turn, liberated the body in some fashion from its normal limitations of placement and movement in daily life. As cultural analyst Tony Bennett elaborates:

> For the most part, however, the [amusement park] addresses—indeed assaults—the body, suspending the physical laws that normally restrict its movement, breaking the social codes that normally regulate its conduct, inverting the usual relations between the body and machinery and generally inscribing the body in relations different from those in which it is caught and held in everyday life.[9]

Particularly, for Chicago's working class men and women, who spent their days laboring on such modern machinery as sewing machines, the factory assembly line, or the mechanized apparatus of the stockyards, the reversal of their everyday relationship to the mechanical may have been pleasurable precisely because it expressed and relieved their *fears* of the machines mastering, assaulting, or even injuring them. As cultural historian John Kasson observes about Coney Island, "Riders could enjoy their own momentary fright and disorientation because they knew it would turn to comic relief; they could engage in what appeared dangerous adventure because ultimately they believed in its safety."[10] Since physical injury in the workplace posed a real and serious threat to laborers, the inscription of "danger" in human-machine relations at the amusement park allowed symbolic expression of those fears in an environment where the outcome was predictably safe.

Riverview also promised the female immigrant a place for her family's summer outings. In the *Chicago Inter-Ocean,* a daily penny newspaper with a largely working class readership, Riverview advertised free weekday admission for women and children. Addressing the laborer who had limited time for leisure and relaxation, the advertisements claimed, "You can spend the whole afternoon and evening with your family and find perfect comfort. THAT'S RIVERVIEW! No 'KEEP MOVING' as in other places. Sit if you want to, there are plenty of seats. A Strenuous Day Today

So Come Out."[11] Riverview suggested that it was in public spaces, rather than in the domestic realm, that working class women could find pleasure in rest while maintaining family unity. For married female wage earners whose labor did not stop once they were outside the factory gates, Riverview's rhetoric implied a modern reorientation among self-identity, space, and the working class family.

Riverview was also an object of bourgeois pleasure, arranged and promoted to middle-class Germans from nearby affluent neighborhoods. Even though the city estimated that there were fewer than three hundred cars on its streets before 1909, Riverview associated some of its pleasures with family automobile outings.[12] The park not only rented out cars but also installed a garage that accommodated over a hundred vehicles. Inside the gates, the immense park featured broad roads (Automobile Course) on which people could tour, reach a remote grove for picnicking, or drive past an Indian Village. Riverview's grand scale and arrangement offered the possibility of segregation and privacy through spectacularized roadside realms of nature.

But even while it catered to "respectable" families, it was also an important site for a working class youth subculture. The Roller Skating Rink and the Loop-the-Loop Bowling Alley were venues for informal heterosocial relations. The Dance Floor, a pavilion that featured live bands, was an especially popular meeting place where contemporary dances encouraged physical disorientation and public intimacy among young men and women. The "spiel" was a dance of wild spinning. "Shaking the shimmy," the "dip," the "turkey trot," and the "bunny hug" all overt symbols of sexual activity, celebrated physical motion and easy familiarity between the sexes.[13]

Even more transgressive was the Bowery, a section along Riverview's boundary that included gambling on games of chance, Salome-the-hootchy-kootchy dancer, a serpentine dancer, a Gypsy camp, and the "girlie" show *Paris by Night*. The show acts transformed foreign cultures into exoticized and sexualized sideshows while objectifying the female body for the pleasure of male visual consumption. As carryovers from early burlesque, they allowed for seeming resistance to "family" values. But they literally "contained" such resistance within a compact area along the park's margins, simply making *explicit* the act of sexual looking that was *implicit* in the park's overall organization. The park incorporated public displays of the body, acts of sexualized and pleasurable looking, and the promise of greater physical contact among strangers even while it promoted family values. As a "laboratory of the new mass culture," the amusement park allowed both middle-class and working class people to rebel against genteel codes of leisure, while at the same time winning their consent to the oppressive mass society by dazzling them with technological spectacles.[14]

Riverview also allowed for greater sexual independence among young single women while introducing them to their new cultural status as both consumers and the objects of consumption. When New York social reformer Belle Israels interviewed several working class girls in 1909 about going alone or with a girlfriend to her area's amusement parks, the girls described the ways that they would try to find young men to "treat" them to the parks' concessions.[15] Like the social reformers who attacked the nickelodeons and linked them to the amusement parks, Israels expressed concern for the sexual behavior encouraged by this economic arrangement at the parks. While acknowledging reformers' fears, social historian Kathy Peiss argues that the young working class woman who went to the park with a girlfriend actually set up a "protective" arrangement whereby she could "strike up innocuous acquaintances with young men" and extend a working girl's culture of female independence "to the resort, whose beaches, boardwalk, and dancing pavilions were arenas for diversion, flirtations, and displays of style."[16] The park, then, contradictorily offered young working class women a chance "to negotiate dependency and claim some choice, autonomy, and pleasure in otherwise dreary lives" while it forwarded an exchange value for female sexuality.[17]

At Riverview, movies were shown between 1906 and 1908 in an Electric Theater, where programs changed twice weekly, and at Hale's Tours of the World, a one-and-a-half story pavilion topped by a large American flag near the main Western Avenue entrance.[18] Hale's Tours occupied a central location in the park next to the three-story carousel that served as a visual focal point and frequent meeting place on the grounds. A grassy parklike space in front of the merry-go-round included benches and gave a wide view of the Tours of the World facade and sign.[19]

Hale's Tours and Scenes of the World, first introduced by entrepreneur George C. Hale at the 1904 St. Louis Exposition, was popular at amusement parks across America and at storefront theaters in cities like New York City, San Francisco, and Chicago. By 1908, there were at least five hundred operating in the United States.[20] Each Hale's Tours was composed of one or two cars, each car able to seat between sixty-five to seventy-two "passengers."[21] Each show lasted approximately ten minutes, and admission was usually ten cents. There were also competitors like Auto Tours of the World and Sightseeing in the Principal Cities and Hruby

PENNY ARCADE, HALE'S TOURS OF THE WORLD, AND MERRY GO ROUND, RIVERVIEW PARK, C. 1908. *Postcard, ICHi-19797. Courtesy Chicago Historical Society.*

& Plummer's Tours and Scenes of the World who provided railway, trolley, or automobile car movie rides like Hale's.[22] Trolley Car Tours Company even promoted its motion simulation ride as a more populist attraction: "Our car is the latest and best in a car device for travels and tours—the most natural way to the masses. Few ride in Pullmans; everybody hits the trolley."[23]

Hale's Tours and its competitors generally offered a point of view from the front or rear of a moving train, creating the illusion of movement into or away from the scene. They capitalized upon previous phantom train ride films (like *Mount Taw RR, No. 3* [Edison Manufacturing Company, 1898], *Frazer Canon* [American Mutoscope & Biograph, 1902], *Mount Stephen* [American Mutoscope & Biograph, 1902] or *The Haverstraw Tunnel* [American Mutoscope & Biograph, 1903]) that offered cowcatcher points of view of a train winding along a track. (Indeed, both Edison Manufacturing Company and American Mutoscope & Biograph reissued many earlier railroad films and advertised them in special Hale's Tours supplements.) In Hale's Tours installations, the railway car theater was rocked from side to side, steam whistles tooted, and the sound of wheels clattering was made in order to simulate railroad travel and to foreground the body itself as a site for sensory experience. Some Hale's Tours programs, like the extant example *The Hold-Up of the Rocky Mountain Express* (American Mutoscope & Biograph, 1906) combined fictions and travelogues that did not uphold a strictly unified cowcatcher point of view while they were screened at the front of a darkened railway car. Hale's Tours, however, was always more than movies; it was also about the physical experience of motion itself, an incorporation of the cinematic into perceptual experience that located meaning in the body of the spectator.

While there are no records to indicate which programs the Riverview Tours of the World featured, there are catalogues (and particularly, catalogues from Chicago film distributors who would have been the concessionaire's most likely source) that describe the available Hale's Tours fare. Hale's Tours scenic trips included filmic journeys to scenic spots in the United States and Canada (including Niagara Falls, the Catskills Mountains, the Rocky Mountains, northern California, the Black Hills, and the Yukon), trips to foreign lands that were especially remote or pre-industrial (China, Ceylon, Japan, Samoa, the Fiji Islands), and even urban trolley or subway rides (e.g., *New York to Brooklyn over Brooklyn Bridge* [unknown, 1899], *Elevated R. R., 110th St. Curve, New York City* [unknown, 1899]).[24] For example, Hale's Tours films typically featured the landscape as the train picks up speed so that the items accelerating into the foreground were the object of information. The films employed both editing and camera movements but usually only after presenting an extended shot (often one to two minutes or longer in a seven- or eight-minute film) organized by the locomotion of the camera. The continuous flow of motion delineated the visual and temporal information within the frame as that of objects rushing toward the camera. The camera was mounted at a slightly tipped angle in order to show the tracks in the foreground as parallel lines that converge at the horizon, an important indicator of depth perspective. Telephone poles, passing under a bridge, tunnels, and other environmental markers in the frame functioned as markers of flow according to the lines of perspective. Passing through tunnels effected a particularly dramatic play of difference of darkness/light, no image/moving image, and interruption/flow. The repetition of all these elements contributed to an overall impression that the perceptual experience of the motion of the camera is a re-creation of the flow of the environment.

Early industry reporters reported rather apocryphal stories of the reception of Hale's Tours. These stories are reminiscent of the reception of

➤ A TRIP ON THE CATSKILL MT. RY. *(American Mutoscope & Biograph, 1906).* THE TRACKS IN THE FOREGROUND APPEAR AS PARALLEL LINES THAT CONVERGE AT THE HORIZON, AN IMPORTANT INDICATOR OF PERSPECTIVAL DEPTH.

the earliest Lumiere films: "The illusion was so good that when trolley rides through cities were shown, members of the audience frequently yelled at pedestrians to get out of the way or be run down. One demented fellow even kept coming back to the same show, day after day. Sooner or later, he figured, the engineer would make a mistake and he would get to see a train wreck." [25] It is noteworthy that in this report spectators do not jump out of the way (as they did in the reports about Lumiere film showings) since they do not understand things coming at them inasmuch as they understand themselves moving forward; they instead yell out at pedestrians in the frame to get out of the way. As Noël Burch says, "These spectators . . . were already in another world than those who, ten years earlier, had jumped up in terror at the filmed arrival of a train in a station: [they] . . . are masters of the situation, they are ready to *go through the peephole.*"[26] Hale's Tours persuaded the spectator to take the bodily place of the subject in the camera's absence.

Hale's Tours did not have to maintain a strict cowcatcher point of view to get across its sensations. The unity between the spectator's point of view and that of the rail traveler was frequently broken. Changes of locale occurred abruptly through editing, the camera position was moved, or the perspective from the front or rear of the train was abandoned altogether. When this happened, the film usually expanded its travel format to offer up views of accompanying tourist attractions or stretched the travelogue with comic or dramatic scenes. A 1906 advertisement in *The New York Clipper* for Hale's Tours listed five "humorous railway scenes" that could be included in Hale's Tours programs.[27] *Trip Through the Black Hills* (Selig Polyscope, 1907) covered "the difficulties of trying to dress in a Pullman berth."[28] In addition, the early film classic, *The Great Train Robbery* (Edison Manufacturing Company, 1903), played in Hale's Tours cars.

It, therefore, was not unusual for the film to cut to the interior of the railroad car, producing a "mirror image" of the social space in which the movie spectator was seated. *The Hold-Up of the Rocky Mountain Express* switches to the car interior not just once but twice to portray social interactions among the passengers and then a train robbery. The film begins with a long shot of the platform of a train station, and then the camera slowly and smoothly moves forward. The point-of-view is the front of a departing train. As the train/camera picks up speed and leaves the station, people on the tracks jump out of the way. The train/camera passes through a town and then into the scenic rural landscape. The voyage through the picturesque snow-covered fields and past trees continues for a few minutes. Then there is an abrupt cut to the inside of a passenger car, obviously produced by a studio set of a passenger car. This is the first shift of address that the film effects: it changes the point of view from looking *out* of the train to *looking in a mirror* (albeit a semiparodic one).

Inside the passenger car, two men sit across from two women. Behind the women, another woman tries to flirt with the men. Oblivious to her efforts, one of the men trades places with the woman opposite him so that the four become paired off in two heterosexual couples. The frustrated flirt instead hits the black porter (an actor in blackface) over the head and knocks him down. The conductor arrives and intervenes. Both railroad employees exit. Next, a tramp crawls out from under the seat behind the couple on the left. Unobserved by the passengers, he sits down next to the lone woman (in effect, producing a third heterosexual coupling

THE HOLD-UP OF THE ROCKY MOUNTAIN EXPRESS (*American Muto-scope & Biograph, 1906*). (1) THE TRAIN LEAVES TOWN; (2) THE SCENIC RURAL LANDSCAPE; (3) INSIDE THE CAR, THE FLIRT FRUSTRATED; (4) THE TRAMP SITS DOWN NEXT TO THE FLIRT; (5) THE HOLD-UP OF THE PASSENGERS; (6) THE BANDITS APPREHENDED.

and realizing her goal, although the humor here resides in the impropriety of this pairing). She reacts in horror and attacks him until the conductor reappears and throws him out of the car.

At this point, the film returns to the cowcatcher point of view. But the camera/train soon stops moving because a log is laid out across the tracks. Two train men enter from the foreground to move the log but instead are held up by outlaws. The film then returns to the interior of the passenger car. Travelers looking out of the window to see the cause of the delay are disturbed by one of the thieves entering the car. He lines up the passengers, robs them, and one of the women faints. The film returns to the point of view of the tracks and depicts the criminals getting away on a handcar; the train starts up and pursues them. Here the point of view of forward locomotion serves narrative rather than picturesque purposes. As the vehicles approach a station, the bandits are apprehended, and the film ends.

Grand Hotel to Big Indian (American Mutoscope & Biograph, 1906) is a variant of the same practice. After a similar extended shot of a cowcatcher traveling point of view along the well-known Horseshoe Loop on the New York State Ulster and Delaware Railway, the film cuts to the train interior where men and women are seated on opposite sides of the aisle. The conductor walks through the car while mattes of traveling landscape "flow" through windows on each side. A porter enters and seats a well-dressed man in a place just vacated by another passenger. The newcomer (the *New York World*'s comic strip character come-to-life Mr. Butt-In) tips his hat to a young girl across the aisle; she gives him the cold shoulder and tells her papa who crosses the aisle to give the masher a hard time. No sooner has that action been completed than the man who initially vacated his seat returns and wants his seat back. A fight in the aisle ensues, it is broken up by the conductor and the porter, and everyone is sent back to their seats. The film then cuts back to the cowcatcher point of view from the exterior of the train.

Other such narrative "interruptions" of the continuous flow of locomotion in this film include a man who cannot get his horse to move off the tracks. Similar to the shot of the train men entering the foreground in *Hold-Up of the Rocky Mountain Express*, the engineer and fireman alight in front of the train and try to help the man pull his horse off the tracks. The engineer squirts oil from a can onto the wheels of the wagon and onto the horse's legs! Mr. Butt-In, the gentleman who caused a comic struggle in the interior, arrives, and another fight ensues. The railroad employees carry off Mr. Butt-In, and the man in the wagon urges his horse

GRAND HOTEL TO BIG INDIAN *(American Mutoscope & Biograph, 1906).* (1) AND (2) COWCATCHER POINTS OF VIEW; (3) INSIDE THE CAR, THE YOUNG GIRL GIVES MR. BUTT-IN "THE COLD SHOULDER"; (4) PAPA GIVES MR. BUTT-IN A HARD TIME; (5) MR. BUTT-IN GETS IN A FIGHT WITH THE MAN WHOSE SEAT HE HAS TAKEN; (6) OUT ON THE TRACKS, THE ENGINEER SQUIRTS OIL ONTO THE WAGON WHEELS AND THE HORSE'S LEGS.

off the tracks. After a pause, the train starts up again and continues on its voyage.

The role of narrativization in both these examples is quite striking since it breaks with the emphasis on flow and perspective of travel in order to display dramatic incidents and bits of social mingling between men and women, different classes, farmers and urbanites, train employees and passengers, ordinary citizens and outlaws. The interior of the railroad car is narrativized as a public arena for social encounters that may themselves become drama. Thus, as Lynn Kirby notes, the railway may become a liminal space in which sexual flirtation instigates events, and brawling frequently offers an inverted means of acceptably civilized resolution of conflict.[29] Although it seems more difficult to narrativize the tracks and car exterior as a similar kind of arena or stage, the films allow for just such a possibility, where the narrativized social encounter (from a horse on the tracks to a train robbery) functions as a significant reorganization of spectatorial address, shifting from direct subject address to an identification with voyeurism. These films were not purely travelogues, then, but were also about the social relations and expectations connected with the experience of travel. They suggest that what was fundamental to the amusement park attraction was not merely the sight of their "destination," the picturesque, foreign, the exotic, the faraway, but the *experience* of being in that place. Thus, Hale's Tours commodified the logic of a new perceptual experience of the inscription of being of the world.

The railway car had already intervened between the traveler and an active sensory experience of landscape to produce a new set of dominant perceptual relations—the visual sensation of the landscape as panoramic. Wolfgang Schivelbusch demonstrates how nineteenth-century travel by rail was a radical cultural event that made the traveler over into a "passenger" whose senses of self, space, and time were radically reorganized.[30] Kirby summarizes Schivelbusch's argument and its relevance for the cinematic spectator such as the "demented fellow" noted above:

> The train can be seen as providing the prototypical experience of looking at a framed, moving image, and as the mechanical double of the cinematic apparatus. Both are a means of transporting a passenger to a totally different place, both are highly charged vehicles of narrative events, stories, intersections of strangers, both are based on a fundamental paradox: simultaneous motion and stillness. These are two great machines of visions that give rise to similar modes of perception, and are geared to shaping the leisure time of a mass society.[31]

Hale's Tours most pointedly incorporated those mechanical pleasures, grafting together railway transport with the pleasure of cinematic consumption. While the wheels and rail of the train were absent, its simulation of travel through the ride unified the cinematic experience with the interior space of the railroad car. The result in Hale's Tours was the product of a dual apparatus—cinema and railroad—that doubly signified the experience of railway tourism.[32]

Hale's Tours, like other automobile and train rides at the amusement park, offered exaggerated, even compressed versions of mechanized travel. It heightened and intensified the relations between body and machine effects, between the individual and fellow travelers (especially through physical closeness and its hints of sexualized intimacy), and between spectatorial eye and panoramic landscape. It transformed the status of a mechanical conveyance into a seemingly limitless commodity of pleasure and excitement.

Hale's Tours's mimetic illusion of travel existed alongside rides that functioned as miniaturized simulacra of the new transportation technologies. For example, the Scenic Railway was an indoor train that traveled through darkened tunnels and past lighted scenery, historical tableaux and grottoes. Down in the Mines was a scenic railway variation that descended into darkened tunnels and passed alongside views of a coal mine in operation. One contemporary journalist describes how the Railway to the Moon, a roller coaster ride, was offered up as a "novel journey" of rail travel, emphasizing mechanical speed:

> The force of gravity is employed in the "up and down-hill" line. Climbing to the top of a stairway, fifty feet or so, you enter a car which rushes down the incline with such speed that it ascends another elevation by its momentum. Descending this, it comes to the end of the road with sufficient speed to turn and run back to the "foot of the stairway on the level track."[33]

In an urban society besieged by mechanized transportation—subways, streetcars, automobiles, commuter trains—the mechanically based ride incorporated the new technologies of transportation within terms of pleasure, exotic adventure, and excitement. The Miniature Railway and the Aerial Tramway, furthermore, allowed the amusement park patron to travel around or over the park as a whole, offering up the site of pleasure itself for pleasurable surveillance.

The very features that made these rides prevalent at amusement parks also made them popular subjects of early cinema. Numerous films were produced of mechanical rides and their patrons' unrestrained behavior at Coney Island and other amusement parks. Films like *Around the Flip-Flap Railroad* (American Mutoscope & Biograph, 1902) capitalized on the motion that was integral to the ride for a kinetic, visually exciting subject of a train doing a vertical 360-degree loop along the track. Indeed, shooting-the-chutes at Coney Island was among the earliest subjects that Edison made for the cinema (*Shooting the Chutes* [Edison Manufacturing Company, 1896]). The ride was reshot several times in the next ten years: *Shoot the Chutes Series* (Edison Manufacturing Company, 1899), *Shooting the Chutes* (American Mutoscope & Biograph, 1902) at a Boston park, *Shooting the Chutes at Luna Park* (American Mutoscope & Biograph, 1903), *Shooting the Chutes at Luna Park, Coney Island* (American Mutoscope & Biograph, 1903), and *Racing Chutes at Dreamland* (American Mutoscope & Biograph, 1904). *Shoot the Chutes Series* is an especially interesting succession of boats sliding down the railway to the pool below it. It presents different points of view of the boats as they descend, including a view from the top where the ride begins. It also offers one view from the camera perched on the prow of the boat as it plunges down the rail in a phantom ride film that anticipates the phantom train ride and Hale's Tours's cowcatcher points of view. It demonstrates, from a very early date, that the illusion of participation in the motion ("going through the peephole") and mechanically produced speed were essential "thrills" to both the amusement park and the cinema.

➤ RACING CHUTES AT DREAMLAND *(American Mutoscope & Biograph, 1904).*

Some of these rides, including Hale's Tours, especially offered the working class a chance to act out fantasies of tourism in those vehicles (automobiles and passenger trains) that were still exclusive perquisites of bourgeois travel. In the United States, long-distance railroad journeys were still primarily the domain of the affluent, and the famous Pullman Car that was advertised as "a steamship on rails" signified luxury travel and class status. As already noted, few families in Chicago could afford to own a private automobile. These new technologies, moreover, may be said to have initiated men and women into their new status within the system of commodity production, converting them from private individuals into a mass culture, consuming machine, travel, and nature alike.

As opposed to the thrill rides and scenic railways, Hale's Tours relied upon less velocity, less physically buffeting assaults, and instead emphasized the stationary body at the center of an *environment* of visual speed and excitement as well as the illusion of travel in an actual worldly location outside the park. In an analysis of cinema shows at late twentieth-century amusement parks that equally applies to the turn of the century, Bennett recognizes the significant difference between the cinema illusion ride and the thrill ride:

> Whereas thrill rides take the normally stationary body and hurtle it through space, [cinema illusion rides] hurtle the vision through space whilst fixing the body as stationary. Yet the cinema shows also compete with the thrill rides by claiming to outdate them, to reproduce all the thrills and excitement of the big rides by means of a more advanced, simpler and safer technology.[34]

Bennett's summary may be aptly applied to Hale's Tours's: it mediated the senses with a cinematic apparatus, the presence of which was displaced onto the architectural apparatus of the railway car ensemble.

Yet, at the turn of the century, the railway travel that Hale's Tours worked so hard to simulate was not necessarily understood by the public as a "simpler and safer technology." Schivelbusch argues that railroad passengers felt ambivalent about train travel and that, despite their thrill at being part of "a projectile shot through space and time," they also had an "ever-present fear of a potential disaster."[35] Schivelbusch also claims that such subliminal fears subsided once the railroad became "a part of normal everyday life."[36] However, since his sources for this are mostly European and British, it is not absolutely clear when such cultural integration was accomplished in the United States and for which groups of people. Certainly, most female immigrants and migrants who moved to Chicago at the turn of the century first experienced the city through the windows of a railroad car and, after their arrivals, their urban travel became increasingly dependent on the subway, streetcar, and elevated train. But, at the same time, the newspapers were filled with stories of streetcar and railway disasters and deaths.[37] Indeed, Kirby persuasively argues that Hale's Tours best unified "the perceptual overlap between the railroad and the cinema" and that the "imagination of disaster" represented both the experience of railway traveler and moviegoing.[38] Thus, spectatorship depended heavily on how people were inscribed in wider discourses and practices related to technology. At the amusement park, the fantasy of seeing technology go out of control and the pleasure in the resulting terror were integral to the spectatorial process.[39]

The privileged role of vision here as the means for organizing pleasure was imbued with a sexual significance. Peiss describes the situation at Coney Island: "The patrons were whirled through space and knocked off balance, their hats blown off, skirts lifted, senses of humor tried. The patrons themselves became the show, proving interest and hilarity to each other. . . . Audience participation, the interaction of strangers, and voyeurism were incorporated."[40] Women and men were positioned as the objects of spectacle as well as each other's gaze, although not necessarily in equivalent ways. Spaces like the Temple of Mirth, a house of mirrors, may have explicitly included such voyeuristic and narcissistic pleasures as the subject of consumable activity whereas other rides more specifically incorporated the exposure of "forbidden" parts of women's bodies for public view.

Many of the movies made of amusement park attractions emphasized the spectacular qualities of the riders while they inscribed spectator positions for the moviegoer, training the moviegoer to the role of the amusement park patron as part of the display and to the integration of sexual surveillance itself as among the pleasures of the amusement park and cinema. For example, *Bamboo Slide* (American Mutoscope & Biograph, 1904) depicts both male and female park-goers sliding down a curving slide at Coney Island. Within the frame, there is a large gathering of men at the end of slide. The all-male crowd of onlookers, watching both the men and the women as they come down the slide, alternate their glances between the riders and the camera. *Steeplechase, Coney Island* (American Mutoscope & Biograph, 1903) depicts a popular amusement park ride of a mechanical horse race along a track. Here, the riders on the horses are all paired-off: on top of each horse is a man and a woman practically seated on his lap. As the competition edges forward, a woman waves her arms, and the men wave their hats at each other.

Among the historical documents that idealize how women's bodies were inscribed within the spaces of an amusement park, three films, in particular, demonstrate how the amusement park connected voyeuristic pleasure to the display of women as sexual spectacle. *Rube and Mandy at Coney Island* (Edison Manufacturing Company, 1903) follows two country bumpkins through their arrival at and participation at the amusement park. The use of two stock objects of ridicule in vaudeville is particularly apt here: the naive, socially backward rustic also represented someone unfamiliar with new technologies and technical procedures. The "bumpkin" or "rube" (short for Reuben) was a figure who unreasonably clung to anachronistic ways in a modern technologized world. As immediate evidence of Rube's and Mandy's status as country bumpkins, they arrive at Coney Island astride their dairy cow. This symbol of nineteenth-century rural farm life separates them from the urbanites who would arrive by train. Their exaggerated dress, makeup, and grotesque gestures further type them as comic outsiders. The film then follows them throughout the park as they try out the park's attractions. For Rube and Mandy, the pleasure of learning with their bodies is repetitively enacted as a humorous mockery of their physical surrender to a series of strange phenomena that disorient them. As backward and unsophisticated, they are more bewildered than pleased at the conclusion of each ride. On occasion, they are even punished: when Rube gets too close to Professor Wormwood's acrobatic Chihuahuas, the professor beats Rube over the head.

In the course of following Rube and Mandy, the film also advertises the amusement park itself and its pleasures in the exhibition of ordinary women as sexual spectacle. It inserts wide panoramic shots of the park. Elsewhere, when a pileup of bodies—both male and female—occurs as customers tumble into each other at the end of a long slide (similar to what is depicted in *Bamboo Slide*), the ride's patrons help each other to their feet, laugh, and smile. They enact pleasurable reactions to close physical contact between the sexes. The camera's point of view of the women who career down the slide reveals their legs as their long skirts are lifted, not only to the cinema spectator of *Rube and Mandy,* but also to gawking male passersby who enter the frame.

In another scene, Mandy walks across a rope bridge raised several feet off the ground. But in this example, the camera assumes a low-angle position that frames Mandy's body centrally in action, rather than showing her from the point of view of the park patrons below her. The choice not to humiliate her by showing the reaction of the amusement park patrons

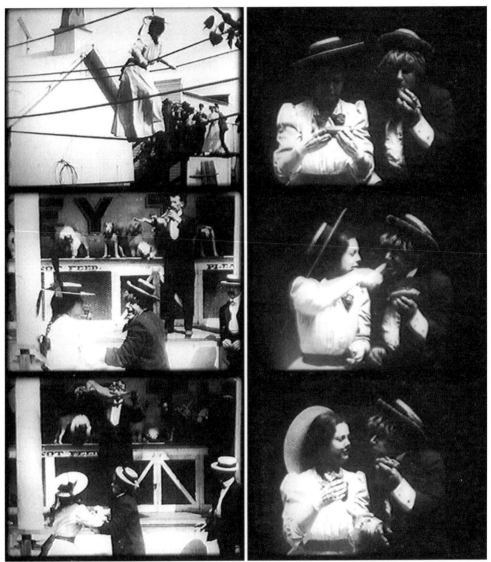

➤ RUBE AND MANDY AT CONEY ISLAND *(Edison Manufacturing Company, 1903).* (1) MANDY WALKS ACROSS THE ROPE BRIDGE; (2) AND (3) RUBE AND MANDY WATCH PROFESSOR WORMWOOD AND HIS PERFORMING DOGS; (4), (5), AND (6) THE EMBLEMATIC SHOT OF RUBE AND MANDY STUFFING THEIR FACES WITH HOT DOGS.

represses the more explicitly illicit act of "looking up a woman's dress" that the ride encouraged. In this way, the film may offer some explanation of the amusement park's expression and transgression of what was permissible public sexual display.

The film ends with an "emblematic shot," a waist-up shot of Rube and Mandy in front of a studio interior flat (such a single shot could be attached by exhibitors either at the beginning or end of a film). The two stuff their faces with Coney Island hot dogs, a new and popular mass-produced urban food. Thus, the couple's only real pleasure occurs not within the realm of the park but in a vulgar display of gluttony. This final moment has allowed Elissa Rashkin to interpret the entire film as incorporating a critique of modernity:

> This type of sensual indulgence is one of the pleasures associated with the "carnivalesque," and emblematic of peasant festivals of the pre-industrial era . . . This type of festivity disappears when formerly rural workers enter industrial society; industrial employment, with its regulated schedule, prevents workers from taking time off for lengthy traditional celebrations, and often polices their day to day behavior, making them conform to whatever standards of cleanliness and sobriety the employer demands. . . . In the wage-based, temporally regulated economy, commercial amusements [like Coney Island] take the place of community celebrations.[41]

Because Rube and Mandy are rubes, they are not yet well enough integrated into urban industrial society to enjoy the amusement park that was produced by and for that society. As Rashkin points out, their overindulgence in hot dogs metaphorically attempts to recover the carnivalesque within the alienating conditions of urban industrialized amusement. *Rube and Mandy,* like several Hale's Tours films, interjects the body of the traveler as a means of mediation between new technologies and travel, between alienation and modern leisure.

Boarding School Girls (Edison Manufacturing Company, 1905) advances the narrative inscription of the female body and gaze at the amusement park. As a comic chase after young women at Coney Island, it aligns the visual pleasure of the female body displayed in motion in the chase genre with the pleasure of sexual surveillance at the amusement park. The film begins with an intertitle of white on black: "The Young Ladies from Miss Knapp's Select School Have an Outing at Coney Island, N.Y." The first three shots depict the finishing school girls descending the front stairs of their brownstone, boarding a horseless carriage, and driving down the street. Miss Knapp, a stereotypical spinster, supervises them as they behave with great decorum, open their parasols, and daintily wave handkerchiefs held in white-gloved hands at passersby. The opening establishes the girls as well-bred and schooled in feminine etiquette, an aspect of bearing and deportment that will shortly be demolished. The girls arrive at Coney Island, disembark from their carriage, and walk two-by-two behind Miss Knapp through the famous gateway of Dreamland. With their parasols held over their heads, they are model examples of the promenade and feminine mantles of reserve. Once inside the park, however, the girls break from the pack and clamber onto a scenic railway. They wave wildly at Miss Knapp as the train departs, and Miss Knapp tries in vain to run after them. As they recede into the background, she wiggles her parasol at them as she pursues the train down the tracks.

This establishes the pattern of the chase that will be repeated across the park's terrain. The girls ride a succession of park attractions and, all the while, they laugh, swing their limbs, and express delight at the ways their bodies are swayed and twisted by the rides. At each ride, Miss Knapp charges into the frame and tries to accost the girls. But she is stymied at each turn by the girls' departure or by the machinery in motion.

For example, the next shot after the girls depart on the scenic railway is a long shot of them hanging onto pulleys as they swing along a horizontal track. The camera is set up at the end of the line so that the girls move from the background into the foreground of the frame. The camera angle allows for their bodies to fill the center of the frame as their skirts flap open to reveal their legs swinging back and forth or kicking out wildly. Chasing after the laughing girls, Miss Knapp appears underneath the suspended track.

The film then cuts to the girls sitting around the circumference of Razzle-Dazzle as it sways and gyrates. Other patrons of the ride even venture to hang by their arms and to swing themselves freely from the hoop in a visually interesting display of acrobatic turns. Miss Knapp dashes into the center of the ring, but the mechanical motion makes her unable to move in any direction and to capture her charges.

After this, the girls try out a succession of rides in Dreamland and Steeplechase parks that subject the body to a series of disorienting effects. They are depicted working their way down the Golden Stairs, a staircase that undulates up and down, making any descent difficult. As the girls haltingly move downward, onlookers provide points of viewer identification for the moviegoer. A man on the left side of frame stares at the camera while a bearded man on the right watches the girls' descent.

⤙ BOARDING SCHOOL GIRLS *(Edison Manufacturing Company, 1905)*. (1) THE BOARDING SCHOOL GIRLS AND MISS KNAPP BOARD THE CARRIAGE; (2) THE DRIVE TO CONEY IS-LAND; (3) THE GIRLS WALK TWO-BY-TWO BEHIND MISS KNAPP; (4) AT THE ENTRANCE TO DREAMLAND, THEY ARE MODEL EXAMPLES OF FEMININE DECORUM; (5) THE CHASE DOWN THE GOLDEN STAIRS; (6) THE GIRLS RIDE INSIDE ROLLING BARRELS WHILE MISS KNAPP RUSHES TO AND FRO; (7) SHOOT-THE-CHUTES; (8) THE GIRLS RIDE THE STEEPLECHASE.

Miss Knapp appears at the stationary stairs on the right and chases after them out of the frame. Then, one by one, the girls slide down a slide, and again onlookers inscribe positions of authorized spectatorship. When the girls next ride inside rolling barrels along a track, Miss Knapp rushes to and fro. The disheveled girls emerge smiling and laughing. The girls try out Shoot-the-Chutes, and the stationary camera depicts their voyage down the incline and across the pool as well as Miss Knapp's in the boat that follows theirs. They try out riding on camels, the Steeplechase, another slide, and a merry-go-round and, in each case, the shot of their ride ends with Miss Knapp's pursuit.

Throughout these sequences, it is not merely the sight of the female body that is meant to produce pleasure but the movement of bodies given over to rides that turn them topsy-turvy. These young female bodies are acted upon, out of control, and given over to shaking and jerking movements that produce a kind of unrestrained, sensual motion *of* the body rather than of individual will or subject control. As park pleasure-seekers, the boarding school girls have shed their ladylike demeanor and self-control for an unrestrained, unfettered display of physical expression. Miss Knapp's inability to participate fully, her efforts to keep herself in restraint, and her pinched appearance and stiff carriage contrast with the relaxed movements of the girls. Through this opposition, the film inverts the usual situation of the chase film: it substitutes a lone figure chasing a pack of young women for a lone figure being chased by a pack of women. This reversal sacrifices none of the visual appeals of the female body in motion, however. The importance of the girls' onscreen presence is precisely their *bodily* presence. The entire surface of their bodies, rather than merely their faces or gestures, signifies their status.

Stagestruck (Edison Manufacturing Company, 1906) seemingly picks up where *Boarding School Girls* leaves off by appropriating the same techniques to transform the cinema of attractions into a more full-fledged narrative cinema. *Stagestruck* begins as a story of three adolescent sisters who are mesmerized by the traveling actor-showman from the big city and who leave their small town for show business careers as dancing Gibson Girls at a cheap Coney Island theater. But the film changes tenor when the girls' farmer parents go to the city in search of their daughters. The farmer and his wife, weary from their hunt, visit Coney Island where they discover the girls on the theater stage. They then chase them through the amusement park, a sequence that occupies an extended period of time and reforms the story into a chase film.

In the first half of the film, events foreshadow the visual displays that will come of the female body at the amusement park. When the showman leans some boards against the girls' second-floor bedroom window so that they can escape, the girls one by one slide down the ramp while the showman watches. Their descent duplicates the bodily action and representation of the park slide in earlier films. It is a significant moment within the narrative since it both enables the young women to pursue a path of action that will get them to the city and initiates their bodily inscription as sexual spectacle and sensory pleasure-seekers, a dual physical status that will culminate in their representation as Gibson Girls and amusement park ride patrons.

After they have completed their descent, their father sticks his head out of the window and gesticulates against their departure. Although he does not attempt to slide down the same boards in pursuit of his daughters, he does follow his daughters. The next shot shows the girls boarding a departing train at the station and their father chasing the train as it heads down the tracks. Through this sequence of events, the father's body is differentiated from the girls' (analogous to Miss Knapp's differentiation from her students) in that his is not the subject of spectacle, projection through space beyond normal physical limitations, or amusement park-styled pleasure-seeking.

After a temporal ellipse (through editing), the girls are shown in a chorus line on a theater stage. They are now quite literally framed as the spectacle for an audience of cheap theater spectators. Like the independent, urban working girls they represent, the sisters have acquired independence through their sexual commodification. Within the restraints of narrative, however, they have achieved their initial desire.

But their desire has also destroyed patriarchal authority and its governance of their sexual behavior. The mother and father quickly discover the girls, and the three young women flee only to be repositioned as the spectacular objects of their parents' pursuit in an extended chase through Coney Island. But, even here, a curious scene ruptures the rhythm and suspends the narrative chase. When the girls encounter a mechanically driven human roulette wheel, they climb onto its flat surface and attempt to stay at its center. They cannot, however, get the better of the device and periodically slip off and fall onto the ground. Each time, they get up and try again. This attempt to "try out" the rides at Coney Island in the middle of a chase sequence reworks the conventional chase of early cinema for the heightened voyeuristic pleasures of amusement park spectatorship. At this moment, the cinema and the amusement park as mutual sites of pleasurable gazing are doubly articulated in the cinematic process of spectatorship and the mimetic representation of the amusement park ride.

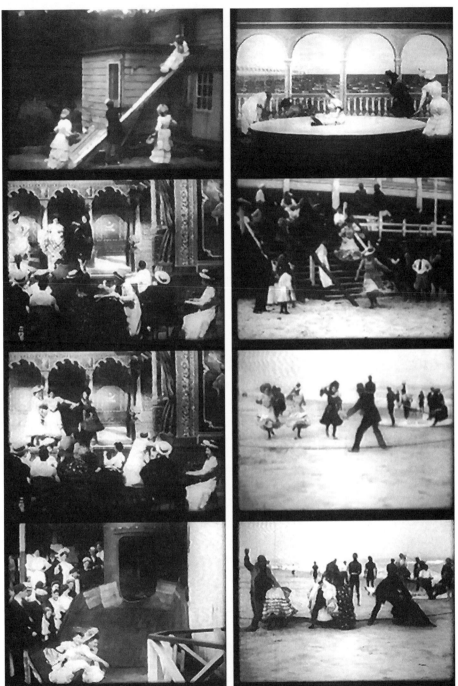

STAGESTRUCK (*Edison Manufacturing Company, 1906*). (1) THE SIS-
TERS' "INITIATION" AS PLEASURE SEEKERS AS THEY ESCAPE FROM THEIR
HOME; (2) THE SISTERS DANCING ONSTAGE AT CONEY ISLAND; (3) THE
SISTERS DISCOVERED BY THEIR PARENTS; (4) THE CHASE THROUGH
CONEY ISLAND; (5) EVERYONE TRIES OUT THE HUMAN ROULETTE WHEEL;
(6) FLEEING ONTO CONEY ISLAND BEACH; (7) AN OBLIGING POLICEMAN
STOPS THE GIRLS; (8) A PUNITIVE ENDING: THE SISTERS GET SPANKED.

This union then gives way to closure at all its discursive levels. On the beach, the girls are caught and soundly spanked. The space of Coney Island and its boardwalk has been represented and advertised, the chase is resolved, family and parental authority are reasserted, and the self-seeking pleasure girls are reinscribed as the sexual objects of transgression. In the spectacular finish, the women are turned into bodies/objects, as they are turned over their parents' and an obliging policeman's knees and spanked in full frontal display for the viewer. However, as Noël Burch muses about the large number of early films that end with beatings, these punitive endings are not *narrative* closures in the sense that the cinema would develop over the next decade whereby the spectator is allowed "to withdraw 'gently' from the diegetic experience."[42] Relying upon an old trick from the circus and music hall, they reverse the pleasures of the film with a shock effect: they literally "kick" the spectator out of the film.

As *Rube and Mandy, Boarding School Girls,* and *Stagestruck* demonstrate, the act of pleasurable and sexual looking, so tacitly a structure of cinematic experience, was likewise an implicit structure of the amusement park. Peiss suggests that the patrons' gazes at each other were an important part of the courtship and flirtation encouraged through the rides, the dance pavilion, and the roller skating rink. Large spectacle displays of pageantry combining actors and scenery (at Riverview, the *Sea Battle of Santiago,* the *Fall of the City of Pompeii,* and *The Great Train Robbery*) and smaller sideshows (Riverview's Aztecs, Chinese Theatre, Turk Show, Plantation Show, and Indian Village, which was later renamed Scenes Among the Sioux) also extended and duplicated the pleasures of looking to the exotic, the remote, and the fantastic. Kasson and Peiss see these displays, in particular, as the culmination of a nineteenth-century entertainment that fed upon middle-class interest in foreign travel. They celebrate the educational potential of these exhibits for the classes that could not travel much beyond the amusement park. These displays, which derive partially from the Midway exhibits at the 1893 Chicago World Columbian Exposition, represented the bodies of nonwhite individuals—both foreign and American—as primitive, docile, and fetishized objects of spectacle. By repetitively coding certain cultures and races as "foreign, exoticized Other," these displays also promoted, through the pleasurable gaze, racial hierarchies to both its middle-class and working class patrons.

In addition, geographic regions that were pre-industrial and populated by nonwhite races were depicted as legitimate objects for visual consumption. Hale's Tours supported this ideology. By simulating railway travel to remote regions, Hale's Tours made distant, unique cultural places into easily accessible spaces. While it democratized tourism by offering views of remote locales to both those who could afford to travel and those who could not, it perpetuated ethnocentric notions about "exotic" lands by making faraway cultures into commodities that could be enjoyed for the price of admission. In this way, the amusement park supported not only American intervention and domination over other peoples but also legitimized American imperialism and consumption of other national spaces.

Riverview as well as Hale's Tours offered culturally acceptable pleasure that expressed conflicting values. It brought together racism and social integration, sexism and sexual independence, class conflict and harmony, family unity and adolescent sociality, fear and absorption of technological changes. Cinema's role in these ideological dramas is especially important. It accustomed the spectator to visual shocks while incorporating and defining a female sexuality in relation to public space, the act of looking, and consumerism.

6

PANDERING
TO PLEASURE

These pictures have brought discredit generally on the moving picture business. . . . The patrons of nickelodeons and moving picture shows are largely women and children, and to gain the better class of trade, such a step of elimination of objectionable pictures has been found necessary.

FRED C. AIKIN, a Chicago film exchange owner, 1908

THROUGHOUT 1907 AND 1908, manufacturer- and distributor-led organizations as well as New York-based and Chicago-based groups vied with each other for control over the increasingly important, financially powerful film industry. Edison Manufacturing Company acted as a catalyst, and the subsequent conflicts that were played out inside business organizations and the courts as well as in the press were resolved in the 1908 formation of the Motion Picture Patents Company (MPPC), headed by Edison. The MPPC was a powerful combination of film manufacturers and distributors who achieved a monopoly over the film business. While the formation of the MPPC and the ways that it changed both the American film industry and the shape of its films is a well-known story, what is not so well known is how it was achieved: through reconfiguring reform rhetoric to serve as a valuable weapon in film industry struggles. Edison claimed that only if *he* was in complete control of the entire film industry could the public be assured of a moral cinema. Thus, Edison hoped to stave off impending regulation of movies at nickelodeons and amusement parks and gain approval for monopoly control by promising self-censorship of films. The claims of Edison and his allies, however, necessitated rebuttal from their competitors. All the leaders of the film industry readily understood the value of this rhetoric and its additional importance for avoiding what they called "oppressive city ordinances."[1] The claims and counter-claims were successful to the extent that they diverted discussion away from concern with the nickelodeons and amusement parks as dangerous social spaces. Cinema as a social phenomenon thus prompted competing film industry forces to produce the first discourses about an ontology of cinema. In the process of formulating arguments contingent on the politics of the changing city, they defined cinema as a modern text of mass culture.

The formation of the MPPC actually took several years, and the most important activities occurred in Chicago. In a course of action modeled after their successful takeover of utility companies in New York City, Thomas Edison and his general manager William Gilmore were attempting to control the means of film production by gaining legal ownership of the technological apparatus—the moving picture camera and projector.[2] For several years, Gilmore had the company buy as many patents as possible on various cameras and projectors. In 1902, he and company patent attorney Frank L. Dyer had filed patent infringement lawsuits against numerous competitors. Rather than simultaneously pursue several pending lawsuits, Dyer pressed the case against Edison's chief East Coast competitor, American Mutoscope & Biograph. Just as the Chicago movie reform campaign got underway, the U.S. Circuit Court of Appeals finally decided that Biograph's equipment did not violate Edison's patents claims (because it did not rely upon the same sprocket-engaging mechanisms), although the decision had the important consequence of legitimating Edison's claims on all other equipment.[3]

Seeing the decision's implications for a victory against all other competitors, Gilmore directed that old patent claims be renewed against two Chicago companies, Selig Polyscope Company and George Kleine Optical Company (Kleine distributed large numbers of imported films as well as Biograph's films) in an effort to attack the film industry at its geographic heart.[4] Movie production itself was spread out in New York City, New Jersey, and Philadelphia as well as in Chicago. But production was only one component of a business that had already evolved into three distinct branches—production, distribution, and exhibition. Film distribution occurred at film exchanges or wholesalers that bought movies from the manufacturers and then rented them to thousands of exhibitors. More than thirty large, well-established film exchanges (including George Kleine, W. H. Swanson, Eugene Cline, and Laemmle Film Service) were headquartered by 1907 in Chicago.[5] Even Edison Manufacturing Company's own film exchange, Edison Display Company, had by 1907 headquartered in Chicago. Chicago may have hosted only one other film manufacturer besides Selig (Essanay Film Manufacturing Company), but, more importantly, it was the country's centralized site for movie distribution.

If Edison Manufacturing Company combined with Selig and other large manufacturers, it could seize power from the exchanges because it would control the majority of product supply. By 1907, this emerging structure of power was already well understood within the film industry, and *Moving Picture World* reported: "Chicago was selected as the field for the first attack for the reason that it is the headquarters of the Kleine interests which form the head and brains of the independent movement for the entire west, and after mature deliberation, it was decided to fire the first gun there."[6] Edison Manufacturing Company's two courtroom bids in Chicago represented a highly visible assault on the film industry at its geographic core.

Thus, Laemmle's supply of free films to Jane Addams's Hull-House nickelodeon in the summer of 1907 may have been portrayed as a civic-minded gesture, but it was also important for staking out the prominence of the distributor rather than the manufacturer as a guardian for public morals in the industry's internal struggle. Laemmle exploited the internationally known reputation of Addams to argue that important controls over the industry should be contained by product differentiation, that the only thing of importance was the exchange's gate-keeping role of disseminating "high-quality" films. In August of 1907, Laemmle ran a three-quarter-page advertisement that featured a lengthy statement signed by Addams below two linked photographs of Addams and himself:

> The five-cent theatre opened by Hull-House in the summer of 1907 depended for its many picture films altogether upon the generosity of Mr. Carl Laemmle of 496 Lake St., Chicago. From his large list of subjects we were able to select fairy stories which delighted the children, foreign scenes which filled our Italian and Greek neighbors with happy reminiscences, dramatizations of great moral lessons contained in such stories as Uncle Tom's Cabin and the Bishop's candlesticks, modern heroism as portrayed by the fireman and the life saving corps, as well as that multitude of simpler domestic scenes which fascinates the spectator, through their very familiarity because they reveal an inner beauty, not suspected before.
>
> It is unfortunate that the five-cent theatre has become associated in the public mind with the lurid and unworthy. Our experience at Hull-House has left no doubt in our minds that in time moving pictures will be utilized quite as the Stereopticon is at present, for all purposes of education and

entertainment and that schools and churches will count the films as among their most valuable equipment.

Jane Addams, President Hull-House, Chicago[7]

By itself, Addams's statement has most frequently been interpreted as a testimonial to the new medium, whereas Laemmle produced it to support the film exchange's position of power within the film industry.

Edison Manufacturing Company responded to Laemmle's advertisements by capitalizing on the cult of personality surrounding Thomas Edison. In Edison Manufacturing Company's publicity statements, Edison-the-man made almost identical pronouncements to those made by Addams: "Nothing is of greater importance to the Success of the motion picture interests than films of good moral tone. . . . The five-cent theatre will prosper according to its moral attitude."[8] Thus, increasingly the issue of the ideological power of the movies over immigrant, juvenile, and female audiences became realigned as a debate over control of the film industry as the solution to public moral regulation.

On October 30, 1907, Edison received a temporary injunction against Selig Polyscope Company, a move expected by industry leaders because it was the same strategy employed by Gilmore and Edison in the company's earlier patent suit against Biograph.[9] The granting of a temporary injunction, according to industry insiders, meant that "in order to continue to fight the case in court it would be necessary for Selig to put up a heavy bond to indemnify the Edison Company in case they won."[10] Given the precedent already established by the U.S. Court of Appeals over the extent of Edison patent claims in his suit against Biograph, there was strong sentiment that "any lawyer would be insane who would recommend his client put up $25,000 and fight."[11] Fearing Edison control over the manufacturers was imminent, the film exchanges arranged a December meeting with Edison executives.[12] They formed the United Film Service Protective Association (UFSPA), a trust that would systematize and regulate nationwide distribution while still giving Edison Manufacturing Company and the Chicago film exchanges a large degree of economic control. When the alliance was announced, its new head wrote a letter to *Moving Picture World* expressing the importance of this industry control for solving the problem of public moral regulation:

All branches of the business realize the urgent necessity for some action toward the general uplifting of the moving picture industry. I believe the forming of this association marks the beginning of the end of the various forms of abuse to which this great industry has been subject, and the abolishment of these abuses means the beginning of the most prosperous era the manufacturers, renters and exhibitors have ever known.

The film manufacturers will, I believe, in the near future make film subjects such as we have never before dreamed of, as they will have the assurance that they will have the members of this association to properly handle and rent their productions at a price in keeping with their value, and they will feel that they can put more time, money and thought into their productions. . . . If the manufacturers will confine their energies to producing comedies, comedy dramas, fairy tales and clean dramas, I believe the present agitation against the moving picture shows in some cities will soon cease.[13]

When, two months later, the Chicago court decided against Selig Polyscope Company, Gilmore demanded even more power in the UFSPA. The short-lived organization re-formed as the Film Service Association (FSA) in order to meet Gilmore's demands and to endorse Edison's claim for equipment ownership. The FSA, which represented more than $50 million in combined manufacturers and distributors capital investments, agreed to pay Thomas Edison royalties that they projected would be between $200,000 and $1 million the first year.[14] The Chicago film exchanges, in particular, acquiesced to Edison Manufacturing Company's demands because any contest would likely result in Edison Manufacturing Company film patent infringement lawsuits against them, and they would necessarily be arguing their cases in the same Chicago circuit court that had just heard the Selig case. For the most part, the Chicago delegation accepted its defeat and swiftly closed ranks to maintain its powerful voting bloc in the association.[15]

The issue of the movies as a medium of mass culture might have been resolved within a newly unified industry there and then except that George Kleine withdrew from the association and set up his own coalition (the Independent Film Association) rather than agree to Gilmore's royalty demands. Because he was Biograph's exclusive distributor, Kleine felt legally secure that his films did not fall within Edison's patent claims. He argued back at the Edison-controlled FSA, "We have always followed the policy of censorship at the root, and have never imported films that could be considered objectionable from any view-point. This is due to our system of inspecting samples of every subject before our stock was shipped from Europe."[16] In response, Dyer filed a patents infringement suit against Kleine in March of 1908. Kleine replied again in kind in the *Moving Picture World*:

A concerted attempt is being made to give the impression that Edison film licensees represent America. . . . By direct statement, by innuendo, by constant repetition, the idea is fostered that this is a patriotic movement fathered by Edison, to retain the plums of the trade for American manufacturers, which the wicked foreigners are trying to filch; that the latter are unknown and their product inferior. Art is the language in which genius speaks; it knows no country, no geographical limitations, because it is universal. Whether in a film, a painting, a symphony, or a statue, the country of origin is as unimportant as the box in which a Paganini may carry a Stradivarius, the pen with which Shakespeare may write Hamlet, or the chisel used by Praxiteles.[17]

Rather than directly attack Edison's and the Chicago film exchanges' joint public claims for a self-imposed control over moral content, Kleine emphasized how their discursive strands forwarded a nativist argument and cleverly shifted the entire debate to the aesthetic significance of the movie experience.[18]

Kleine asserted that cinema's ontological basis—that the very essence of cinema—was the technological simulation of reality and that only through the powerful economic check of laissez-faire competition (the opposite of Edison's monopoly controls) could cinema's true nature become increasingly realized. He wrote to *Variety* on March 25, 1908: "Does the answer rest in the necessity of finding some means to justify and validate the attempt to restrict the number of film subjects placed upon the market and to legalize certain other operations which would otherwise be considered in restraint of trade?"[19] In this argument, the revival of the illustrated travel lecture and the scenic helped to support his case. Kleine locally produced an illustrated travel lecture that was an unrivaled film spectacle, a show that he used in 1908 to test the verisimilitudinous limits of motion pictures.

Henry Lee's Mimic World was a ninety-minute program of short fictional subjects, songs, and motion picture scenics from around the world accompanied by fifty singers and vocal artists, narration by popular stage actor Joseph Kilgour, organ music, and a Cameraphone (a phonograph that was synchronized with the projector for mechanically producing vocal impressions). A *Chicago Tribune* reporter described the event in great detail:

The pictured play [the fictional shorts] is either a drama or a farce, and the story of this is told by the actor (Joseph Kilgour) who stands at the side of the screen; while practically every action displayed on the screen is audibly duplicated back of the screen on the stage.

The pictured incident [the scenic] may deal with sports in Australia or the shipment of ice from Norway to England, or perhaps the singing of several songs by a music hall soubrette in London. The element of realism is the same as that introduced in the plays. When songs are the feature two invisible phonographs, one to reproduce the instrumental accompaniment, the other the voice of the singer, make the moving picture a "cameraphone" and the entertainment unique.[20]

Mimic World improved upon the usual illustrated travel lecture, unified by the lecturers' live narration, because it employed three projectors for uninterrupted, continuous images and because it added voluminous sound effects produced both by actors behind the screen and by the Cameraphone.

The program played in June of 1908 for one week at the 4,000-seat Auditorium Theatre. As the *Variety* reporter proclaimed, "The idea of converting the magnificent Auditorium into a mammoth moving picture house attracted wide attention."[21] The lengthy program carried a ticket price that was as much as a legitimate theater performance and played exclusively four times daily in a theater that catered to middle-class patrons. According to the *Chicago Tribune*, the event was well attended.[22] But, most importantly, *Mimic World* synchronized sound and image in what was described by its reviewers as a new realist cinema. Among a number of showmen in the United States and Europe who were utilizing phonographs attached by cable to motion picture projectors, Lee sold Kleine just such a synchronized sound film extravaganza at the moment when Kleine was trying to inscribe a superior position to Edison.

The critical reception of Lee's "talking picture" allied technological innovation with realism as the legitimate end of cinema. In an era when individual film reviews were unusual enough, both the *Chicago Tribune* and *Variety* wrote lengthy reviews about the verisimilitude of Lee's spectacle. The *Chicago Tribune* declared that *Mimic World* "sought to perfect the moving picture show."[23] The *Variety* reporter repetitively attested to *Mimic World*'s sound and image verisimilitude:

[An] interesting contribution is a panoramic view of Australia, showing *with marvelous accuracy* crafts navigating steadily and while the whistles blow and the stream roars voluminously with all the effects of *realism*, a street in Sydney is reached.

The camera has depicted one of the most *natural* episodes reproduced on canvas. While a crowd surges to and fro on the main thoroughfare, a fire alarm is sounded. The spectators are in an uproar and the terrific noise of fire gongs is heard. Maddened horses attached to fire fighting apparatuses dash along, leaving the excited crowds in commotion.

The most remarkable effect was the *natural* sound accompanying the streams of water pouring from the hose.

A veritably remarkable picture, with utmost *sound-realism* was the rapidly speeding train. Even the rustling of the steam *could be heard distinctly*, so technically precise were the attending details. [emphasis mine][24]

The review makes it seem likely that the film's sounds were exceptional, isolated, and loud. The writer repeatedly describes a high auditory volume, using such words as "commotion," the "roar" of the water, and the "terrific noise" of the fire gong. The *Chicago Tribune* reviewer likewise devoted a lengthy paragraph to cataloguing the various sound effects.[25] While realism usually expresses its "authenticity" through an organization that does not foreground the apparatus itself, the film may have forwarded sound as an important aspect of realistic reproduction precisely by marking the capacity to *produce* sound itself.[26]

Mimic World enlarged discussion of technological improvement. One industry trade paper ran a brief editorial that it was "glad to note that he [Kleine] had taken his first chance at 'tooting his own horn.'" (George Spoor from Essanay [the other Chicago film manufacturer] announced that he, too, would use a new invention to produce "talking pictures.")[27] By championing ontological realism, Kleine appeared to be working to convince the public as well as the industry that better movies depended upon the competition of an open marketplace. He fixed the significance of cinema less in relationship to ideological issues and controls over immigrant and female morals than in its capacity as a mechanically produced art form:

> Cinematography shall reach the position of dignity and popular recognition to which it is entitled. To bring about this very desirable consummation, we must encourage the *natural trend* of the business. . . . Of course, it is nice to call the Auditorium show "the limit" of the moving picture's possibilities but bigger things yet may develop. The future of the film is almost unlimited. [emphasis mine][28]

Kleine argued that cinema's "natural direction" was an unchecked market, which would stimulate competing interests to develop better technology for an increasingly spectacular naturalism. Such a direction would only be possible if Edison and the Edison-controlled FSA did not gain control over the industry thereby reducing competition incentives. At stake, said Kleine, was not only the future of the film industry but the future of cinema as an art form.

At the same time that *Mimic World* was garnering industry praise for its Chicago success, Edison Manufacturing Company invited a *Variety* reporter to interview Thomas Edison. A mere two weeks after it provided extensive coverage of *Mimic World* and heralded Kleine's purpose and aesthetic mission, *Variety* printed an exclusive interview with the reclusive inventor and corporate titan. The awestruck reporter related Edison's new "*personal* interest in the strictly commercial side of the business" so that he could champion the movies' ideological role in the immigrant's welfare:

> The poor man is able to indulge himself and his whole family in a wholesome entertainment now at 10 cents apiece. The cost of even third-class amusement of any other sort puts it beyond his reach, for the difference between 10 cents and a quarter apiece for a whole family is a considerable item. Just as the phonograph puts the best music in the home of the poor man, so the moving picture supplies him with an entertainment that is at once within his taste and understanding and is varied enough to be a mental stimulant and an education.[29]

Throughout the lengthy interview, Edison championed industry control by manufacturers as the way to guarantee the movies' beneficial role in working class *family* culture. He reasoned that it was distributors (and importers like Kleine) who had bought foreign films featuring "hangings, murders and violent deaths [which] should be barred from the sheet" and who were the bane of the industry.[30] He promised more artistic output from American manufacturers: "Now that that [sic] is in a way to reach settlement the betterment of film subjects will follow."[31] In this way, Edison countered Kleine's rhetoric at the same time that he neatly folded industry control into a nativist argument promoting American values that served the purposes of both charity workers and industry moguls.

Soon after this rhetorical battle was staged in the industry newspapers, the Chicago judge who had earlier ruled on the Selig case issued a temporary injunction against Kleine. Both Edison and Kleine employees concluded that the case would end in Kleine's defeat. So Kleine, American Mutoscope & Biograph executives, and Edison representatives began to meet privately during the summer of 1908 and continued to do so throughout the autumn.[32] Rumors of a consolidation appeared in industry trade papers as early as August.[33] In December of 1908, Kleine and Edison announced that they would combine the FSA, Biograph, and Kleine in the Motion Picture Patents Company (MPPC). Kleine's reconciliation with the Edison interests and the Chicago film exchanges within the already formed Edison corporate structure led to the dissolution of his competitively formed rhetoric of realism.[34] However, by championing cinema's importance as art, Kleine proclaimed the realist position that would eventually come to dominate for much of the twentieth century. He offered some of the earliest defenses that cinema's indexical relationship to the world would achieve realism only so long as the technology kept improving cinema's legibility.

The newly formed monopoly presented a cohesive system for controlling manufacture and distribution only for the moment. In the years that the MPPC exercised authority, it was continuously challenged. Ultimately, the federal courts ruled in 1915 that the MPPC was an illegal trust. But by the time that happened, the film industry had become dependent on an assembly-line mode of manufacture whereby plot, setting, character, and action were all formulaically laid out in controlled conditions of movie studios (rather than depending on the eccentricities and vagaries of itinerant filmmakers and crews). Studio producers could more rationally, efficiently and cheaply turn out mass numbers of variations of fictional subjects because they could plan and rely upon repetitive use of the same stages, actors and personnel, props, and equipment. (Thus, there was no place in such a system for production of Hale's Tours–like material shot all over the world.) The cinema that emerged in the early teens was dominated by the fictional film and longer individual movies.

The debates over a morally redemptive cinema that defined the medium based on either film content or on the indexical quality of a photographic-based medium helped to provide discursive support for such a system. They refigured the ontological nature of cinema from the local experience that included all the social aspects of the exhibition space to a purely audio-visual text produced in the phantasmagoria of cinema. After 1908, this cinema seemed increasingly tangible in new, larger theaters devoted to movie exhibition where house lights were kept low, rowdy behavior and audience interaction discouraged and disciplined, and fictional films with live musical accompaniments flourished. The experience of cinema became celebrated as an individualistic, self-absorbed, all-encompassing fantasy.

CONCLUSION

Mother . . . I will *not* go home! I will *not* be good! I will *not* reform!

CHARACTER IN A DIME NOVEL, 1891

We see thousands of girls walking up and down the streets on a pleasant evening with no chance to catch a sight of pleasure even through a lighted window, save as those lurid places provide it. Apparently the modern city sees in these girls only two possibilities, both of them commercial: first, a chance to utilize by day their new and tender labor power in its factories and shops, and then another chance in the evening to extract from them their petty wages by pandering to their love of pleasure.

JANE ADDAMS, *The Spirit of Youth and City Streets,* 1910

URBAN COMMERCIAL CULTURE at the turn of the last century involved the new visibility of independent women, complicated a scripting of female victims and predatory procurers, and enlarged those entertainment pastimes that catered to the sizable number of factory workers, clerks, shopgirls, and domestics. Nowhere was this more evident than in Chicago, model American city and self-conscious beacon to the world. Chicago reformers and businessmen alike understood the importance of its commercial diversions, especially in spaces like the department store shopping zone on State Street, the 1893 Columbian Exposition, downtown and neighborhood nickelodeons, and the city's amusement parks. In their efforts to produce, manage, and control commercial culture, they addressed the relevancy of female identity formation to pleasure seeking. There may have been other, more important functions for all these spaces than promoting themselves as inviting urban environments for women. But none was so integral to the definition of the modern as the ways in which these urban institutions promised women the freedom of mobile spectatorship, the imaginary openness and privilege of the flâneur's city. Because the urban environment did fundamentally address women's desires as well as the question of her purposeless mobility, one may uncover how history recast a female flâneuse. At stake is nothing less than a more accurate perception of the ways that we think about the spaces of modernity and their attendant modes of vision, as well as the constitution of a modern *feminine* subject.

Female flâneurs were supposed to be impossible, but women wandering on formerly forbidden streets made this ideal problematic. What this disjuncture requires is a critique of flânerie. Feminist scholars have already begun to muddy the question of the flâneuse. They base their arguments on a definition of flânerie as a set of subjective relations within expressions of institutional and discursive power, or, in short, the ideology of social power and its gendered construction. Some (e.g., Janet Wolff, Anke Gleber) see flâneuserie as an impossibility given the ideologies by which women's mobility was constrained; others (particularly Susan Buck-Morss and Anne Friedberg) argue that prostitutes or shoppers were female flâneurs.[1] Cultural history generates different conclusions. Arguments such as Friedberg's and Buck-Morss's about the scattered presence, high visibility, and unrestrictive mobility of certain categories of urban female pedestrians are exaggerated. The appearances and movements of prostitutes and shoppers were carefully regulated and supervised. Because women enjoyed access to the city street did not mean that gender hierarchies were being overturned. Popular representations of women's public appearances on city thoroughfares and at the 1893 Chicago Columbian Exposition established both the real and ideal cities as stages for female spectacle. The very organization of space, visual sightlines, displays, and circulation patterns within these settings as well as within department stores, nickelodeons, and amusement parks—urban areas expressly designed for female movement—not only qualified the range of a woman's participation but moderated her public appearances, because they also taught her that she was the object of public surveillance. It matters little whether the subjects were prostitutes streetwalking, women window shopping, female tourists, or girls pleasure-seeking in the park. None had the limitless, unfettered freedom of mobility and visual consumption that is associated with flânerie.

The figure of the prostitute registered prominently in the flâneur's fantasy of the city, and she was a significant legacy for turn-of-the-century urban culture. She made frequent appearances in late nineteenth- and early twentieth-century urban realist literature and paintings, in reformers' tracts, the cheap press, vaudeville, and the movies. She was almost required by the culture, as literary critic Mark Seltzer points out, because the "fallen girl" provided "a way of at once embodying and bringing to book, in both senses, the desire to see and the project of making 'the social' visible."[2] Seltzer automatically accepts the denomination of the prostitute as a "fallen girl," thus reifying the nineteenth century's rigidly structured binary distinction between the whore and the lady.

Dismantling this binary opposition is essential because the prostitute has been employed in representational practices to discipline *all* women. Turn-of-the-century discourse established the mutual interdependency of the prostitute and the pure woman through a series of overlapping dualities of space, subjectivity, physicality, and visuality. The public (the streets) was deemed oppositional to the private; social conditioning was opposed to the rigors of individualism; motion was contrasted with stillness; seeing was countered with being seen. But these fictional, idealist forms of representation—the "need" to have a prostitute/fallen girl as a counterpoint to the morally pure lady—neglect how these oppositions were more casually acted out in daily life, how classifications were broken and transgressed, and even how categorical boundaries could be fluid and changeable. The streetwalker or prostitute as a lifelong "career" criminal easily identified is precisely a fictional figure, an abstraction constructed as a disciplinary model for all women and not the equivalent of social practices wherein numerous women entered into prostitution on occasional, irregular, or even casual bases.[3] Prostitution was more typically something young women did to supplement otherwise meager incomes. The girls in the rooming house districts, the factories, and the shops drifted into and out of prostitution or lived intermittently off men or simply followed new patterns of courtship that allowed men to treat them to commercial entertainments and to buy them trinkets. Prostitution took several, often ambiguous forms ranging from streetwalking or "being in the life" to serially monogamous live-in relationships (being a "kept woman") to "treating."

The streetwalker, the female shopper, and the categories of urban pleasure-seeking women in between were defined not through their continuous, aimless, observational rambling but through their purposefulness and the timing of their appearances. The different elements of motion and stillness in the woman's sanctioned urban walk had important effects and repercussions for her public claims to identity. She was governed by a rhythm of action, waiting or standing, and recovered motion, by seeing and being seen by others. These elements introduce aspects of the importance of self-presentation that do not belong to flânerie. Female urban consciousness, then, is less connected to flânerie and a radical subjectivity and more to the rituals of urban commodity consumption.

For example, the department store windows that solicited women's attention and desire contrasted "still lives" of mannequins and commodities with the passersby in motion. The transparency and reflections of the glass walls made visible simultaneously moving people, contemplative window shoppers, and frozen objects. The store interiors, sometimes regarded as shoppers' Edens, were settings not only for commodity spectacles but also for surveillance of the female inhabitants. Inside and out, the department store reminded both female shoppers and those watching the shoppers of the reduction of persons to immobility and of the relationships between persons and things.

This model of mobile spectatorship is equally applicable to viewing the display of goods, people, and culture at the 1893 Columbian Exposition. The Exposition may have made available to female tourists the kind of urban ramble that many of them found lacking in the American city. However, it defined such flâneuserie within its controlled displays of commodities and attractions, producing a mobile spectatorship that remade the vagaries of the real city into a safe playground for containing both gender and racial differences.

Cinema capitalized on this historically specific kind of spectatorship connected to women's urban spatial experience. This spectatorship was neither ahistorical nor static but socially constituted through cultural practices. Cinema benefited from the shopper's and tourist's training to see and be seen through a complex set of subject-object relations. At the moving pictures, women were images for consumption in the theatrical space of the movie theater while they were also the most important patrons. For many critics, however, women became central to motion pictures as desiring subjects only in the teens when the film industry coupled their desiring gaze in moviegoing with possession of commodified fantasies in fan magazines, the star system, and merchandising tie-ins.[4] However, as Miriam Hansen correctly notes, these links between the department store, the screen space of the movie theater, and the objects of movie culture are speculative and tenuous, for there is no historical evidence that women's shopping gaze and identity at the department store was identical to women fans' consumption of movie culture in the teens.[5]

Women's status as moviegoers, though, from the beginning continuously shifted between being addressed as subject and object, between looking and being-looked-at. Inasmuch as early cinema embodied women's active processes of looking as bound up in tensions between power and containment, it gave expression to the ideological dilemma of the newly important female spectator in the public sphere. It posed a model for feminine consciousness in the relationship it exerted between her body and the world, between what a woman is to herself and to her culture, and between a woman's confrontation and reintegration of images that are simultaneously both herself and Other.

Nickelodeons and amusement parks best illustrated the ambivalent ways in which women could lay claims to new urban spaces. While theaters and parks may be understood as alternative spots for accommodating working class, nonwhite, and immigrant women's desires and for resisting dominant culture, they also further naturalized woman's place as a public sexual spectacle. They promoted a sexual economy organized around woman's position as the object of male desire even when she was ostensibly the desiring subject. Middle-class social reformers and charity workers may not have understood this in precisely these terms since their beliefs about female sexual independence and behavior were linked to a particular bourgeois moralism. Their interest stemmed from their need to impose middle-class values on an unruly underclass so as to control new urban populations. Their objections about commercial amusements as sexualized social spaces ultimately contributed to the gentrification of some of these spaces. Their concerns implicitly recognized that commercial amusements depended in multiple and varying ways on women's position as an exchange commodity in modern industrial culture.

My discussion of cinema's role in the reorganization of woman-oriented urban culture offers a broader reach, both chronologically and in terms of the variety of social phenomena addressed, than previous feminist studies on gender and early cinema. It takes the pre-1908 era seriously. Both Hansen and Janet Staiger have argued that nickelodeons during 1906-1909 provided women an alternative space, that reformers participated in a campaign of class uplift for those very spaces, and that the cinema that resulted after 1908 was organized around a passive female spectator.[6] The result encouraged a reception that was highly uniform, individualistic, and atomistic in remaking movie spaces into safe spaces for a female virtual mobility. Staiger's focus, however, is less on the long-lasting importance of the period before 1908 than on the transformative power of the 1908–1915 years for putting into place a cinematic mode of address that spoke to women's current social situations while it addressed them as passive spectators. Both Staiger and Judith Mayne have emphasized the movies between 1909 and 1915 that addressed women's desires and then disciplined those desires.[7] They come up with four major categories of films: those whose plots channeled female independence back into marriage; those that depicted an active, assertive female sexuality as unnatural and predatory (e.g., the "vamp" films); those that dramatized the urban sexual dangers awaiting potential female victims (e.g., "white slavery" films like *The Inside of the White Slave Traffic* and *Traffic in Souls,* both 1913); and those that represented the perilous consequences of overconsumption (e.g., *The Cheat,* 1915). Staiger and Mayne steadfastly underscore film's organization as a developing, coherent representational system for mirroring social tensions and issues rather than conceptualize cinema as an institution participating in a reorganization of public cultural space.[8]

While Hansen closely and sensitively considers cinema as a social phenomenon, she is finally interested in a concept of spectatorship that does not depend upon actual reception practices. She consistently stakes out the historical development of a concept of spectatorship as an effect of efforts to control reception and the broader historical context. She also suggests that the kind of passive spectatorship as fans and consumers traditionally associated with female identification and preoccupation with the movies requires two important qualifiers: it was historically implemented unevenly over a long time in many different locations, and it was always a reaction to the massive crisis unleashed by women's ascendancy to new experiences when they invaded public space.[9] But her project, too, is ultimately to provide a history of the systematized cinematic regulation of looking that is fully in place by the 1920s. She does identify specific historical pockets of resistance that demonstrate classical cinema's inability in the 1920s to fully contain its spectators, for example, Chicago's African-American, Polish, and Italian neighborhood audiences and Rudolph Valentino's female fans.[10]

In all these cases, cinema before 1908 is at best a foreshadowing of that which seems most compelling: the hegemony of the dominant paradigm of cinema and cinema spectatorship. These film historians maintain that, once cinema was invented, it had to contend with the female spectator and, in the process, her engagement and involvement led to cinema's emergence as a mass culture industry. Their tendency to focus exclusively on nickelodeon moviegoing rather than on the *fuller range* of places where movies showed and on the broader spectrum of women's mobile spectatorship permits a continuous line of linking movie theater precursors that serve as an explanations for the rise of dominant movie culture in the teens.

More is at stake in a broadly based synthesis of cinema's indebtedness to modes of vision than cinema's preparations for classical Hollywood cinema. At the turn of the century, the collective rules of cultural governance were being formulated that shaped movies' meaningful integration into women's everyday lives. Cinema's modern status resides in its force as a social phenomenon that addressed the role that female sexuality should play in public. This is a new definition of what cinema was, and it proposes the primacy of cinema's importance as a social rather than as a physical phenomenon. Cinema's function as a social phenomenon dictated its development, technical achievements, and even the discourse that defined its physical status before cinema achieved long-term physical stability.

My focus has not been a diachronic study of cinema during the period between its earliest manifestations at the end of the nineteenth century and its stabilization two decades or so later. Traditional film history's periodization (and feminist film criticism's as well) of silent cinema has been tripartite: the invention of the apparatus and the resulting cinema of attractions until about 1908; the development of the feature film, ending about the time World War I did; and the Golden Twenties as a decade of stabilization when Hollywood became a dominant international cultural force. This scheme of development presumes a priori that classical cinema will triumph and that it will be supported by the passive, even, ideally, feminine spectator. But since critics generally agree that cinema prior to 1908 had not yet achieved stability, a retrospective focus on only those elements that contributed to stability ignores the promise of other features that may have been heterodox or that raise novel questions about cinema's initiation of a modern feminine identity.

My synchronic view of the ways in which women invaded urban spaces both in imaginary and actual realms uncovers a set and range of practices through which the cinema admitted women. Cinema offered itself as an important site for women's participation, and was itself defined in doing so. Because the uncertain status of women and their visual location figured largely in the ongoing reorganization of culture at the time, these cultural phenomena had a particularly decisive effect on cinema's practices. Cinema gained new importance by defining itself through this most immediate of contemporary problems. Neither the growth of the nickelodeon nor cinema's borrowing of representational practices from other media is sufficient means by which to understand these complex processes. A richer understanding of them requires full alertness to cinema's efforts to define itself as a place of amusement within the spatial, social, and economic practices of turn-of-the-century America.

Cinema was central to a cultural reorganization involving women, their public identities, and urban space, and it effected enormous transformations in both women's imaginary and social geographies. From the outset, cinema accomplished this neither by neglecting nor repressing women's desires. It exerted an important effect on the body, particularly the female body, not merely through visible shocks made possible by the apparatus itself but through the implementation of the apparatus in particular kinds of social spaces. Women at the amusement parks and in theaters responded not only according to the contexts of these situations but also in relationship to how they had been taught to learn with their bodies in other commercial spaces they inhabited—the street, the department store, the fair. What the culture taught them was that their social and public opportunities for mobility and participation were permissible, even desirable, for determining a New Woman who could serve consumer culture. It was no simple coincidence that the social phenomenon of cinema invited women to find pleasure in their bodies and experience unrestrained passions while it simultaneously constructed them as the object of (male) desire and of immature emotions that needed to be tamed and controlled. This double-edged process of subjectivity and objectification was fundamental to recuperating female desire so that it could function in the service of patriarchy.

N O T E S

Introduction

1. Rick Altman, "The Silence of the Silents," *The Musical Quarterly* (Summer 1997), 689.

2. See Charles Musser, *The Emergence of Cinema: The American Screen to 1907* (Berkeley and Los Angeles: University of California Press, 1990); Charles Musser, *Before the Nickelodeon: Edwin S. Porter and The Edison Manufacturing Company* (Berkeley and Los Angeles: University of California Press, 1991); Richard Abel, *The Ciné Goes to Town: French Cinema, 1896–1914* (Berkeley and Los Angeles: University of California Press, 1994); Miriam Hansen, *Babel & Babylon: Spectatorship in American Silent Film* (Cambridge, Mass.: Harvard University Press, 1991); Giuliana Bruno, *Streetwalking on a Ruined Map: Cultural Theory and the City Films of Elvira Notari* (Princeton, N.J.: Princeton University Press, 1993); Noël Burch, *Life to Those Shadows,* trans. Ben Brewster (Berkeley and Los Angeles: University of California Press, 1990); Tom Gunning, "The Cinema of Attractions: Early Film, Its Spectator, and the Avant-Garde," in *Early Cinema: Space, Frame, Narrative,* ed. Thomas Elsaesser (London: British Film Institute, 1990), 56–62; *Wide Angle* 8, nos. 3–4 (1986), 63–70; Judith Mayne, "'Primitive' Narration," in *The Woman at the Keyhole: Feminism and Women's Cinema* (Bloomington: Indiana University Press, 1990), 157–183.

3. Journals with recent special issues devoted to early cinema include *Iris,* no. 11 (1990) on early cinema audiences; *Iris,* no. 22 (1997) on the lecturer in early cinema; *Persistence of Vision,* no. 9 (1991) on early cinema. Anthologies include Richard Abel, ed., *Silent Film* (New Brunswick, N.J.: Rutgers University Press, 1996); Leo Charney and Vanessa Schwartz, eds., *Cinema and the Invention of Modern Life* (Berkeley and Los Angeles: University of California Press, 1995); Roland Cosandey and André Gaudreault, eds., *Images across Borders* (Lausanne: Editions Payet, 1995); Roland Cosandey, André Gaudreault, and Tom Gunning, eds., *An Invention of the Devil?: Religion and Early Cinema* (Lausanne: Editions Payet, 1992); Thomas Elsaesser, ed., *Early Cinema: Space, Frame, Narrative* (London: British Film Institute, 1990); Jay Leyda and Charles Musser, eds., *Before*

Hollywood: Turn-of-the-Century Film from American Archives (New York: American Federation of the Arts, 1986). The Pordenone Silent Film Festival, begun in 1981, annually screens selected silent films from archives around the world, and it sponsors the journal *Griffithiana*, devoted in large part to film history relevant to screenings at the annual Pordenone, Italy, festival. Domitor is an international society of film scholars dedicated to the study of early cinema, and its biannual conference proceedings have been published as essay collections (see entries above under Roland Cosandey).

4. Ray Rosenzweig, *Eight Hours for What We Will: Workers and Leisure in an Industrial City, 1870–1920* (Cambridge: Cambridge University Press, 1983), 217.

5. Elizabeth Ewen, *Immigrant Women in the Land of Dollars: Life and Culture on the Lower East Side, 1890–1925* (New York: Monthly Review Press, 1985), 224.

6. For a discussion of the definition of the city in the late nineteenth century, see James Gilbert, *Perfect Cities: Chicago's Utopias of 1893* (Chicago: University of Chicago Press, 1991), 16–18.

7. U.S. Bureau of the Census, *Twelfth Census of the United States Population, Part 1,* 10 vols. (Washington, D.C.: United States Census Office, 1901), 1: cxxii; the information regarding the 1890 U.S. census is from Gilbert, *Perfect Cities,* 16.

8. U.S. Bureau of the Census, *Twelfth Census of the United States Population,* 1:cxxii.

9. Knight, Leonard & Co., *Guide to the Columbian World's Fair* (Chicago: Knight, Leonard, 1892), 2.

10. Joanne J. Meyerowitz, *Women Adrift: Independent Wage Earners in Chicago, 1880–1930* (Chicago: University of Chicago Press, 1988), 5.

11. Ibid.

12. Theodore Dreiser, *Sister Carrie* (1900; reprint, New York: New American Library, 1961), 19. Dreiser lived in Chicago from 1887 until the early 1890s. He worked for a time there as a feature writer for the *Chicago Globe.* Dreiser returned to Chicago in 1893 to cover the Chicago World's Columbian Exposition for the *St. Louis Republic.* By the end of the decade, he had moved to New York City, where he worked as a journalist and began *Sister Carrie* in 1899.

13. Judith R. Walkowitz has forcefully written about a somewhat similar trend in Victorian London, and some of her descriptions also apply to the situation in Chicago: "Women's presence in this public world provoked a heightened sense of sexual antagonism and reinforced assumptions of sexual difference, particularly the prevailing Victorian association of sexual desire with maleness." Judith R. Walkowitz, *City of Dreadful Delight: Narratives of Sexual Danger in Late-Victorian London* (Chicago: University of Chicago Press, 1992), 7.

14. Meyerowitz, *Women Adrift,* xix.

15. Elizabeth Wilson, *The Sphinx in the City: Urban Life, the Control of Disorder, and Women* (Berkeley and Los Angeles: University of California Press, 1991), 7.

16. David Scobey, "Anatomy of the Promenade: The Politics of Bourgeois Sociability in Nineteenth-Century New York," *Social History* 17, no. 2 (1992), 203–227.

17. Walkowitz, *City of Dreadful Delight,* 17–18.

18. Ibid., 21.

19. For discussions on sexual difference and flânerie, see Bruno, *Streetwalking on a Ruined Map,* 49–51; Anne Friedberg, "Les Flâneurs du Mal(l): Cinema and the Postmodern Condition," *PMLA* 106 (May 1991), 419–431; Susan Buck-Morss, "The Flâneur, the Sandwichman, and the Whore: The Politics of Loitering," *New German Critique* 39 (1986), 99–140; Janet Wolff, "The Invisible Flâneuse: Women and the Literature of Modernity," in *Feminine Sentences: Essays on Women & Culture* (Berkeley and Los Angeles: University of California Press, 1990), 34–50; Wilson, *Sphinx in the City,* 55–56.

20. M. G. Van Rensselaer, "At the Fair," *The Century Magazine* 46, no. 1 (May 1893), 11.

21. Walter Benjamin, quoted in Buck-Morss, "The Flâneur, the Sandwichman, and the Whore," 104.

22. In addition to Bruno, Friedberg, Buck-Morss, Wolff, and Wilson already cited, see Jonathan Crary, *Techniques of the Observer: On Vision and Modernity in the Nineteenth Century* (Cambridge, Mass.: MIT Press, 1990), 21.

23. Buck-Morss, "The Flâneur, the Sandwichman, and the Whore," 104–105.

24. Dana Brand, *The Spectator and the City in Nineteenth-Century American Literature* (Cambridge: Cambridge University Press, 1991), 77.

25. Buck-Morss, "The Flâneur, the Sandwichman, and the Whore," 119.

26. Walkowitz, *City of Dreadful Delight,* 21.

27. Anke Gleber, "Women on the Screens and Streets of Modernity: In Search of the Female Flâneur," in *The Image in Dispute: Art and Cinema in the Age of Photography,* ed. Dudley Andrew (Austin: University of Texas Press, 1997), 72–73.

28. Mark Seltzer, *Bodies and Machines* (New York: Routledge, 1992), 98–99.

29. Buck-Morss, "The Flâneur, the Sandwichman, and the Whore," 125.

30. Richard Maltby, "The Social Evil, the Moral Order, and the Melodramatic Imagination, 1890–1915," in *Melodrama: Stage Picture Screen,* ed. Jacky Bratton, Jim Cook, and Christine Gledhill (London: British Film Institute, 1994), 216.

31. Guy Szuberla, "A City Comes of Age," *Journal of American History* 79 (December 1992), 1101.

Chapter 1. Urban Travels: Fantasies of Flâneurs and Flirts

1. George Ade, "The Stenographic Proposal," in *In Babel* (New York: McClure, Phillips, 1903), 257–265.

2. Ibid., 259.

3. George Ade, "From the Office Window," in *Stories of the Streets and of the Town: From "The Chicago Record" 1893–1900* (Chicago: The Caxton Club, 1941), 167–171.

4. Ibid., 170.

5. Ibid.

6. Ibid., 170–171.

7. Ibid., 171.

8. James Gilbert, *Perfect Cities: Chicago's Utopias of 1893* (Chicago: University of Chicago Press, 1991), 50.

9. Ibid., 51.

10. See *Rand McNally & Co.'s Handy Guide to Chicago and the World's Columbian Exposition* (Chicago: Rand McNally, 1893), especially chap. 10, "A Ramble at Night," 68–72 and 104–111; *Chicago By Night* (Chicago: Rand McNally, 1893).

11. *Rand McNally & Co.'s Handy Guide to Chicago,* 105. However, Timothy J. Gilfoyle points out in his study of sex commercialization in nineteenth-century New York City that in the latter half of the nineteenth century there were guidebooks that "described for the veteran and newcomer alike the most enticing haunts of the sexual underworld." Timothy J. Gilfoyle, *City of Eros: New York City, Prostitution, and the Commercialization of Sex, 1790–1920* (New York: Norton, 1992), 130. Such guidebooks probably existed for Chicago as well by the century's end. However, Rand McNally's guidebooks are important here because they were aimed at a more general, heterogeneous, and diverse group of tourists.

Another kind of "guidebook" was published in 1894—William Stead's *If Christ Came to Chicago,* a moralist's call to clean up Chicago. This tract provided maps of the locations of Chicago's brothels, gambling dens, and saloons! In effect, Stead's book was yet another attempt to bifurcate the city into spatial zones of vice and virtue and to argue for ways to control or contain the vice. William Stead, *If Christ Came to Chicago* (Chicago: Laird & Lee, 1894).

12. *Rand McNally & Co.'s Handy Guide to Chicago,* 105.

13. Theodore Dreiser, "Last Day at the Fair," *St. Louis Republic,* 23 July 1893, 6; reprinted in *Theodore Dreiser, Journalism,* ed. T. D. Nostwich, 2 vols. (Philadelphia: University of Pennsylvania Press, 1988), 1:135.

14. Sarah Jane Kimball, diary, 27 September 1893, 29, Sarah Jane Kimball Papers, State Historical Society of Iowa, Iowa City, Iowa.

15. *Rand McNally & Co.'s Handy Guide to Chicago,* 72.

16. Guy Szuberla, "Ladies, Gentlemen, Flirts, Mashers, Snoozers, and the Breaking of Etiquette's Code," *Prospects* 15 (1990), 172.

17. Ibid.

18. Reginald Wright Kauffman, *The House of Bondage* (1910; reprint, Upper Saddle River, N.J.: The Gregg Press, 1968), 3.

19. Ibid., 15.

20. Szuberla, "Ladies, Gentlemen, Flirts, Mashers, Snoozers, and the Breaking of Etiquette's Code," 179.

21. *Life* 8, 23 September 1886, 177.

22. *Life* 11, 12 January 1888, 25, quoted in Szuberla, "Ladies, Gentlemen, Flirts, Mashers, Snoozers, and the Breaking of Etiquette's Code," 178.

23. *Life* 2, 19 November 1893, 274; quoted in ibid., 188.

24. *Life* 8, 4 November 1886, 274.

25. Szuberla, "Ladies, Gentlemen, Flirts, Mashers, Snoozers, and the Breaking of Etiquette's Code," 178–179.

26. Sigmund Krausz, *Street Types of Chicago with Literary Sketches by Well-Known Authors* (Chicago: Max Stern, 1892). Typologies, defining character types through physical characteristics, were increasingly fashionable at the turn of the century. They also provided urban authorities (particularly police departments) with scientific pretensions to epistemological control by making the visible social body legible. Alan Sekula describes the central roles of photography and the archive in establishing the scientific authority of typologies. Alan Sekula, "The Body and the Archive," *October* 39 (Winter 1986), 3–64.

27. Krausz, *Street Types of Chicago,* 159.

28. Ibid., 158.

29. Ibid., 163.

30. Theodore Dreiser, *Sister Carrie* (1900; reprint, New York: New American Library, 1961), 54.

31. Ibid., 55.

32. Szuberla, "Ladies, Gentlemen, Flirts, Mashers, Snoozers, and the Breaking of Etiquette's Code," 190.

33. Dreiser, *Sister Carrie,* 26.

34. Ibid., 27.

35. Ibid.

36. Tom Gunning, "'Now You See It, Now You Don't': The Temporality of the Cinema of Attractions," *The Velvet Light Trap* 32 (Fall 1993), 8.

37. Tom Gunning, "The Cinema of Attractions: Early Film, Its Spectator, and the Avant-Garde," in *Early Cinema: Space, Frame, Narrative,* ed. Thomas Elsaesser (London: British Film Institute, 1990), 57–58.

38. For a fuller discussion of exhibitionism, women's bodily display, and cinema, see Miriam Hansen, *Babel & Babylon: Spectatorship in American Silent Film* (Cambridge, Mass.: Harvard University Press, 1991), 35–44.

39. This separates these films from the facial gesture films, like *Photographing a Female Crook* (American Mutoscope & Biograph, 1904), *A Subject for the Rogue's Gallery* (American Mutoscope & Biograph, 1904), and *Facial Expression* (Edison Manufacturing Company, 1902), that isolated women's faces as they contorted, grimaced, and rolled their eyes.

40. Judith Mayne, *The Woman at the Keyhole: Feminism and Women's Cinema* (Bloomington: Indiana University Press, 1990), 157–183.

41. Walter Benjamin, "The Work of Art in the Age of Mechanical Reproduction," in *Illuminations,* ed. Hannah Arendt, trans. Harry Zohn (New York: Schocken Books, 1969), 228.

42. Janet Staiger, *Bad Women: Regulating Sexuality in Early American Cinema* (Minneapolis: University of Minnesota Press, 1995), 57, 58.

43. Robert C. Allen, *Horrible Prettiness: Burlesque and American Culture* (Chapel Hill: University of North Carolina Press, 1991), 244.

44. Ibid., 271.

45. Barbara N. Cohen-Stratyner, *Biographical Dictionary of Dance* (New York: Schirmer Books, 1982), 66.

46. Ibid.

47. M. Alison Kibler, "Female Varieties: Gender and Cultural Hierarchy on the Keith Vaudeville Circuit, 1890–1925" (Ph.D. diss., University of Iowa, 1995), *passim*.

48. Ibid.

49. Allen, *Horrible Prettiness,* 273.

50. Mayne, *The Woman at the Keyhole,* 161–164. Tom Gunning qualifies Mayne's argument by noting that, while the film can be seen as a proto-narrative, it is still largely and categorically "display" since the woman's display neither instigates a series of incidents nor functions to reveal character traits. He contrasts this woman's display with that of Marilyn Monroe's similarly uplifted skirt in *The Seven Year Itch* since the latter film provides a moment of spectacle that functions narratively to create character traits that explain later narrative actions. Gunning, "'Now You See It, Now You Don't,'" 9.

51. Gilfoyle suggests that the main thoroughfare may have been moving slowly uptown in the early 1900s. Gilfoyle, *City of Eros,* 203.

52. *The American Film Institute Catalog of Motion Pictures Produced in the United States: Film Beginnings, 1893–1910, A Work in Progress,* comp. Elias Savada (Metuchen, N.J.: Scarecrow Press, 1995), 1174.

53. Gilfoyle, *City of Eros,* 204.

54. Gunning, "'Now You See It, Now You Don't,'" 9.

55. Ibid., 12.

56. Ibid., 9.

57. Suzanne L. Kinser, "Prostitutes in the Art of John Sloan," *Prospects* 9 (1984), 234.

58. Ibid., 241.

59. Ibid., 240.

60. John Sloan, diary, 20 May 1908, quoted in *John Sloan 1871–1951* (Boston: Boston Book & Art, 1971), 103.

61. Gilfoyle, *City of Eros,* 222–223.

62. Ibid., 223.

63. Anonymous source, quoted in Gilfoyle, *City of Eros,* 205.

Chapter 2. The Fair View: The 1893 Chicago World's Columbian Exposition

1. There is some dispute over whether there actually was a kinetoscope at the fair. Charles Musser quotes film historian Terry Ramsaye saying that no peephole kinetoscopes were shown at the fair; Charles Musser, *Before the Nickelodeon: Edwin S. Porter and The Edison Manufacturing Company* (Berkeley and Los Angeles: University of California Press, 1991), 498–499 (n. 15). In his history of the

kinetosocope, Gordon Hendricks says that at least one machine—the model shown at the Brooklyn Institute—was part of the Edison phonograph exhibit; Gordon Hendricks, *The Kinetoscope: America's First Commercially Successful Motion Picture Exhibitor* (New York: Arno Press, 1966), 40–45. But, Musser argues that Hendricks bases his account on advance publicity, and so he goes with Ramsaye's conclusions, based on an interview with Norman Raff. World's Columbian Exposition historians acknowledge this dispute but maintain there was a single kinetoscope present. They have implied that because there are no photographs ("truth-in-seeing" is being invoked here!), some historians have doubted the veracity of the claim. Stanley Appelbaum, who has worked extensively with the Exposition collections at the Chicago Historical Society, concludes that "reports are numerous and circumstantial" that a kinetoscope was hooked up to a phonograph at the Edison Manufacturing Company exhibit in the Electricity Building. He sees the discrepancy in reporting due to the difference between Edison's plans to have an entire bank of machines and the result that probably only one machine appeared. Stanley Appelbaum, *The Chicago World's Fair of 1893: A Photographic Record* (New York: Dover, 1980), 47. In addition, George Spoor, one of the founders of Essanay Film Manufacturing Company, has been cited on numerous occasions as having been influenced to get into the business by the kinetoscope at the Chicago Columbian Exposition.

2. The obvious gender coding in the two types of activities, as Linda Williams has persuasively demonstrated, "was thus never purely scientific . . . [providing] an illustration of Foucault's point that the power exerted over bodies in technology is rendered pleasurable through technology." Linda Williams, *Hard Core: Power, Pleasure, and the "Frenzy of the Visible"* (Berkeley and Los Angeles: University of California Press, 1989), 39. Charles Musser supports this view in his discussion of a Muybridge lecture given in Orange, New Jersey, on February 25, 1888. Musser cites a letter to the editor of the *Orange Journal* that questioned the "propriety of exhibiting semi-nude human figures to a promiscuous [i.e., male and female] assembly," and Musser concludes that Muybridge intended to challenge sexual mores and to "provoke such a reaction from his audiences." Charles Musser, *The Emergence of Cinema: The American Screen to 1907* (Berkeley and Los Angeles: University of California Press, 1990), 53.

Williams's important conclusion, however, is complicated somewhat by a rhetoric of class hierarchy that Muybridge and the images made available in the public lectures. The mechanics who performed the manual labor and many of the women identified in the lectures as artists' models who earned their living by exhibiting their bodies for view were typed by employment as lower classes being made available for the gaze of middle- and upper-class patrons. Such rigid hierarchizing was convoluted somewhat by Muybridge's explanations that some of both male and female models were well-respected members of society, including teachers, society matrons, the premier dancer of a Philadelphia theater, an art instructor, a fencing master. Although Muybridge justified full nudity or near nudity as being in the service of science and art, the revelations of the bodies in his lectures also offered a transgressively sexual public sight, especially in their intimate views of respectably bourgeois men and women.

The implications of this situation are illustrated in one instance reported during Muybridge's lecture at the Philadelphia Academy of Fine Arts several years earlier. When a gentleman and a lady walked across the front of the hall during an intermission, a student in attendance made a cutting remark that compared the two to the naked models just seen. As the report goes, the student's remark "brought down the house" (Robert B. Haas, *Muybridge: Man in Motion* [Berkeley and Los Angeles: University of California Press, 1976], 149). The story, whether true or not, explicitly identifies the extension of a spectator's attention from the screen to passersby or audience members made over into sexualized spectacle through the very act of moving within the theatricalized space in front of the screen as itself a social arena. If, as Mark Seltzer argues, Muybridge's human motion studies abstracted the human form into a progressive series of poses and movements, they arguably did so through a semiotics of sexualized appearances that heightened their rhetoric of a public sexuality constructed by both intimate revelations and generalized motions. Mark Seltzer, *Bodies and Machines* (New York: Routledge, 1992), 12–16.

3. Appelbaum, *The Chicago World's Fair of 1893*, 102.

4. M. B. Van Rensselaer, "At the Fair," *The Century Magazine* 46, no. 1 (May 1893), 6–7.

5. Neil Harris, "Great American Fairs and American Cities: The Role of Chicago's Columbian Exposition," in *Cultural Excursions: Marketing Appetites and Cultural Tastes in Modern America* (Chicago: University of Chicago Press, 1990), 118; James Gilbert, *Perfect Cities: Chicago's Utopias of 1893* (Chicago: University of Chicago Press, 1991), 75–130.

6. Alan Trachtenberg, *The Incorporation of America: Culture and Society in the Gilded Age* (New York: Hill & Wang, 1982); Robert Rydell, *All the World's a Fair: Visions of Empire at American International Expositions, 1876–1916* (Chicago: University of Chicago Press, 1984), 38–71; John Kasson, *Amusing the Million: Coney Island at the Turn of the Century* (New York: Hill & Wang, 1978), 11–28.

7. Harris, "Great American Fairs and American Cities," 120.

8. For a discussion of the official Exposition photography and its incorporation of preferred vantage points, see Peter B. Hales, "Photography and the World's Columbian Exposition: A Case Study," *Journal of Urban History* 15 (May 1989), 247–273. Summaries of photographic representations of the Exposition may be found in Diane Kirkpatrick, *The Fair View: Representations of the World's Columbian Exposition of 1893* (Ann Arbor: University of Michigan Museum of Art, 1993); and Julie K. Brown, *Contesting Images: Photography and the World's Columbian Exposition* (Tucson: University of Arizona Press, 1994).

9. Marian Shaw, *World's Fair Notes: A Woman Journalist Views Chicago's 1893 Columbian Exposition* (1893; reprint, St. Paul: Pogo Press, 1992), 15.

10. Harris, "Great American Fairs and American Cities," 120.

11. See Hales, "Photography and the World's Columbian Exposition," 247–273.

The Chicago Columbian Exposition was the first fair to be so extensively documented and publicized in photography. Photographers Charles Arnold and William Henry Jackson both took official views for the Exposition's board of directors, although most of Jackson's photographs were not used by the board. In addition, there was a Government Board Committee on Photography, which documented the Exposition for the U.S. government.

Moses P. Handy, as director of the Department of Publicity and Promotion, was in charge of authorizing all others who wished to photograph the fair. Those who did pay the fees for the requisite license were generally entrepreneurs like Benjamin West Kilburn, who published a number of stereoscopic views of the Exposition. Others published lantern slides or photograph albums. There were photographers who received licenses to use the new Kodak amateur camera on the grounds. However, these photographers used the new format principally for producing collections of souvenir books, e.g., *Glimpses of the World's Fair: A Selection of Gems of the White City Seen Through a Camera* (Chicago: Laird & Law, 1893); F. Dundas Todd, *World's Fair Through a Camera: Snap Shots by an Artist* (St. Louis: Woodward and Tiernan, 1893).

Kirkpatrick and Brown also discuss the number of amateur photographers/tourists who used new Kodak hand-held cameras to photograph the fair. (Kodak introduced a hand-held camera for the general market in 1888.) However, few of these photographs survive, and both Brown's and Kirkpatrick's discussions rely more heavily on stereo cards and chromolithographs of men and women carrying Kodak cameras than on the photographs made by amateurs. But it is important that Kirkpatrick still concludes, "Many amateur photographs consciously echoed the formal official depictions . . . as did most representations on memorial coins, souvenir ribbons and spoons, and even the covers of sheet music and books." Kirkpatrick, *The Fair View,* 10. Thus, she suggests that the amateurs had already learned to see in the ways laid out for them by the authorized views. This bolsters my overall argument about the significant role that such representations played in organizing the visual reception of the Exposition.

12. Although the Movable Sidewalk was located near the lakeside entrance and could ostensibly help move people more quickly and efficiently to and from that entrance, numerous novels and travelers' accounts indicate that they used the sidewalk expressly for viewing the fair.

13. Shaw, *World's Fair Notes,* 23.

14. *Pictorial Album and History of the World's Fair and Midway* (Chicago: Harry T. Smith, 1893), Chicago World's Columbian Exposition Collections, Prints and Photographs, Chicago Historical Society, Chicago, Illinois.

15. Ibid.

16. Lillie Brown-Buck, *Amy Leslie at the Fair* (Chicago: W. B. Conkey, 1893), 39–40.

17. Gilbert, *Perfect Cities,* 118.

18. Shaw, *World's Fair Notes,* 56.

19. Brown-Buck, *Amy Leslie at the Fair,* 99.

20. Charles M. Stevens, *The Adventures of Uncle Jeremiah and Family at the Great Fair: Their Observations and Triumphs* (Chicago: Laird & Lee, 1893), 65–68.

21. Robert Mushet, *Chicago Yesterday and Today: A Guide to the Garden City and the Columbian Exposition* (Chicago: Donohue & Henneberry, 1893), 19.

22. Mable L. Treseder, quoted in Gilbert, *Perfect Cities,* 126.

23. *Pictorial Album and History of the World's Fair and Midway,* n.p.

24. Shaw, *World's Fair Notes,* 58.

25. Ibid., 58–59.

26. Theodore Dreiser, "Third Day at the Fair," *St. Louis Republic,* 20 July 1893, 4; reprinted in *Theodore Dreiser, Journalism,* ed. T. D. Nostwich, 2 vols. (Philadelphia: University of Pennsylvania Press, 1988), 1:128.

27. Brown-Buck, *Amy Leslie at the Fair,* 66.

28. Ibid., 100.

29. *Pictorial Album and History of the World's Fair and Midway,* n.p.

30. Ibid.

31. Ibid.

32. Paul Greenhalgh, *Ephemeral Vistas: The Expositions Universelles, Great Exhibitions, and World's Fairs, 1851–1939* (Manchester: Manchester University Press, 1988), 98.

33. Ibid.

34. Ibid.

35. Rydell, *All the World's a Fair,* 38–71; Gilbert, *Perfect Cities,* 75–130 *passim;* Greenhalgh, *Ephemeral Vistas,* 97–102.

36. Ida B. Wells-Barnett and Frederick Douglass, "The Reason Why the Colored American Is Not in the World's Columbian Exposition," in *Selected Works of Ida B. Wells-Barnett,* ed. Trudier Harris (New York: Oxford University Press, 1991), 46–137. The pamphlet documented this exclusionary process as well as lynch, convict lease, and miscegenation laws; details of numerous lynchings; and African-American achievements in arts, science, and commerce since the abolition of slavery. A thorough discussion of the pamphlet and Wells and Douglass's indictment of the fair's racism is in Gail Bederman, "Civilization, the Decline of Middle-Class Manliness, and Ida B. Wells's Anti-Lynching Campaign (1892–94)," in *Gender and American History Since 1890,* ed. Barbara Melosh (New York: Routledge, 1993), 212–217.

37. Wells-Barnett and Douglass, "The Reason Why the Colored American Is Not in the World's Columbian Exposition," 52, 58.

38. John Flinn, as quoted in Gilbert, *Perfect Cities,* 116. *Scribner's Magazine* described the Dahomey as "uncleanly, unkempt . . . forbidding and repulsive." *Frank Leslie's Popular Magazine* proclaimed, "Sixty-nine [Dahomeyans] are here in all their barbaric ugliness, blacker than buried midnight and as degraded as the animals which prowl the jungles of their dark land." Quoted in Ginalie Swaim with Becky Hawbaker and Lisa Moran, "Iowans at the 1893 World Columbian Exposition," *The Palimpset* 74, no. 4 (Winter 1993), 169.

39. Brown-Buck, *Amy Leslie at the Fair*, 81.

40. Miles Orvell, *The Real Thing: Imitation and Authenticity in American Culture, 1880–1940* (Chapel Hill: University of North Carolina Press, 1989), 35.

41. Kirkpatrick, *The Fair View*, 6.

42. Clara Louise Burnham, *Sweet Clover, a Romance of the White City* (Boston: Houghton, Mifflin, 1894). Burnham, who was the successful author of several romance novels, was incidentally the wife of the Exposition's famous planner, Daniel Burnham.

43. Ibid., 279.

44. Ibid., 194–202.

45. Ibid., 364–368.

46. Van Rensselaer, "At the Fair," 6.

47. Sarah Jane Kimball Papers, State Historical Society of Iowa, Iowa City, Iowa.

48. See, for example, Brown-Buck, *Amy Leslie at the Fair*, 48; Charles Graham, *Chicago Tribune Art Supplements in Two Parts: World's Columbian Exposition* (n.p., n.d.), *passim;* Charles Graham, *The World's Fair in Water Colors* (Springfield, Ohio: Mast, Crowell & Kirkpatrick, 1893).

49. F. Robertson, untitled illustration, in Brown-Buck, *Amy Leslie at the Fair*, 48.

50. Graham, *Chicago Tribune Art Supplements.*

51. Ibid.

52. Theodore Dreiser, "Last Day at the Fair," *St. Louis Republic*, 23 July 1893, 6; reprinted in *Theodore Dreiser, Journalism*, 1:136.

53. Fatimah Tobing Rony, "Those Who Squat and Those Who Sit: The Iconography of Race in the 1895 Films of Felix-Louis Regnault," *Camera Obscura* 28 (1992), 272.

54. Ibid., 272–273.

55. Ibid.

56. Emmanuelle Toulet, "Cinema at the Universal Exposition, Paris 1900," *Persistence of Vision* 9 (1991), 10–36.

Chapter 3. Eve in the Garden of Desire: The Department Store and the Woman Who Looks

1. Susan Porter Benson, *Counter Cultures: Saleswomen, Managers, and Customers in American Department Stores, 1890–1940* (Urbana and Chicago: University of Illinois Press, 1986), 82–83.

2. Begun as a joint venture by well-known real-estate baron Potter Palmer, Marshall Field, and Levi Z. Leiter, Marshall Field's specialized in quality merchandise, a one-price, price-tagging system, and a money-back guarantee. The business was so successful that, in 1868, Field and Leiter bought out Palmer and moved to their first palatially built store on State Street. When the store burned to the ground in the Chicago Fire of 1871, they kept the business going for two years in temporary locations until a new store was opened on Washington and State

streets in 1873. That building burned in 1877, and they rebuilt in 1879. The new store introduced electric illumination, a central switchboard and telephone lines to every department, and show windows for visual displays of merchandise.

3. Lloyd Wendt and Herman Kogan, *Give the Lady What She Wants! The Story of the Marshall Field & Company* (Chicago: Rand McNally, 1952), 218.

4. The Mandel Brothers began as a dry goods store in 1855 at Clark and Van Buren streets (some eight blocks away from the original Marshall Field's store). When this store, too, burnt in the 1871 fire, Field himself persuaded the brothers to relocate to State Street in 1877 to help create a new retail center.

5. An 1892 tourist guidebook, *A Week in Chicago* (Chicago: Rand McNally, 1892), devoted three pages single-spaced to hyperbolic enumeration of the amounts of materials (I-beams, columns, plaster, etc.) that went into the Big Store's construction. It also offered statistics about the store's size, number of employees, etc., as well as detailed information about the departments and services.

6. A. M. Rothschild and Company advertisement, *Chicago Tribune,* 5 July 1896, 34.

7. Started by Edward J. Lehmann in 1875, The Fair was so immediately successful that it expanded regularly over the next twenty years. The Fair, however, was more the forerunner for the twentieth-century five-and-dime store than for the department store as a palace of consumption. In fact, The Fair was eventually bought and taken over by the five-and-dime chain S. S. Kresge.

8. Wendt and Kogan, *Give the Lady What She Wants!,* 160.

9. Soon after, however, the Madison and State streets store (it is still being used as a department store) was sold to Carson, Pirie Scott & Company, another State Street department store that had recently lost its lease.

10. Rachel Bowlby even goes so far as to claim that the "transformation of merchandise into a spectacle" offers an important precedent to the cinema; Rachel Bowlby, *Just Looking: Consumer Culture in Dreiser, Gissing, and Zola* (New York: Methuen, 1985), 6.

11. Elizabeth S. Abelson, *When Ladies Go a-Thieving: Middle-Class Shoplifters in the Victorian Department Store* (New York: Oxford University Press, 1989), 11.

12. Robert W. Twyman, *History of Marshall Field & Co., 1852–1906* (Philadelphia, 1954), 60, quoted in Porter Benson, *Counter Cultures,* 19.

13. Porter Benson, *Counter Cultures,* 82.

14. Theodore Dreiser, *Sister Carrie* (1900; reprint, New York: New American Library, 1961), 26–27.

15. Abelson, *When Ladies Go a-Thieving,* 11.

16. Anne Friedberg, *Window Shopping: Cinema and the Postmodern* (Berkeley and Los Angeles: University of California Press, 1993), 42.

17. Porter Benson, *Counter Cultures,* 20.

18. Hilda Satt Polacheck, *I Came a Stranger: The Story of a Hull-House Girl,* ed. Dena J. Polacheck Epstein (Urbana and Chicago: University of Illinois Press, 1989), 59.

19. Dreiser, *Sister Carrie,* 26–27.

20. Porter Benson, *Counter Cultures,* 20.

21. "Wide-Awake Retailing," *Dry Goods Economist* 56, 17 May 1902, 59, quoted in Porter Benson, *Counter Cultures,* 90.

22. Rosalind Williams, "The Dream World of Mass Consumption," in *Rethinking Popular Culture: Contemporary Perspectives in Cultural Studies,* ed. Chandra Mukerji and Michael Schudson (Berkeley and Los Angeles: University of California Press, 1991), 204.

23. Among the critics who discuss this phenomenon, see especially Rosalind Williams, *Dream Worlds: Mass Consumption in Late Nineteenth-Century France* (Berkeley and Los Angeles: University of California Press, 1982); Giuliana Bruno, *Streetwalking on a Ruined Map: Cultural Theory and the City Films of Elvira Notari* (Princeton, N.J.: Princeton University Press, 1993), 52.

24. Abelson, *When Ladies Go a-Thieving,* 28, 35.

25. Ibid., 41.

26. See: Friedberg, *Window Shopping,* 66–68; Charles Eckert, "The Carole Lombard in Macy's Window," *Quarterly Review of Film Studies* 3, no. 1 (Winter 1978), 4–5; Mary Ann Doane, *The Desire to Desire: The Woman's Film of the 1940s* (Bloomington: Indiana University Press, 1987), 24; Jane Gaines, "The Queen Christina Tie-Ups: Convergence of Show Window and Screen," *Quarterly Review of Film and Video* 11, no. 1 (Winter 1989); Jeanne Allen, "The Film Viewer as Consumer," *Quarterly Review of Film Studies* 5, no. 4 (Fall 1980), 482.

27. Abelson, *When Ladies Go a-Thieving,* 75, citing Ellen Andrews to James Andrews, 20 May 1884.

28. Tudor Jenks, "Before Shop Windows," *Outlook* 51, 27 April 1895, 688, quoted in ibid., 70.

29. "Obituary: Arthur Fraser," *Women's Wear Daily,* 8 July 1947, 71, quoted in Abelson, *When Ladies Go a-Thieving,* 71.

30. Abelson, *When Ladies Go a-Thieving,* 71.

31. Wendt and Kogan, *Give the Lady What She Wants!,* 215.

32. For Baum's career as a window dresser, see William Leach, *Land of Desire: Merchants, Power, and the Rise of a New American Culture* (New York: Vintage Books, 1993), 41, 55–61; Friedberg, *Window Shopping,* 66.

33. L. Frank Baum, *The Art of Decorating Dry Goods Windows and Interiors* (Chicago, 1900), 87, 109, 128, quoted in Leach, *Land of Desire,* 60.

34. Friedberg, *Window Shopping,* 66–68.

35. Bruno, *Streetwalking on a Ruined Map,* 51

36. Ibid., 50.

37. Ibid., 50–52.

38. Laura Mulvey, "Visual Pleasure and Narrative Cinema," *Screen* 16 (1975), 6–18.

39. Judith Mayne, *The Woman at the Keyhole: Feminism and Women's Cinema* (Bloomington: Indiana University Press, 1990), 157–183; Mary Ann Doane, "Technology's Body: Cinematic Vision in Modernity," *differences: A Journal of Feminist Cultural Studies* 5, no. 2 (1993), 1–23.

40. Mayne, *The Woman at the Keyhole,* 175.

41. Ibid., 174.

42. Ibid., 178. Also see Mayne's well-argued critique of Tom Gunning's division of early cinema between "exhibitionist" and "voyeurist," as too simple an opposition that does not take into account the heterogeneous ways that the gendering of early cinema participates in this as a master trajectory.

43. Charles Keil, "The Story of Uncle Josh Told: Spectatorship and Apparatus in Early Cinema," *Iris* 11 (Summer 1990), 69. It is also worth noting here, perhaps, that the wife hires a male secretary to replace the female one, making the common assumption of heterosexual orthodoxy that a man is also and always another inappropriate or unlikely object of male desire.

44. Several film scholars have discussed keyhole films: Tom Gunning, "What I Saw from the Rear Window of the Hotel des Folies-Dramatiques, or the Story Point of View Films Told," in *Ce que je vois de mon ciné: La représentation du regard dans le cinéma des premiers temps,* ed. André Gaudreault (Paris: Méridiens Klincksieck, 1988), 33–44; Miriam Hansen, *Babel & Babylon: Spectatorship in American Silent Film* (Cambridge, Mass.: Harvard University Press, 1991), 40–41; Noël Burch, *Life to Those Shadows,* trans. Ben Brewster (Berkeley and Los Angeles: University of California Press, 1990), 222–224; Elena Dagrada, "Through the Keyhole: Spectators and Matte Shots in Early Cinema," *Iris* 11 (Summer 1990), 95–106.

45. Gunning, "What I Saw from the Rear Window," 39–40; Burch, *Life to Those Shadows,* 222.

46. Dagrada, "Through the Keyhole," 101.

47. Gunning, "What I Saw From the Rear Window," 37–38.

48. Burch, *Life to Those Shadows,* 222.

49. Mayne, *The Woman at the Keyhole,* 170–171.

50. Mayne discusses two other through-the-keyhole films that similarly feature female voyeurs—*Die Rache der Frau Schultze* (*Mrs. Schultze's Revenge,* 1905) and *La Fille de bain indiscrète* (*The Indiscreet Bathroom Maid,* Pathé Frères, 1902). When Frau Schultze cannot sleep because her musician neighbor is playing his piano, she spies on him through the keyhole in the door separating their rooms. She sends a fly through the keyhole and watches as the neighbor wreaks havoc in his apartment as he tries to swat the fly. The "indiscreet maid" is a female bath attendant who peeks through a series of transoms in a hotel and watches the male occupants of the rooms. For Mayne, the women subjects of these films illustrate "not only the pleasure of [women] peering through keyholes but also and especially the desire to manipulate the scene." Mayne, *The Woman at the Keyhole,* 177. These women are not punished; however, they also cannot cross the threshholds into the spaces of the objects of their looks. Unlike in other "Peeping Tom" films that regularly end with the male's punishment for looking at a female subject, both women emerge triumphant at the films' conclusions: Frau Schultze expresses satisfaction at the group of men who have arrived and put an end to her neigh-

bor's racket; the "indiscreet maid" laughs at the comedic scene in the last bathroom. Their desire may not be able to motivate the kind of reverse angle to the room interior that Mayne sees as so important for the paradigm of a classical Hollywood cinema vocabulary (the conclusion of *A Search for the Evidence*), but the power of their role may also not be so neatly accounted for within that same paradigm.

51. While different versions of films circulated or were often abbreviated by exhibitors, it is unlikely that in Mayne's viewing she saw an expurgated version. In the version of *A Search for the Evidence* held at the Library of Congress, the film ends differently than as Mayne describes: the detective and the wife enter the room. *The Early Motion Pictures Catalogue to the Paper Print Collection in the Library of Congress* describes the conclusion as "the wife and her escort attempt to break into the room." Kemp Niver, *Early Motion Pictures: The Paper Print Collection in the Library of Congress* (Washington, D.C.: Library of Congress, 1985), 291. The *Biograph Bulletin* that appeared upon the film's initial release in 1903 also describes the end as "the detective and the wife breaking in and an exciting denouement when the wife confronts the woman." *Biograph Bulletin,* no. 14, 21 September 1903, reprinted in Kemp. R. Niver, ed., *Biograph Bulletins 1896–1908* (Los Angeles: Artisan Press, 1971), 102. Indeed, since the highly moralistic and "exciting" conclusion was advertised by Biograph as a drawing card, it is unlikely that exhibitors would have snipped it off.

52. *Biograph Bulletin,* no. 9, 29 August 1903, reprinted in Niver, ed., *Biograph Bulletins 1896–1908,* 89.

53. Hansen, *Babel & Babylon,* 40–41.

54. Ibid., 173; also see Judith Mayne, "Uncovering the Female Body," in *Before Hollywood: Turn-of-the-Century American Film,* ed. Jay Leyda and Charles Musser (New York: Hudson Hills Press, 1987), 66.

55. Hansen, *Babel & Babylon,* 39.

56. It might be worth noting that the Biograph catalogue entry for this particular film provides only a rough description of what actually occurs and assigns her a more passive role and him a more active one: "Showing a pretty girl (figure large) at a window looking for the approach of her lover with a pair of field glasses. She is greatly disappointed at his non-appearance, as her face plainly shows, but he creeps in by her side and announces his presence by a kiss." This description suggests the degree to which it was possible for a spectator to interpolate female desire as waiting, and to infer female passivity and male activity despite the film's assertion of female agency. See *Biograph Bulletin,* no. 14, 21 September 1903, reprinted in Niver, ed., *Biograph Bulletins 1896–1908,* 104.

57. See, for example, Dagrada, "Through the Keyhole," 100.

58. See Richard Abel, *The Ciné Goes to Town: French Cinema 1896–1914* (Berkeley and Los Angeles: University of California Press, 1994), 120–121, for more on *Le Déjeuner du Savant.*

59. *In My Lady's Boudoir; Lucky Kitten; The Rose; He Loves Me, He Loves Me Not; Sweets for the Sweet; A Welsh Rabbit.*

60. Mayne suggests the importance of this male figure is a "telling embodiment of the equivalence between cinematic pleasure and voyeuristic fantasies," building sexist gender hierarchies into the rudimentary processes of cinematic ways of showing and telling; Mayne, *The Woman at the Keyhole*, 69. Tom Gunning, however, notes that the film was produced by American Mutoscope & Biograph Company for their mutoscope viewer (a peep-show device that used a series of flipped cards) for individual viewing and not for cinema. Moreover, Gunning takes into account the importance of how the film frustrates "full satisfaction" for the man on the street who stands in for the film viewer when Suzie pulls down the window shade before removing all her clothes; Tom Gunning, "Pull Down the Curtains Suzie," in *Before Hollywood*, 114.

61. For a critique of this blind spot, see Jackie Stacey, "Desperately Seeking Difference," *Screen* 28, no. 1 (Winter 1987), 48–61.

62. Ibid.

63. *Biograph Bulletin*, no. 55, 27 November 1905, 13, reprinted in Niver, ed., *Biograph Bulletins 1896–1908*, 203.

64. Hansen, *Babel & Babylon*, 57.

65. *Moving Picture World*, 25 May 1907, 178.

66. Hansen, *Babel & Babylon*, 52–53.

67. See Lucy Fischer, "The Lady Vanishes: Women, Magic, and the Movies," in *Film Before Griffith*, ed. John Fell (Berkeley and Los Angeles: University of California Press, 1983), 339–354, for an extended discussion on a set of psychoanalytic implications regarding early trick films that are about "magical" appearances and disappearances of women and their transformations between live and object forms. Fischer covers a large number of Georges Méliès's films as well as several early Edison films.

68. Abelson, *When Ladies Go a-Thieving*, 174.

69. Edward A. Filene, quoted in Porter Benson, *Counter Cultures*, 76.

70. Several critics have remarked on this in passing. Miriam Hansen said, "The lady thief goes about her business just as unnoticeable to us as to the customers within the diegesis." *Babel & Babylon*, 34. William Everson said, "The interior shot of the department store is so 'busy,' with so many identically dressed women bustling around in a protracted long shot, that the audience is given no guidance at all as to where to look or what is going on." Quoted in Charles Musser, *Before the Nickelodeon: Edwin S. Porter and The Edison Manufacturing Company* (Berkeley and Los Angeles: University of California Press, 1991), 297.

71. Musser, *Before the Nickelodeon*, 296–297.

72. Ibid., 297.

73. Ibid., 298.

74. This order observed in the print from the Library of Congress Paper Print Collection is not quite the same order as described in the Edison Film Catalogue, where the wealthy woman arrives at the police station before the beginning of the story of the poor woman.

75. Musser, *Before the Nickelodeon*, 299.

Chapter 4. Dangers of the House of Dreams: Women, Nickelodeons, and Early Movie Reform

1. Richard Maltby, "The Social Evil, the Moral Order, and the Melodramatic Imagination, 1890–1915," in *Melodrama: Stage Picture Screen,* ed. Jacky Bratton, Jim Cook, and Christine Gledhill (London: British Film Institute, 1994), 218.

2. Kinetoscopes had been offering moving pictures in individual peephole devices for two years prior to 1896 at phonograph parlors.

3. "Hopkins' South Side Theatre," *Chicago Tribune,* 5 July 1896, 36.

4. Hopkins Theater advertisements throughout July 1896 list the movie bill; see *Chicago Tribune,* 5 July 1896, 36; *Chicago Tribune,* 12 July 1896, 36; *Chicago Tribune,* 19 July 1896, 31; *Chicago Tribune,* 26 July 1896, 34.

5. A local reporter said, "It is difficult to obtain even standing room at Hopkins' Theater these afternoons and evenings, and the popularity is due in a great measure to the exhibition of Edison's vitascope. The introduction of this scientific achievement in the art of reproduction of living scenes has attracted the attention and patronage of many people who never before attended the continuous and popular form of entertainment," "Hopkins South Side Theater," *Chicago Tribune,* 19 July 1896, 31.

6. James S. McQuade, "Chicago Reports Many Variations in Pictures Shows," *Moving Picture World* no. 3, 15 July 1916, 413.

7. *Chicago Chronicle,* 17 November 1896, quoted in *Biograph Bulletins 1896–1908,* ed. Kemp R. Niver (Los Angeles: Artisan Press, 1971), 18.

8. See Charles Musser, *The Emergence of Cinema: The American Screen to 1907* (Berkeley and Los Angeles: University of California Press, 1990), 133–189, for an excellent discussion of the technical developments of machines, the competition, the production and types of entertainment as they were becoming available.

9. Ibid., 241.

10. Hopkins Theater display advertisement, *Chicago Tribune,* 7 February 1898, 5.

11. See, for example, Hopkins Theater display advertisements, *Chicago Tribune,* 20 February 1898, 32; *Chicago Tribune,* 1 March 1898, 5; *Chicago Tribune,* 6 March 1898, 38.

12. "Cheer for the Flag," *Chicago Tribune,* 21 February 1898, 3. Charles Musser quotes a New York City newspaper's summary of the *Tribune's* report on the Hopkins showing: "There was fifteen minutes of terrific shouting . . . when the battleships Maine and Iowa were shown in the biograph manoeuvering off Fortress Monroe. The audience rose, cheered and cheered again, and the climax was reached when a picture of Uncle Sam under the flag was thrown on the canvas." "Chicago Enthusiasts," *New York World,* 24 February 1898, 3, quoted in Musser, *Emergence of Cinema,* 241.

13. See, for example, Hopkins Theater display advertisements, *Chicago Tribune,* 3 April 1898, 46; *Chicago Tribune,* 24 April 1898, 46.

14. "The Drama," *Chicago Tribune,* 1 May 1898, 43.

15. Schiller Theater display advertisement, *Chicago Tribune,* 15 May 1898, 42; *Chicago Tribune,* 29 May 1898, 33; *Chicago Tribune,* 5 June 1898, 36.

16. Vaudeville listings ("Attractions for the Week"), *Chicago Tribune,* 1 May 1898–31 August 1898, *passim.*

17. Ibid. The Chicago-based Kleine Optical Company and the Sears, Roebuck and Company as well as the Stereopticon and Film Exchange, the L. Manasse Company, and others sold magic lantern and stereopticon slides of Cuban and Philippino travel and battle scenes to theaters; Cloduado A. del Mundo, Jr., "Cinema and Colonialism: Philippine Cinema During the American Colonial Period" (Ph.D. diss., University of Iowa, 1994), 42.

18. Clark Street Museum listing, *Chicago Tribune,* 29 May 1898, 32.

19. It was customary for the company service to include the projector, the operator, and the pictures even though only the machine usually received billing in the vaudeville program and in its advertisements.

20. McQuade, "Chicago Reports Many Variations in Pictures Shows," 413.

21. Musser, *Emergence of Cinema,* 287.

22. Ibid., 288.

23. Ibid., 290.

24. McQuade, "Chicago Reports Many Variations in Picture Shows," 414.

25. Ibid.

26. "Nickel Theatre Pays Well; Small Cost and Big Profit," *Chicago Tribune,* 8 April 1906, 3.

27. Carl Laemmle, quoted in Musser, *Emergence of Cinema,* 422.

28. Paul Gulick, "Carl Laemmle Made Start in Chicago 'Store Show,'" *Moving Picture World,* no. 3, 15 July 1916, 420.

29. "Nickel Theatre Pays Well," 3.

30. "In Chicago," *Billboard,* 16 March 1907, 32.

31. Louise de Koven Bowen, *Safeguards for City Youth at Work and at Play* (New York: Macmillan, 1914), 13.

32. Lewis E. Palmer, "The World in Motion," *Survey* 22, 5 June 1909, 356.

33. "The Nickelodeons," *Variety,* 14 December 1907, 33.

34. U.S. Bureau of the Census, *Thirteenth Census of the United States: Population, 1910: General Report and Analysis,* 11 vols. (Washington, D.C.: Government Printing Office, 1913), 1:208.

35. Ibid., 81.

36. For a discussion on the role of movie theaters in immigrant and working-class life, see Roy Rosenzweig's *Eight Hours for What We Will: Workers and Leisure in an Industrial City, 1870–1920* (Cambridge: Cambridge University Press, 1983), 191–221, and Elizabeth Ewen's *Immigrant Women in the Land of Dollars: Life and Culture on the Lower East Side, 1890–1925* (New York: Monthly Review Press, 1985), 208–224; also, see Judith Mayne, "Immigrants and Spectators," *Wide Angle* 5, no, 2 (1982), 32–41.

37. Viola Paradise, "The Jewish Immigrant Girl in Chicago," *Survey* 26, 6 September 1913, 701.

38. See Kenneth L. Kusmer, "Functions of Organized Charity in the Progressive Era: Chicago as a Case Study," *Journal of American History* 60, no. 3 (December 1973), 657–678.

39. Eugene T. Lies, quoted in ibid., 665.

40. "Censors Inspect Nickel Theaters," *Chicago Tribune,* 1 May 1907.

41. Musser, *Emergence of Cinema,* 447.

42. The first published report in the country on penny arcades and cheap theaters written by a prominent Chicago charity worker singled out nickelodeons as an "objectionable" form of recreation; Sherman C. Kingsley, "The Penny Arcade and the Cheap Theatre," *Charities and the Commons,* no. 18, 8 June 1907, 295–297.

43. "Nickel Theaters Under Two Fires," *Chicago Tribune,* 28 December 1908, 1.

44. See, for example, ibid.

45. Joseph Medill Patterson, "The Nickelodeons," *The Saturday Evening Post,* 23 November 1907, 10.

46. "Film Shows Busy; Panic Stops One," *Chicago Tribune,* 15 April 1907, 4.

47. Jane Addams, *The Spirit of Youth and the City Streets* (New York: Macmillan, 1910), 86.

48. "Nickel Theaters Crime Breeders," *Chicago Tribune,* 13 April 1907, 3.

49. "Film Shows Busy; Panic Stops One," 1.

50. De Koven Bowen, *Safeguards for City Youth,* 14.

51. "Censoring the Movies," *Chicago Tribune,* 2 May 1907, 8.

52. "Film Shows Busy: Panic Stops One," 4.

53. "Cheap Shows a Lure; Police Aim a Blow," *Chicago Record-Herald,* 1 May 1908, 1.

54. Sherman C. Kingsley, quoted in "Would Suppress Vicious Theaters," *Chicago Tribune,* 28 April 1907, 10.

55. "Nickel Theaters Crime Breeders," 3.

56. Palmer, "The World in Motion," 357.

57. "In Chicago," 33; "Cheap Shows a Lure," 1.

58. Kathy Peiss, *Cheap Amusements: Working Women and Leisure in Turn-of-the-Century New York* (Philadelphia: Temple University Press, 1986), 139–162.

59. "Nickel Theaters Crime Breeders," 3.

60. Miriam Hansen, *Babel & Babylon: Spectatorship in American Silent Film* (Cambridge, Mass.: Harvard University Press, 1991), 93–94.

61. See, for example, Paradise, "The Jewish Immigrant Girl in Chicago," 701.

62. Palmer, "The World in Motion," 356.

63. Hansen, *Babel & Babylon,* 118.

64. Mary Ann Doane, "Technology's Body: Cinematic Vision in Modernity," *differences: A Journal of Feminist Cultural Studies* 5, no. 2 (1993), 15.

65. Hansen, *Babel & Babylon,* 92.

66. U.S. Bureau of the Census, *Thirteenth Census of the U.S.*, 1:208. For census purposes, the single category "Negro" included "Negroes, mulattos, blacks, and anyone of African heritage," according to census reports. For further summary discussion of migration patterns to Chicago in the first decades of the twentieth century, see Jacqueline Jones, *Labor of Love, Labor of Sorrow: Black Women, Work, and the Family, From Slavery to the Present* (Chapel Hill: University of North Carolina Press, 1986), 152–195. She notes that large-scale migration from the South to Chicago only emerged after 1910 and culminated in the Great Migration during World War I.

67. Hazel V. Carby, "Policing the Black Woman's Body in an Urban Context," *Critical Inquiry* 19 (Summer 1992), 740.

68. Ibid., 740.

69. Ibid., 752.

70. For a lively discussion on the Levee from the 1890s until World War II, see Richard Lindberg, *Chicago by Gaslight: A History of Chicago's Netherworld 1880–1920* (Chicago: Academy Chicago Publishers, 1996), 111–156.

71. For types of employment and employment statistics, see Jones, *Labor of Love*, 104.

72. Addams, *Spirit of Youth*, 86–87.

73. De Koven Bowen, *Safeguards for City Youth*, 23.

74. Addams, *Spirit of Youth*, 88.

75. "Film Shows Busy; Panic Stops One," 4.

76. Kingsley, "The Penny Arcade and the Cheap Theatre," 295–297.

77. Kathleen D. McCarthy, "Nickel Vice and Virtue: Movie Censorship in Chicago, 1907–1915," *Journal of Popular Film* 5, no. 4 (1976), 38.

78. "The Five Cent Theaters," *Chicago Tribune*, 10 April 1907, 8.

79. "Film Shows Busy; Panic Stops One," 3.

80. "The Five Cent Theaters," 4.

81. "Nickel Theaters Crime Breeders," 3.

82. "Cheap Shows a Lure," 3.

83. "Traces Crime to Nickel Theater," *Chicago Tribune*, 14 April 1907, 3.

84. For further discussion, see Richard Abel: "'Pathé Goes to Town': French Films Create a Market for the Nickelodeon," *Cinema Journal* 35, no. 1 (Fall 1995), 3–26.

85. Richard Abel, *The Ciné Goes to Town: French Cinema, 1896–1914* (Berkeley and Los Angeles: University of California Press, 1994), 103.

86. Musser, *Emergence of Cinema*, 449–489.

87. "A Vitagraph Film," *Billboard*, 26 April 1907, 27.

88. "Film Shows Busy; Panic Stops One," 1.

89. Musser, *Emergence of Cinema*, 406.

90. Addams, *Spirit of Youth*, 93–94.

91. "Film Shows Busy; Panic Stops One," 4.

92. Ibid., 1.

93. Ibid.

94. Ibid.

95. Ibid.

96. Ibid., 4.

97. Henri Bousquet, ed., *Catalogue Pathé des Années 1896 à 1914, 1907* (Paris: Henri Bousquet, 1993), 7.

98. "Film Shows Busy; Panic Stops One," 4.

99. Noël Burch, *Life to Those Shadows,* trans. Ben Brewster (Berkeley and Los Angeles: University of California Press, 1990), 172–173.

100. "Les spectateurs se plairont à reconnaître ces quelques types de révoltés sociaux qui, malgré les répressions terribles qui la loi exerce contre eux, ne désarment jamais, même devant la mort." Henri Bousquet, ed. *Catalogue Pathé des Années 1896 à 1914, 1896 à 1906* (Paris: Henri Bousquet, 1993), 919.

101. "Houston Authorities Object to Picture of Thaw-White Tragedy," *Moving Picture World,* 20 April 1907, 102. In a report of police shutting down an exhibition of *The Unwritten Law,* "the mirrored bedroom scene" was especially singled out.

102. Musser, *Emergence of Cinema,* 479.

103. "Nickel Theaters Crime Breeders," 3.

104. "The Hunger for Amusement," *Chicago Daily News,* 19 April 1907, 8.

105. "Sh-h! The Sleuths Are on the Trail," *Chicago Inter-Ocean,* 5 May 1907, 4.

106. "Censoring the Shows," *Chicago Daily News,* 2 May 1907, 8.

107. *Chicago Daily News,* 20 April 1907, 9.

108. Max Schmidt, "Immoral Pictures!" *Chicago Daily News,* 7 May 1907, 9.

109. A. L. Cooley, "Low-Priced Theaters," *Chicago Daily News,* 13 May 1907, 9.

110. Frank Krueger, "He Likes the 5-Cent Shows," *Chicago Daily News,* 1 May 1907, 9.

111. Ibid.

112. "A Clarion Note," *Moving Picture World,* 20 April 1907, 101, reprints the *Chicago Tribune* editorial "The Five Cent Theaters" from April 10, 1907, and Kleine's letter to the *Tribune,* also dated April 10, 1907.

113. George Kleine, quoted in "A Clarion Note," 101–102.

114. Ibid., 102.

115. "Defends Moving Pictures," *Billboard,* 4 May 1907, 13.

116. "Chicago Tribune ATTACKS Moving Pictures!" *Billboard,* 27 April 1907, 34.

117. Ibid.

118. "A Clarion Note," 102.

119. "Social Workers Censor Shows," *Chicago Tribune,* 3 May 1907, 3.

120. Ibid.

121. Moya Luckett, "Cities and Spectators: A Historical Analysis of Film Audiences in Chicago, 1910–1915" (Ph.D. diss., University of Wisconsin at Madison, 1995), 20.

122. George Spoor, quoted in "Spoor Discusses," *Views and Film Index,* 7 November 1908, 6.

123. "What Is the Trouble?" *Views and Films Index,* 13 June 1908, 4. Also see, "Wicked Five-Cent Theatres," *Moving Picture World,* 23 November 1907, 615.

124. H. H. Buckwalter, a film manufacturer, quoted in "1908 to See Rise," *Views and Films Index,* 18 January 1908, 3.

125. Quoted in Eileen Bowser, *The Transformation of Cinema: 1907–1915* (Berkeley and Los Angeles: University of California Press, 1990), 41. It is important to note here that after Chicago's 1907 campaign, there was a campaign against nickelodeons in New York City. For a summary of the specifics, see Janet Staiger, *Bad Women: Regulating Sexuality in Early American Cinema* (Minneapolis: University of Minnesota Press, 1995), 86–115. *Moving Picture World*'s proposal in 1909 was most likely in response to *both* cities.

126. Untitled editorial, *Views and Films Index,* 5 December 1908, 3.

127. See Musser, *Emergence of Cinema,* 446–447, for discussion of the illustrated travel lecture. See William Uricchio and Roberta Pearson, *Reframing Culture: The Case of the Vitagraph Quality Films* (Princeton, N.J.: Princeton University Press, 1993), for the definitive study on making and marketing "quality films" and on improving the educational quality of motion pictures as a means for garnering a middle-class audience.

128. Musser, *Emergence of Cinema,* 378.

129. For discussions of the contribution of the chase film to the emerging vocabulary and syntax of narrative cinema, see Burch, *Life to Those Shadows,* 147–150, 156, 160, 172–176; Abel, *The Ciné Goes to Town,* 109–177.

130. Hansen, *Babel & Babylon,* 46.

131. Untitled editorial, *Moving Picture World,* 29 June 1907, 262–263.

132. Ibid.

133. Laemmle even bragged in a company advertisement that he brought more new Pathé films than anybody else to Chicago; Laemmle display advertisement, *Billboard,* 4 May 1907, 31.

134. McCarthy, "Nickel Vice and Virtue," 45

135. Louise de Koven Bowen, *Five and Ten Cent Theaters: Two Investigations* (Chicago: The Juvenile Protective Association, 1911), 3–4.

136. Untitled editorial, *Moving Picture World,* 29 June 1907, 262.

Chapter 5. Through the Peephole: Cinema at the Amusement Park

1. "Park Notes," *Billboard,* 3 February 1906, 20.

2. Stan Barker, "Paradises Lost," *Chicago History* 22, no. 1 (March 1993), 28.

3. A discussion about amusements parks owned by traction companies who were content to break even on their parks so long as the parks supported street car ridership and revenues occurs in "Parks & Fairs," *Variety,* 18 July 1908, 14.

4. "Millions in Chicago Park," *Billboard,* 16 March 1907, 81. For advertisements, see *Chicago Sunday Tribune,* 2 June 1907, sec. 10, 2. An advertisement in the *Chicago Daily News* reported that the park had set the world's attendance record the previous day at 368,712. See *Chicago Daily News,* 17 June 1907, 4.

5. F. C. McCarahan, "Chicago Amusements," *Billboard,* 10 August 1907, 7.

6. City of Chicago, Department of Development and Planning, *Historic City: The Settlement of Chicago* (Chicago: Department of Development and Planning, 1976), 66.

7. "Riverview: Chicago's Newest Outdoor Resort, Opens with Novel Features," *Chicago Daily American,* 3 July 1904, Riverview Park clippings file, Chicago Historical Society, Chicago, Illinois.

8. Frederic Thompson, "Amusing the Million," *Everybody's Magazine* 19 (September 1908), 385.

9. Tony Bennett, "A Thousand and One Troubles: Blackpool Pleasure Beach," in *Formations of Pleasure,* ed. Tony Bennett et al. (London: Routledge, 1983), 147–148.

10. John Kasson, *Amusing the Million: Coney Island at the Turn of the Century* (New York: Hill & Wang, 1978), 82.

11. Riverview Park advertisement, *Chicago Inter-Ocean,* 30 May 1907, 12.

12. Department of Development and Planning, *Historic City: The Settlement of Chicago,* 64.

13. Kathy Peiss, *Cheap Amusements: Working Women and Leisure in Turn-of-the-Century New York* (Philadelphia: Temple University Press, 1986), 101–102.

14. The appellation "laboratory of the new mass culture" originates with Kasson, *Amusing the Million,* 8.

15. Belle Lindner Israels, "The Way of the Girl," *Survey* 22, 3 July 1909, 486–497.

16. Peiss, *Cheap Amusements,* 127.

17. Ibid., 55.

18. Movies showed at other local parks, too. White City featured the Kinodrome as early as the season of 1906; *Variety,* 9 June 1906, 13. The Chutes ran moving pictures of the 1906 San Francisco earthquake at its Niemeyer's Theatre during the summer of 1906; *Variety,* 1 June 1906, 10.

19. Film scholars have generally considered Hale's Tours as an overture toward cinematic realism or, more recently, as a way to mask the presence of the apparatus and discursively promote a transparent view of reality. As early as 1957, Raymond Fielding wrote, "Except for the lack of color, the illusion was quite convincing. . . . [Hale's Tours] represented one of the earliest examples in a long series of continuing attempts by film producers to duplicate or simulate certain aspects of perceived reality." Raymond Fielding, "Hale's Tours: Ultrarealism in the Pre-1910 Motion Picture," in *Before Griffith,* ed. John L. Fell (Berkeley and Los Angeles: University of California Press, 1983), 123.

Twenty-five years later, Charles Musser echoed Fielding, "These attempts to expand the range of perception to include sound, colour and bodily sensation further heightened the illusion of film as a transparent medium. Charles Musser, "The Nickelodeon Era Begins: Establishing the Framework for Hollywood's Mode of Representation," *Framework,* nos. 22–23 (1983), 9.

Even though they take into account the relationships between the environment of the railway car and the cinematic material, both authors treat Hale's Tours primarily within a teleology of cinematic realism.

20. B. S. Brown, "Hale's Tours and Scenes of the World," *Moving Picture World,* no. 3, 15 July 1916, 373.

21. Ibid., 372.

22. "Auto Tours of the World and Sightseeing in the Principal Cities," *Billboard,* 27 January 1906, 23. Hruby & Plummer's Tours and Scenes of the World advertised "a moving picture show in a knock-down portable canvas car, boat, vehicle or ordinary tent," complete with mechanical apparatus for simulating motion, movie screen and projector, and movies; display advertisement, *Billboard,* 3 March 1906, 25.

24. "Here Is the Real Thing" display advertisement, *Billboard,* 24 March 1906, 39.

25. See, for example, the following display advertisements: "Hale Tour Films, Selig Polyscope 'Latest Films,'" *Views and Films Index,* 20 April 1907, 5; "Hale Tour Runs," *Biograph Bulletin,* no. 73, 30 June 1906, reprinted in *Biograph Bulletins 1896–1908,* ed. Kemp R. Niver (Los Angeles: Artisan Press, 1971), 250–252.

25. E. C. Thomas, "Vancouver, B.C., Started with 'Hale's Tours,'" *Moving Picture World,* 15 July 1916, 373.

26. Noël Burch, *Life to Those Shadows,* trans. Ben Brewster (Berkeley and Los Angeles: University of California Press, 1990), 39.

27. Edison Manufacturing Company advertisement, *New York Clipper,* 28 April 1906.

28. Fielding, "Hale's Tours: Ultrarealism in the Pre-1910 Motion Picture," 128.

29. Lynn Kirby, "The Urban Spectator and the Crowd in Early American Train Films," *Iris* 11 (Summer 1990), 49–62.

30. Wolfgang Schivelbusch, *The Railway Journey: Trains and Travel in the 19th Century,* trans. Anselm Hollo (New York: Urizen, 1977).

31. Lynn Kirby, "Male Hysteria and Early Cinema," *Camera Obscura* 17 (1988), 113.

32. The spatial relations within the Hale's Tours car, however, did not accurately reproduce the experience of the railroad car whereby the panoramic views pass alongside the passenger. Instead, the perceptual illusion was visual movement into and out of deep space. The cognitive cues as well as the surrounding environment encouraged spectatorial processes that may have oscillated between the effects of panoramic views and screen space.

33. Rollin Lynde Hartt, "The Amusement Park," *Atlantic* 99 (May 1907), 668.

34. Bennett, "A Thousand and One Troubles," 151.

35. Schivelbusch, *The Railway Journey,* 130–131.

36. Ibid., 131.

37. For a description of typical urban conveyance stories of disaster and for an analysis of their significance for the cinematic imagination, see Ben Singer's essay,

"Modernity, Hyperstimulus, and the Rise of Popular Sensationalism," in *Cinema and the Invention of Modern Life,* ed. Leo Charney and Vanessa Schwartz (Berkeley and Los Angeles: University of California Press, 1995), 72–99.

38. Kirby, "Male Hysteria and Early Cinema," 113–131.

39. In this context, Raymond Fielding's concern that the decline of Hale's Tours after 1908 was due to women's discomfort from the rocking sensation and close confinement is unwarranted. Fielding, "Hale's Tours," 129. Indeed, close physical proximity and containment marked numerous rides throughout the amusement park. Many rides regimented seating by couples or groups, encouraging physical contact between the sexes especially when the seating spaces were small and the ride one of speed or force. It is more likely that travelogue films became increasingly harder to obtain after 1908 when a newly monopolized movie industry focused on narrative fiction because it could more economically and efficiently pre-plan such products on a mass basis in indoor studios.

40. Peiss, *Cheap Amusements,* 134–135.

41. Elissa Rashkin, "Vision, Transgression, and Discipline: Tourism in Early U.S. Cinema" (unpublished essay, December 1991), 20.

42. Burch, *Life to Those Shadows,* 191, 193.

Chapter 6. Pandering to Pleasure: The Power of the Film Industry

1. See "Position of the Kleine Optical Co.," *Moving Picture World,* 7 March 1908, 182.

2. Edison's corporate empire represented a new economic hierarchy of control for the twentieth century. The constituent companies themselves depended less upon their "boss" than upon professional business executives and lawyers as their overseers. The motion-picture-producing Edison Manufacturing Company was largely run by Gilmore and company patent attorney Frank L. Dyer. Beneath them was a labyrinthian operating structure made up of middle management specializing in accounting, legal issues, public relations, advertising, marketing, and sales.

3. "Edison vs. American Mutoscope and Biograph Company," *Moving Picture World,* 9 March 1907, 4.

4. Dyer said that the Kleine lawsuit was another attempt to thwart Biograph. "Why They Chose Chicago," *Variety,* 21 March 1908, 15.

5. "Motion Picture Business Enjoys a Frenzied Boom," *Moving Picture World,* 14 September 1907, 439.

6. "The Film Service Situation The Lines Are Being Drawn Tighter," *Moving Picture World,* 4 April 1908, 287.

7. *Views and Films Index,* 10 August 1907, 10.

8. See, for example, the full front-page photograph and accompanying statement, *Moving Picture World,* 31 December 1907, 1.

9. See Janet Staiger, "Combination and Litigation: Structures of U.S. Film Distribution, 1891–1917," *Cinema Journal* 23, no. 2 (Winter 1983), 41–72.

10. Letter from Frank J. Marion to Kleine Optical Company, 14 March 1907, Box 29, George Kleine Papers, Manuscript Collections, Library of Congress, Washington, D.C.

11. Ibid.

12. When representatives from 104 film exchanges nationwide met in December, the Chicago exchanges quickly constituted a powerful voting bloc. Although Chicago-based exchanges accounted for only 14 of the 104 member companies, practically all of them had voting branch offices resulting in an alliance that was one-third of the total vote. Since only one company based outside of Chicago held more than one vote, no other company or regional group of companies had enough votes to create a competitive bloc. "At the Convention," *Views and Films Index,* 21 December 1907, 4–5.

13. James B. Clark, Letter, *Moving Picture World,* 21 December 1907, 681.

14. "$1,000,000 a Year Edison Royalties," *New York Times,* 12 February 1908, 5.

15. One should not underestimate the efforts among film industry leaders, especially Edison representatives, to exclude Jewish distributors like Laemmle from this consolidation of power. One New York industry representative wrote to George Kleine asking him to support his slate of candidates for FSA offices, noting that "Edison Co. will simply back out if . . . the Hebrews get the running of the association." Letter from F. J. Marion, Kalem Company, 20 November 1907, Box 29, George Kleine Papers.

16. "Position of the Kleine Optical Co.," *Moving Picture World,* 7 March 1908, 182.

17. "Geo. Kleine Replies to Critics," *Moving Picture World,* 4 April 1908, 288.

18. See Richard Abel, "'Pathé Goes to Town': French Films Create a Market for the Nickelodeon," *Cinema Journal* 35, no. 1 (Fall 1995), 3–26, for foreign versus nativist issues in the Edison interests gaining control.

19. Letter from George Kleine, typescript, 25 March 1908, Box 26, Historical Patent Fight, George Kleine Papers.

20. "The Mimic World," *Chicago Tribune,* 1 June, 1908, 8.

21. Frank Weisberg, "The Limit in Moving Pictures, Success at Auditorium," *Variety,* 6 June 1908, 11.

22. "The Mimic World," 8.

23. Ibid.

24. Weisberg, "The Limit in Moving Pictures," 11.

25. "The Mimic World," 8.

26. Later in film history, it became usual to express "innovation" in this way. Stereo sound, wide-screen technologies, and color were all introduced in the United States in several Hollywood films that foregrounded sound placement, panoramic vistas, or intense color. Only at those moments when service to the narrative was less important than the economic imperative of establishing a new technological realism has the apparatus generally become so visibly or audibly inscribed.

27. "Chicago Film Manufacturer Has Revolutionary Scheme," *Variety*, 6 June 1908, 11.

28. Weisberg, "The Limit in Moving Pictures," 11.

29. "'A Square Deal for All' Is Thomas Edison's Promise," *Variety*, 20 June 1908, 12.

30. Ibid.

31. Ibid.

32. Edison's largest concession to Kleine and Biograph appears to have been Gilmore's resignation. Soon after the meetings began, Gilmore left on a European family vacation; "Gilmour [sic] Sails," *Variety*, 11 July 1908, 11. While he was abroad, the company reported that he had retired; "Edison and Gilmore Part," *New York Times*, 26 July 1908, section 2, 7. Industry insiders speculated that Biograph, Kleine, and Edison were working on a merger and Gilmore's retirement was to make room for Biograph executives who would want some of the key positions in any new corporate structure; "Moving Picture Peace Strongly Rumored About," *Variety*, 15 August, 1908, 11. But between June and October of 1908, the meetings went largely unreported in the popular and trade presses and thereafter received only scant coverage. The lack of reports concerning the Kleine-Edison meetings suggests not the absence of any activity but a controlled structure of absence in order to reposition the film industry as a unified structure.

33. "Moving Picture Peace Strongly Rumored About," 11.

34. At the same time, New York City civic officials stepped up a local censorship campaign against its local theaters, and the newly formed MPPC swiftly and efficiently offered a unified response of self-regulatory control over content.

Conclusion

1. Janet Wolff, "The Invisible Flâneuse: Women and the Literature of Modernity," in *Feminine Sentences: Essays on Women & Culture* (Berkeley and Los Angeles: University of California Press, 1990), 34–50; Anke Gleber, "Women on the Screens and Streets of Modernity: In Search of the Female Flâneur," in *The Image in Dispute: Art and Cinema in the Age of Photography*, ed. Dudley Andrew (Austin: University of Texas Press, 1997), 55–85; Anne Friedberg, "Les Flâneurs du Mal(l): Cinema and the Postmodern Condition," *PMLA* 106 (May 1991), 419–431; Susan Buck-Morss, "The Flâneur, the Sandwichman, and the Whore: The Politics of Loitering," *New German Critique* 39 (1986), 99–140.

2. Mark Seltzer, *Bodies and Machines* (New York: Routledge, 1992), 98–99.

3. For accounts of prostitution in this regard, see, especially, Timothy J. Gilfoyle, *City of Eros: New York City, Prostitution, and the Commercialization of Sex, 1790–1920* (New York: Norton, 1992); Joanne J. Meyerowitz, *Women Adrift: Independent Wage Earners in Chicago, 1880–1930* (Chicago: University of Chicago Press, 1988); Judith R. Walkowitz, *City of Dreadful Delight: Narratives of Sexual Danger in Late-Victorian London* (Chicago: University of Chicago Press, 1992);

Sharon Wood, "Wandering Girls and Leading Women: Sexuality and Urban Public Life in Davenport, Iowa, 1880–1910" (Ph.D. diss., University of Iowa, 1994).

4. For a summary of this position, see Mary Ann Doane, "Technology's Body: Cinematic Vision in Modernity," *differences: A Journal of Feminist Cultural Studies* 5, no. 2 (1993), 1–23; Miriam Hansen, *Babel & Babylon: Spectatorship in American Silent Film* (Cambridge: Harvard University Press, 1991), 121–124.

5. Hansen, *Babel & Babylon,* 121–122.

6. Ibid., 1–125; Janet Staiger, *Bad Women: Regulating Sexuality in Early American Cinema* (Minneapolis: University of Minnesota Press, 1995), 54–98.

7. Staiger, *Bad Women,* 116–178; Judith Mayne, *The Woman at the Keyhole: Feminism and Women's Cinema* (Bloomington: Indiana University Press, 1990), 174–175.

8. An exceptional work that does consider cinema's participation in the reorganization of public cultural space and feminine identity in the post-1908 period is Shelley Stamp Lindsey, *Screening Spaces: Placing Women at the Motion Pictures, 1908–1917* (Princeton, N.J.: Princeton University Press, forthcoming). Her definition of cinema, more along the lines of this study, even opens up other categories of feature films as equally important for taking up issues of modern female identities, in particular, suffrage films and "drag" or cross-dressing films.

9. Ibid., 123.

10. Hansen, *Babel & Babylon,* 100, 243–294.

SELECTED BIBLIOGRAPHY

Archival Sources

Chicago Historical Society, Chicago, Illinois. Chicago World's Columbian Exposition Collections, Prints and Photographs.
———. Riverview Park, Manuscript Collections and Prints and Photographs.
Library of Congress, Washington, D.C. Detroit Photographic Collection, Prints and Photographs.
———. George Kleine Papers, Manuscript Collections.
———. Paper Print Collection of Early Motion Pictures, 1894–1912, Motion Picture, Broadcasting, and Recorded Sound Division.
State Historical Society of Iowa, Iowa City, Iowa. Sarah Jane Kimball Papers.

Newspapers

Billboard, 1906–1912
Chicago Daily American, 1904–1908
Chicago Daily News, 1907–1908
Chicago Inter-Ocean, 1907–1908
Chicago Record-Herald, 1907–1908
Chicago Tribune, 1896–1908
Moving Picture World, 1907–1916
New York Times, 1896–1908
Variety, 1907–1908
Views and Films Index, 1907–1909

Primary Sources

Addams, Jane. *The Spirit of Youth and the City Streets.* New York: Macmillan, 1910.
Ade, George. "From the Office Window." In *Stories of the Streets and of the Town: From "The Chicago Record" 1893–1900,* 167–171. Chicago: The Caxton Club, 1941.

————. "The Stenographic Proposal." In *In Babel*, 257–265. New York: McClure, Phillips, 1903.

Brown, B. S. "Hale's Tours and Scenes of the World." *Moving Picture World*, no. 3, 15 July 1916, 373.

Brown-Buck, Lillie. *Amy Leslie at the Fair*. Chicago: W. B. Conkey, 1893.

Burnham, Clara Louise. *Sweet Clover, a Romance of the White City*. Boston: Houghton, Mifflin, 1894.

Chicago By Night. Chicago: Rand McNally, 1893.

de Koven Bowen, Louise. *Five and Ten Cent Theaters: Two Investigations*. Chicago: The Juvenile Protective Association, 1911.

————. *Safeguards for City Youth at Work and at Play*. New York: Macmillan, 1914.

Dreiser, Theodore. "Last Day at the Fair." *St. Louis Republic*, 23 July 1893, 6. Reprinted in *Theodore Dreiser, Journalism*, edited by T. D. Nostwich, 2 vols, 1:134–138. Philadelphia: University of Pennsylvania Press, 1988.

————. *Sister Carrie*. 1900. Reprint. New York: New American Library, 1961.

————. "Third Day at the Fair." *St. Louis Republic*, 20 July 1893, 4. Reprinted in *Theodore Dreiser, Journalism*, edited by T. D. Nostwich, 1:126–129. Philadelphia: University of Pennsylvania Press, 1988.

Glimpses of the World's Fair: A Selection of Gems of the White City Seen Through a Camera. Chicago: Laird & Law, 1893.

Graham, Charles. *Chicago Tribune Art Supplements in Two Parts: World's Columbian Exposition*. N.p, n.d.

————. *The World's Fair in Water Colors*. Springfield, Ohio: Mast, Crowell & Kirkpatrick, 1893.

Hartt, Rollin Lynde. "The Amusement Park." *Atlantic* 99 (May 1907), 667–677.

Israels, Belle Lindner. "The Way of the Girl." *Survey* 22, 3 July 1909, 486–497.

Kauffman, Reginald Wright. *The House of Bondage*. 1910. Reprint, Upper Saddle River, N.J.: The Gregg Press, 1968.

Kingsley, Sherman C. "The Penny Arcade and the Cheap Theatre." *Charities and the Commons*, 18, 8 June 1907, 295–297.

Knight, Leonard & Co. *Guide to the Columbian World's Fair*. Chicago: Knight, Leonard, 1892.

Krausz, Sigmund. *Street Types of Chicago with Literary Sketches by Well-Known Authors*. Chicago: Max Stern, 1892.

McQuade, James S. "Chicago Reports Many Variations in Pictures Shows." *Moving Picture World*, no. 3, 15 July 1916, 413–415.

Mushet, Robert. *Chicago Yesterday and Today: A Guide to the Garden City and the Columbian Exposition*. Chicago: Donohue & Henneberry, 1893.

Niver, Kemp R., ed. *Biograph Bulletins 1896–1908*. Los Angeles: Artisan Press, 1971.

Palmer, Lewis E. "The World in Motion." *Survey* 22, 5 June 1909, 355–365.

Paradise, Viola. "The Jewish Immigrant Girl in Chicago." *Survey* 26, 6 September 1913, 699–704.

Pictorial Album and History of the World's Fair and Midway. Chicago: Harry T. Smith, 1893.

Rand McNally & Co.'s Handy Guide to Chicago and the World's Columbian Expostion. Chicago: Rand McNally, 1893.

Shaw, Marian. *World's Fair Notes: A Woman Journalist Views Chicago's 1893 Columbian Exposition.* 1893. Reprint, St. Paul: Pogo Press, 1992.

Stevens, Charles M. *The Adventures of Uncle Jeremiah and Family at the Great Fair: Their Observations and Triumphs.* Chicago: Laird & Lee, 1893.

Thompson, Frederic. "Amusing the Million." *Everybody's Magazine* 19 (September 1908), 378–387.

Todd, F. Dundas. *World's Fair Through a Camera: Snap Shots by an Artist.* St. Louis: Woodward and Tierman, 1893.

Van Rensselaer, M. G. "At the Fair." *The Century Magazine* 46, no. 1 (May 1893), 3–13.

A Week in Chicago. Chicago: Rand McNally, 1892.

Wells-Barnett, Ida B., and Frederick Douglass. "The Reason Why the Colored American Is Not in the World's Columbian Exposition." In *Selected Works of Ida B. Wells-Barnett,* edited by Trudier Harris, 46–137. New York: Oxford University Press, 1991.

Secondary Sources

Abel, Richard. *The Ciné Goes to Town: French Cinema, 1896–1914.* Berkeley and Los Angeles: University of California Press, 1994.

———. "'Pathé Goes to Town': French Films Create a Market for the Nickelodeon." *Cinema Journal* 35, no. 1 (Fall 1995), 3–26.

Abelson, Elizabeth S. *When Ladies Go a-Thieving: Middle-Class Shoplifters in the Victorian Department Store.* New York: Oxford University Press, 1989.

Allen, Robert C. *Horrible Prettiness: Burlesque and American Culture.* Chapel Hill: University of North Carolina Press, 1991.

Altman, Rick. "The Silence of the Silents." *The Musical Quarterly* (Summer 1997), 648–718.

Andrew, Dudley, ed. *The Image in Dispute: Art and Cinema in the Age of Photography.* Austin: University of Texas Press, 1997.

Appelbaum, Stanley. *The Chicago World's Fair of 1893: A Photographic Record.* New York: Dover, 1980.

Barker, Stan. "Paradises Lost." *Chicago History* 22, no. 1 (March 1993), 26–49.

Benjamin, Walter. "The Work of Art in the Age of Mechanical Reproduction." In *Illuminations,* edited by Hannah Arendt, translated by Harry Zohn, 217–251. New York: Schocken Books, 1969.

Bennett, Tony. "A Thousand and One Troubles: Blackpool Pleasure Beach." In *Formations of Pleasure,* ed. Tony Bennett et al., 138–155. London: Routledge, 1983.

Benson, Susan Porter. *Counter Cultures: Saleswomen, Managers, and Customers in American Department Stores, 1890–1940.* Urbana and Chicago: University of Illinois Press, 1986.

Bowser, Eileen. *The Transformation of Cinema: 1907–1915.* Berkeley and Los Angeles: University of California Press, 1990.

Brand, Dana. *The Spectator and the City in Nineteenth-Century American Literature.* Cambridge: Cambridge University Press, 1991.

Brown, Julie K. *Contesting Images: Photography and the World's Columbian Exposition.* Tucson: University of Arizona Press, 1994.

Bruno, Giuliana. *Streetwalking on a Ruined Map: Cultural Theory and the City Films of Elvira Notari.* Princeton, N.J.: Princeton University Press, 1993.

Buck-Morss, Susan. *The Dialectics of Seeing: Walter Benjamin and the Arcades Project.* Cambridge, Mass.: MIT Press, 1991.

———. "The Flâneur, the Sandwichman, and the Whore: The Politics of Loitering." *New German Critique* 39 (1986), 99–140.

Burch, Noël. *Life to Those Shadows.* Translated by Ben Brewster. Berkeley and Los Angeles: University of California Press, 1990.

Carby, Hazel V. "Policing the Black Woman's Body in an Urban Context." *Critical Inquiry* 19 (Summer 1992), 738–755.

Charney, Leo, and Vanessa Schwartz, eds. *Cinema and the Invention of Modern Life.* Berkeley and Los Angeles: University of California Press, 1995.

Crary, Jonathan. *Techniques of the Observer: On Vision and Modernity in the Nineteenth Century.* Cambridge, Mass.: MIT Press, 1990.

Dagrada, Elena. "Through the Keyhole: Spectators and Matte Shots in Early Cinema." *Iris* 11 (Summer 1990), 95–106.

Doane, Mary Ann. "Technology's Body: Cinematic Vision in Modernity." *differences: A Journal of Feminist Cultural Studies* 5, no. 2 (1993), 1–23.

Elsaesser, Thomas, ed. *Early Cinema: Space, Frame, Narrative.* London: British Film Institute, 1990.

Ewen, Elizabeth. *Immigrant Women in the Land of Dollars: Life and Culture on the Lower East Side, 1890–1925.* New York: Monthly Review Press, 1985.

Fell, John L., ed. *Before Griffith.* Berkeley and Los Angeles University of California Press, 1983.

Friedberg, Anne. "Les Flâneurs du Mal(l): Cinema and the Postmodern Condition." *PMLA* 106 (May 1991), 419–431

———. *Window Shopping: Cinema and the Postmodern.* Berkeley and Los Angeles: University of California Press, 1993.

Gaudreault, André, ed. *Ce que je vois de mon ciné: La représentation du regard dans le cinéma des premiers temps.* Paris: Méridiens Klincksieck, 1988.

Gilbert, James. *Perfect Cities: Chicago's Utopias of 1893.* Chicago: University of Chicago Press, 1991.

Gilfoyle, Timothy J. *City of Eros: New York City, Prostitution, and the Commercialization of Sex, 1790–1920.* New York: Norton, 1992.

Greenhalgh, Paul. *Ephemeral Vistas: The Expositions Universelles, Great Exhibitions, and World's Fairs, 1851–1939.* Manchester: Manchester University Press, 1988.

Gunning, Tom. "'Now You See It, Now You Don't': The Temporality of the Cinema of Attractions." *The Velvet Light Trap* 32 (Fall 1993), 3–12.

Hales, Peter B. "Photography and the World's Columbian Exposition: A Case Study." *Journal of Urban History* 15 (May 1989), 247–273.

Hansen, Miriam. *Babel & Babylon: Spectatorship in American Silent Film.* Cambridge, Mass.: Harvard University Press, 1991.

Harris, Neil. *Cultural Excursions: Marketing Appetites and Cultural Tastes in Modern America.* Chicago: University of Chicago Press, 1990.

Jones, Jacqueline. *Labor of Love, Labor of Sorrow: Black Women, Work, and the Family, From Slavery to the Present.* Chapel Hill: University of North Carolina Press, 1986.

Kasson, John. *Amusing the Million: Coney Island at the Turn of the Century.* New York: Hill & Wang, 1978.

Keil, Charles. "The Story of Uncle Josh Told: Spectatorship and Apparatus in Early Cinema." *Iris* 11 (Summer 1990), 63–76.

Kibler, M. Alison. "Female Varieties: Gender and Cultural Hierarchy on the Keith Vaudeville Circuit, 1890–1925." Ph.D. diss., University of Iowa, 1995.

Kinser, Suzanne L. "Prostitutes in the Art of John Sloan." *Prospects* 9 (1984), 231–254.

Kirby, Lynn. "Male Hysteria and Early Cinema." *Camera Obscura* 17 (1988), 113–131.

———. *Parallel Tracks: The Railroad and Silent Cinema.* Durham: Duke University Press, 1997.

———. "The Urban Spectator and the Crowd in Early American Train Films." *Iris* 11 (Summer 1990), 49–62.

Kirkpatrick, Diane. *The Fair View: Representations of the World's Columbian Exposition of 1893.* Ann Arbor: University of Michigan Museum of Art, 1993.

Kusmer, Kenneth L. "Functions of Organized Charity in the Progressive Era: Chicago as a Case Study." *Journal of American History* 60, no. 3 (December 1973), 657–678.

Leach, William. *Land of Desire: Merchants, Power, and the Rise of a New American Culture.* New York: Vintage Books, 1993.

Leyda, Jay, and Charles Musser, eds. *Before Hollywood: Turn-of-the-Century Film from American Archives.* New York: American Federation of the Arts, 1986.

Lindberg, Richard. *Chicago by Gaslight: A History of Chicago's Netherworld 1880–1920.* Chicago: Academy Chicago Publishers, 1996.

Luckett, Moya. "Cities and Spectators: A Historical Analysis of Film Audiences in Chicago, 1910–1915." Ph.D. diss., University of Wisconsin at Madison, 1995.

McCarthy, Kathleen D. "Nickel Vice and Virtue: Movie Censorship in Chicago, 1907–1915." *Journal of Popular Film* 5, no. 4 (1976), 37–55.

Maltby, Richard. "The Social Evil, the Moral Order and the Melodramatic Imagination, 1890–1915." In *Melodrama: Stage Picture Screen,* edited by Jacky Bratton, Jim Cook, and Christine Gledhill, 214–230. London: British Film Institute, 1994.

Mayne, Judith. "Immigrants and Spectators." *Wide Angle* 5, no. 2 (1982), 32–41.

———. *The Woman at the Keyhole: Feminism and Women's Cinema.* Bloomington: Indiana University Press, 1990.

Meyerowitz, Joanne J. *Women Adrift: Independent Wage Earners in Chicago, 1880–1930.* Chicago: University of Chicago Press, 1988.

Musser, Charles. *Before the Nickelodeon: Edwin S. Porter and The Edison Manufacturing Company.* Berkeley and Los Angeles: University of California Press, 1991.

———. *The Emergence of Cinema: The American Screen to 1907.* Berkeley and Los Angeles: University of California Press, 1990.

———. "The Nickelodeon Era Begins: Establishing the Framework for Hollywood's Mode of Representation." *Framework,* nos. 22–23 (Autumn 1983), 4–11.

Niver, Kemp. *Early Motion Pictures: The Paper Print Collection in the Library of Congress.* Washington, D.C.: Library of Congress, 1985.

Orvell, Miles. *The Real Thing: Imitation and Authenticity in American Culture, 1880–1940.* Chapel Hill: University of North Carolina Press, 1989.

Peiss, Kathy. *Cheap Amusements: Working Women and Leisure in Turn-of-the-Century New York.* Philadelphia: Temple University Press, 1986.

Rony, Fatimah Tobing. "Those Who Squat and Those Who Sit: The Iconography of Race in the 1895 Films of Felix-Louis Regnault." *Camera Obscura* 28 (January 1992), 263–289.

Rosenzweig, Ray. *Eight Hours for What We Will: Workers and Leisure in an Industrial City, 1870–1920.* Cambridge: Cambridge University Press, 1983.

Rydell, Robert. *All the World's a Fair: Visions of Empire at American International Expositions, 1876–1916.* Chicago: University of Chicago Press, 1984.

Schivelbusch, Wolfgang. *The Railway Journey: Trains and Travel in the 19th Century.* Translated by Anselm Hollo. New York: Urizen, 1977.

Scobey, David. "Anatomy of the Promenade: The Politics of Bourgeois Sociability in Nineteenth-Century New York." *Social History* 17, no. 2 (1992), 203–227.

Sekula, Alan. "The Body and the Archive." *October* 39 (Winter 1986), 3–64.

Seltzer, Mark. *Bodies and Machines.* New York: Routledge, 1992.

Stacey, Jackie. "Desperately Seeking Difference." *Screen* 28, no. 1 (Winter 1987), 48–61.

Staiger, Janet. *Bad Women: Regulating Sexuality in Early American Cinema.* Minneapolis: University of Minnesota Press, 1995.

———. "Combination and Litigation: Structures of U.S. Film Distribution, 1891–1917." *Cinema Journal* 23, no. 2 (Winter 1983), 41–72.

Swaim, Ginalie, with Becky Hawbaker and Lisa Moran. "Iowans at the 1893 World's Columbian Exposition." *The Palimpset* 74, no. 4 (Winter 1993), 161–187.

Szuberla, Guy. "Ladies, Gentlemen, Flirts, Mashers, Snoozers, and the Breaking of Etiquette's Code." *Prospects* 15 (1990), 169–196.

Toulet, Emmanuelle. "Cinema at the Universal Exposition, Paris 1900." *Persistence of Vision* 9 (1991), 10–36.

Trachtenberg, Alan. *The Incorporation of America: Culture and Society in the Gilded Age.* New York: Hill & Wang, 1982.

Uricchio, William, and Roberta Pearson. *Reframing Culture: The Case of the Vitagraph Quality Films.* Princeton, N.J.: Princeton University Press, 1993.

Walkowitz, Judith R. *City of Dreadful Delight: Narratives of Sexual Danger in Late-Victorian London.* Chicago: University of Chicago Press, 1992.

Williams, Linda. *Hard Core: Power, Pleasure, and the "Frenzy of the Visible."* Berkeley and Los Angeles: University of California Press, 1989.

Williams, Rosalind. "The Dream World of Mass Consumption." In *Rethinking Popular Culture: Contemporary Perspectives in Cultural Studies,* edited by Chandra Mukerji and Michael Schudson, 198–235. Berkeley and Los Angeles: University of California Press, 1991.

Wilson, Elizabeth. *The Sphinx in the City: Urban Life, the Control of Disorder, and Women.* Berkeley and Los Angeles: University of California Press, 1991.

Wolff, Janet. *Feminine Sentences: Essays on Women & Culture.* Berkeley and Los Angeles: University of California Press, 1990.

Wood, Sharon. "Wandering Girls and Leading Women: Sexuality and Urban Public Life in Davenport, Iowa, 1880–1910." Ph.D. diss., University of Iowa, 1994.

GENERAL INDEX

Page numbers in italics refer to illustrations.

FILM INDEX

Page numbers in italics refer to illustrations.

ABOUT THE AUTHOR

Lauren Rabinovitz is a professor of American studies and film studies at the University of Iowa. She is the author of *Points of Resistance: Women, Power, and Politics in the New York Avant-Garde Cinema, 1943–71,* co-author of the award-winning CD-ROM *The Rebecca Project,* and co-editor of *Seeing Through the Media: The Persian Gulf War.*